Foundational Issues in Natural Language Processing

System Development Foundation Benchmark Series

Max Brady, editor
Robotics Science, 1989

Max V. Mathews and John R. Pierce, editors
Current Directions in Computer Music Research, 1989

Philip R. Cohen, Jerry Morgan, and Martha E. Pollack, editors
Intentions in Communication, 1990

Eric L. Schwartz, editor
Computational Neuroscience, 1990

Peter Sells, Stuart M. Shieber, and Thomas Wasow, editors
Foundational Issues in Natural Language Processing, 1991

Foundational Issues in Natural Language Processing

edited by Peter Sells, Stuart M. Shieber, and Thomas Wasow

System Development Foundation Benchmark Series

A Bradford Book
The MIT Press
Cambridge, Massachusetts
London, England

This book was set in Palatino by Asco Trade Typesetting Ltd., Hong Kong and printed and bound in the United States of America.

Library of Congress Cataloging-in-Publication Data

Foundational issues in natural language processing / edited by Peter Sells, Stuart M. Shieber, and Thomas Wasow.
    p.   cm.—(System Development Foundation benchmark series)
    "A Bradford book."
    Includes bibliographical references and index.
    ISBN 0-262-19303-5
    1. Computational linguistics.   I. Sells, Peter, 1957–   .   II. Shieber, Stuart M. III. Wasow, Thomas.   IV. Series.
P98.F65   1991
410'.285—dc20   91-599
                                                                      CIP

Contents

List of Contributors

Robert C. Berwick
Artificial Intelligence Laboratory
Massachusetts Institute of
  Technology
Cambridge, MA

Janet Dean Fodor
Graduate Center
City University of New York
New York, NY

Aravind K. Joshi
Department of Computer and
  Information Science
Moore School
University of Pennsylvania
Philadelphia, PA

William C. Rounds
Computer Science and Engineering
  Division
Electrical Engineering and
  Computer Science Department
University of Michigan
Ann Arbor, MI

K. Vijay-Shanker
Department of Computer Science
University of Delaware
Newark, DE

David Weir
Department of Electrical
  Engineering and Computer
  Science
The Technological Institute
Northwestern University
Evanston, IL

Introduction

Research on natural language processing involves at least four distinct but closely related areas of study. They are (1) investigating the psychological processes involved in human language understanding; (2) building computational systems for analyzing natural language input (and/or producing natural language output); (3) developing theories of natural language structure; and (4) determining the mathematical properties of grammar formalisms.

(1) and (2) are obvious lines of research, differing in their emphasis on whether the goal is to understand human language use or to simulate human linguistic behavior on a machine. In order for these efforts to have some principled basis, they must incorporate (or perhaps embody) theoretical claims about the appropriate units of description for utterances and what relations among those units are linguistically significant. In other words, significant work in areas (1) and (2) builds on (and, ideally, contributes to) work in area (3). In all three of these lines of research, there is a tendency to develop rich systems of formalism and terminology. Area (4) plays a vital clarifying role in the enterprise, by specifying rigorously what the relations are among different-looking models of natural language structure and processing.

The literature abounds with examples of work that demonstrates the interrelatedness of these areas of research, bringing considerations from one to bear on the problems of another. A particularly clear illustration is provided by Chomsky's argument in the 1950s (see Chomsky 1956, 1957) that finite-state grammars were inadequate models of natural language syntax. Let us review that argument, highlighting the roles of (1)–(4) and the relations among them (and, in the process, perhaps stretching the historical record just a little).

A *finite-state grammar* is a rewriting system, with rules of the following forms (where capital letters are nonterminal symbols and lowercase letters are terminal symbols): $A \rightarrow a$ and $A \rightarrow Ba$. The language generated by such a grammar is the set of strings of terminal symbols that can be generated beginning with the designated nonterminal symbol S and applying rules from the grammar in any order. Such a language is called a *finite-state language.* It is evident that every finite-state grammar is equivalent to an automaton, described as follows by Chomsky (1957:18–19):

> Suppose that we have a machine that can be in any one of a finite number of different internal states, and suppose that this machine switches from one state to another by producing a certain symbol (let us say, an English word). One of these states is an initial state; another is a final state. Suppose that the machine begins in the initial state, runs through a sequence of states (producing a word with each transition), and ends in the final state. Then we call the sequence of words that has been produced a "sentence". Each such machine thus defines a certain language; namely, the set of sentences that can be produced in this way.

Chomsky (1957:20) goes on to say:

> This conception of language is an extremely powerful and general one. If we can adopt it, we can view the speaker as being essentially a machine of the type considered. In producing a sentence, the speaker begins in the initial state, produces the first word of the sentence, thereby switching into a second state which limits the choice of the second word, etc. Each state through which he passes represents the grammatical restrictions that limit the choice of the next word at this point in the utterance.

What we have, then, is a very simple theory of grammar, a corresponding machine model that could easily be implemented on real computers (even those of the mid-1950s), and the suggestion that this model might be given a psychological interpretation. Simple as it is, this approach to natural language processing was not made entirely of straw. Chomsky (1957:20) says that this "is essentially the model of language" developed in Hockett 1955, and it is possible to find statements in the psychological literature of the time to indicate that it was taken seriously as an account of human verbal behavior. For example, Lashley (1951:182) quotes the following characterization of language behavior from Washburn 1916: "a combination of movements so linked together that the stimulus furnished by the actual performance of certain movements is required to bring about other movements."

It is not difficult to prove that certain sets of strings are not finite-state languages. For example, "mirror-image languages"—that is, infinite sets of strings, each of which is a palindrome (such as {*a, b, aa, bb, aaa, bbb, aba, bab, aaaa, bbbb, abba, baab,* ...})—are not finite state. More generally, any language whose sentences can have an unbounded number of nested dependencies is beyond the expressive power of finite-state grammars or the equivalent machines. The heart of Chomsky's argument against finite-state grammars was the claim that natural languages permit precisely this sort of dependency.

English, he observed (Chomsky 1957:22), includes constructions like those in (1), where the S's represent clauses.

(1) a. If S_1, then S_2.
     b. Either S_1 or S_2.

Other combinations, such as *Either S_1 then S_2, are not possible, showing that there is a dependency between the words in each of these pairs. Moreover, sentences of the forms in (1) can be substituted for the S's in these schemata, yielding patterns like If either S_1 or S_2, then S_3. In principle, this process can be iterated, resulting in strings of arbitrary length with unbounded numbers of these dependent elements, nested in just the manner known to be beyond the descriptive power of finite-state grammars.

We note in passing that neither Chomsky nor we present actual English sentences (as opposed to schematic patterns) in support of this argument. We return to the significance of this omission below. For now, we wish to emphasize the form of the argument: a mathematical result and an observation about the well-formed sentences of English are combined to discredit a theory of grammar and models of natural language processing (both psychological and computational) built on that theory. This is a prototype for arguments connecting mathematical linguistics, grammatical theory, psycholinguistics, and computational linguistics.

The elegance of Chomsky's argument led others to seek similar results. Few, if any, have been as celebrated, in part because developing comparably powerful arguments for or against less simplistic theories proved more difficult. However, the literature contains many examples, of which we will briefly describe four.

Putnam (1961) argued that natural languages (assumed to be sets of sentences, which in turn were taken to be strings of words) must be decidable. This was based on the observation that people are very good at distinguishing well-formed sentences from arbitrary strings of words. Since the human brain is, according to Putnam, a finite computing device, it follows that there must be an effective procedure for each language capable of deciding which strings are sentences of the language. Putnam coupled this with an argument that the theory of transformational grammar prevalent at the time allowed grammars that would generate undecidable languages. The latter argument was based on the observation that transformational grammars could mimic arbitrary Turing machine operations by means of insertions and deletions. Hence, Putnam concluded, transformational grammar as it was being developed at the time was too powerful a theory of natural language syntax. Here mathematical and psychological considerations were combined to argue against a linguistic theory.

Postal emulated Chomsky's argument more directly. Citing results (Chomsky 1959) showing that context-free grammars could not generate languages with arbitrary cross-serial dependencies—that is, dependencies of the form $a_1 a_2 a_3 \ldots a_n \ldots b_1 b_2 b_3 \ldots b_n \ldots$ (where the dependencies hold between the a's and b's with the same subscripts)—Postal (1964a) claimed that the Northern Iroquoian language Mohawk had a construction of precisely this form. Postal (1964b) went on to argue that a multitude of then popular grammatical theories were in fact merely unformalized versions of context-free grammar. He did not go on to draw the associated psychological and computational inferences, though others did (see, for example, Chomsky 1964: sec. I; Hopcroft and Ullman 1979:78).

Gazdar (1981:155) argued on the basis of psycholinguistic and computational considerations *for* taking context-free grammar seriously as a theory of natural language syntax. The fact that context-free languages can be parsed in time (at worst) proportional to the cube of the length of the input (Earley 1970) comports well with the observation that humans are very efficient at processing natural language input, as well as with the aim of constructing fast natural language understanding systems. These mathematical, psychological, and computational observations served as initial motivation for the grammatical theory known as Generalized Phrase Structure Grammar (see Gazdar et al. 1985 for a detailed exposition of this theory, as well as arguments for it based on linguistic considerations).

A somewhat different combination of mathematical, psychological, and linguistic considerations can be found in work on learnability, notably the work of Wexler and Culicover (1980). Starting from the observation that natural languages are learned by young children, they developed a precise definition of learnability. They went on to propose a set of constraints on a version of transformational grammar that would jointly suffice to permit a proof that the languages such grammars generate were learnable—in fact, learnable from simple data.

Other examples could be cited. The point, however, should by now be clear: the four areas of research cited in the opening paragraph have often been related to one another in the literature. On the other hand, such connections have also often been questioned, and inferences like those described in the preceding paragraphs are regarded by many with considerable skepticism. A number of factors contribute to the difficulty of making persuasive arguments relating psycholinguistics, computational linguistics, grammatical theory, and mathematical linguistics.

First, and most widely discussed, is the fact that a grammar does not determine a processing system (either human or electronic). The performance of a language processor depends on many factors other than the knowledge embodied in a grammar. Observable behaviors—including both grammaticality judgments and measures of processing complexity like reaction times—are influenced by such extragrammatical factors as memory limitations, parsing strategies, lexical retrieval mechanisms, and the like. Hence, any argument purporting to connect data on language processing to grammatical theory is open to serious question.[1]

Indeed, it is not even clear that an optimal processing system should include a discrete part that can be identified as the grammar. Much work has assumed that it should; Chomsky (1965:9), for example, states, "No doubt, a reasonable model of language use will incorporate, as a basic component, the generative grammar that expresses the speaker-hearer's knowledge of the language." This assumption has been questioned on a number of occasions (see, for example, Bever 1970; Katz 1981), and the issue remains a vexed one. It is addressed in the present volume in the chapters by Berwick and Fodor.

Second, the appropriate notions of complexity for evaluating natural language processing systems are not given a priori. Chomsky's argument against finite-state grammar reviewed earlier takes generative capacity as its complexity measure, but this is a very crude metric. For example, though deterministic and nondeterministic finite-state machines accept precisely the same languages, a deterministic machine may require exponentially more states than a nondeterministic one for a given language.

In the past decades, theoretical computer science has provided a variety of complexity measures more delicate than generative capacity. However, these measures may depend crucially on the form of the system. Hence, arguments relating grammatical theory to processing can make use of these measures only if they make strong assumptions about how the grammar is embedded in the processing system. For example, Berwick and his collaborators have shown that generalized phrase structure grammars, although equivalent in generative capacity to context-free grammars, fare far worse with respect to some other complexity metrics, thus weakening considerably the force of Gazdar's argument cited above. Rounds's chapter in the present volume surveys some of the mathematical tools available for the comparison of natural language systems, as well as some of the ways in which care must be taken in their application.

Third, the mathematical results employed in arguments of the sort we are considering tend to be worst-case, limiting arguments. Familiar context-free languages, for example, can be parsed in linear time—far faster than the cubic time worst-case result available for the class as a whole. The mathematical results, therefore, may not always be a useful guide to the performance of real processing systems.

The issue comes up even in connection with Chomsky's argument against finite-state grammars. That argument depends crucially on the grammaticality of sentences with arbitrarily many nested dependencies. In fact, speakers tend to have great difficulty with sentences containing more than two nested dependencies. For example, even a sentence like (2) is quite awkward, though it was carefully constructed to exhibit three nested dependencies without becoming utterly incomprehensible.

(2)   If Pat both sees either Chris or Sandy and talks to one of them, then we should leave.

Further nesting would render it completely unacceptable. Moreover, one could argue that, because every human has only a finite amount of memory, natural languages *must* be finite state, for any language accepted by an automaton with fixed finite memory can be shown to be finite state. Consequently, Chomsky's argument (and most others modeled on it) requires that we dismiss as irrelevant factors like memory limitations. Since such factors are very relevant to the performance of real processing systems, the significance of the limiting proofs is called into question.

In short, the connections among grammatical theory, mathematical linguistics, and the operation of real natural language processing systems are complex ones. Drawing conclusions in one domain on the basis of considerations from another typically involves making simplifying assumptions that are easily called into question. This does not mean that the four lines of inquiry in question should proceed completely independently of one another. If the construction of computational natural language systems is to be of scientific as well as practical significance, it must be related in some way to human linguistic processing. And if the latter is to be studied in a systematic way, experiments must be based on a rigorous and principled theoretical foundation. In spite of the difficulties inherent in trying to relate the formal properties of grammatical theories to the observable properties of language-processing systems, the alternative to facing up to these difficulties is mere seat-of-the-pants guesswork. For this reason, work continues on the relationship among these four areas, and much of the best research on natural language processing—including the research presented in this volume—concerns itself with those relationships.

The chapters by Rounds and by Joshi, Vijay-Shanker, and Weir deal with the relationship of mathematical results about grammar formalisms to linguistic issues. Rounds discusses the relevance of complexity results to linguistics and computational linguistics, providing useful caveats about how results might be misinterpreted, plus pointers to promising avenues of future research. Joshi, Vijay-Shanker, and Weir survey results showing the equivalence (in terms of generative capacity) of several different grammatical formalisms, all of which are "mildly context sensitive." Central to their results are a number of variants on tree-adjoining grammars, a formalism they and several collaborators have developed and applied to natural language phenomena.

The chapter by Fodor is concerned with the relationship of grammatical or computational models to psychological processes in the minds of speakers. Fodor discusses how psycholinguistic results can bear on the choice among competing grammatical theories, surveying a number of recent experiments and their relevance to issues in grammatical theory.

The chapter by Berwick considers the relationship between issues in linguistic theory and the construction of computational parsing systems. Berwick examines what it means to implement a theory of grammar in a computational system. He argues for the advantages of a "principle-based" approach over a "rule-based" one and surveys several recent parsing systems based on Government-Binding Theory.

The four chapters contain revised versions of material presented at a conference held in January, 1987, in Santa Cruz, California. The conference was sponsored by the Center for the Study of Language and Information, with funds provided by the System Development Foundation. In addition to the four papers published here, there were presentations by Lauri Karttunen and Don Hindle. Karttunen explored unification-based approaches to grammatical analysis and their appeal from both linguistic and computational perspectives. Hindle reported on his work with Mitch Marcus on the computational and psychological advantages of deterministic parsing models.

The issues addressed in this volume are difficult ones. They will continue to be debated for decades to come. These works represent the current state of the art as articulated by some of the leading thinkers in the multidisciplinary field of natural language processing.

Note

1. This argument applies to all kinds of performance data, including native speakers' judgments of acceptability. Although it is standard for generative grammarians to take such judgments as providing especially direct access to some internalized grammar, no justification for this practice has ever been offered.

References

Bever, T. 1970. "The Cognitive Basis for Linguistic Structures." In J. R. Hayes (ed.) *Cognition and Language Learning*. New York: Wiley.

Chomsky, N. 1956. "Three Models for the Description of Language." *I.R.E. Transactions on Information Theory* IT-2:113–124. Reprinted, with corrections, in R. Luce, R. Bush, and E. Galanter (eds.) *Handbook of Mathematical Psychology, Volume II*. New York: Wiley (1965).

Chomsky, N. 1957. *Syntactic Structures*. The Hague: Mouton.

Chomsky, N. 1959. "On Certain Formal Properties of Grammars." *Information and Control* 2:137–167. Reprinted in R. Luce, R. Bush, and E. Galanter (eds.) *Handbook of Mathematical Psychology, Volume II*. New York: Wiley (1965).

Chomsky, N. 1964. "Current Issues in Linguistic Theory." In J. A. Fodor and J. Katz (eds.) *The Structure of Language*. Englewood Cliffs, New Jersey: Prentice-Hall.

Chomsky, N. 1965. *Aspects of the Theory of Syntax*. Cambridge, Massachusetts: MIT Press.

8   Introduction

Earley, J. 1970. "An Efficient Context-free Parsing Algorithm." *Communications of the ACM* 13:94–102.

Gazdar, G. 1981. "Unbounded Dependencies and Coordinate Structure." *Linguistic Inquiry* 12:155–184.

Gazdar, G., E. Klein, G. Pullum, and I. Sag. 1985. *Generalized Phrase Structure Grammar.* Oxford: Blackwell.

Hockett, C. 1955. *A Manual of Phonology.* Baltimore: Waverly Press.

Hopcroft, J., and J. Ullman. 1979. *Introduction to Automata Theory, Languages, and Computation.* Reading, Massachusetts: Addison-Wesley.

Katz, J. 1981. *Language and Other Abstract Objects.* Totowa, New Jersey: Rowman and Littlefield.

Lashley, K. 1951. "The Problem of Serial Order in Behavior." In S. Saporta (ed.) *Psycholinguistics.* New York: Holt, Rinehart and Winston.

Postal, P. 1964a. "Limitations of Phrase Structure Grammar." In J. A. Fodor and J. Katz (eds.) *The Structure of Language.* Englewood Cliffs, New Jersey: Prentice-Hall.

Postal, P. 1964b. *Constituent Structure: A Study of Contemporary Models of Syntactic Description.* Bloomington, Indiana: Research Center for the Language Sciences.

Putnam, H. 1961. "Some Issues in the Theory of Grammar." In G. Harman (ed.) *On Noam Chomsky.* Garden City, New York: Anchor Books.

Washburn, M. F. 1916. *Movement and Mental Imagery.* Boston: Houghton Mifflin.

Wexler, K., and P. Culicover. 1980. *Formal Principles of Language Acquisition.* Cambridge, Massachusetts: MIT Press.

Chapter 1

The Relevance of Computational Complexity Theory to Natural Language Processing

William C. Rounds

1 Introduction

Mathematical models in linguistics often have a peripheral status. The creator of a model may not completely understand the theory being modeled, and the user of a model may not understand its idealizations and presuppositions. The result may be that the model is generally ignored, or that its predictions are used too literally. It is therefore necessary for the creators of models to document exactly their intentions for the models, and for the users of the models to be aware of these intentions and to realize what assumptions and idealizations are made. This chapter is an attempt to explain informally the intuitions behind complexity theory in computer science, with a view toward discovering in what ways the results of this theory may be used productively in computational linguistics and linguistics more generally. Several papers have recently appeared invoking complexity techniques and deriving complexity results for various linguistic theories. These (generally excellent) papers deserve to have their presuppositions carefully examined, so that their conclusions may be properly applied.

One of the first formalizations of a linguistic theory was the paper by Peters and Ritchie (1973) on the generative capacity of transformational grammars. Their model is intended to capture the intuitions of transformational grammar as exactly as possible, given the extensive literature available at the time, and focusing principally on the *Aspects* model (Chomsky 1965). Peters and Ritchie were especially careful to document their intentions in making this model, with the result that its conclusions (that any recursively enumerable set could be generated) forced a major reassessment of the notion of "natural language grammar."

Complexity results in linguistics usually involve several parameters and often speak about more than simple notions of weak generative capacity. The problems of documentation are thus more difficult than those faced by Peters and Ritchie. However, identifying the right complexity parameters can still clarify some real issues for a linguistic theory. The papers by Ristad (1986a) and Barton (1985, 1986) are good examples. Ristad's results point to aspects of generalized phrase structure theory (Gazdar et al. 1985) that may lead to computational difficulties, and Barton's results point out similar problems in immediate dominance/linear precedence (ID/LP) parsing and in morphology.

These results have been summarized by Barton, Berwick, and Ristad (1987). I recommend that the reader consult this book for a full explanation of the notions I touch on in this chapter. Many of the points I make here are reiterated there.

The presuppositions of an already established theory, such as complexity theory, are perhaps the properties of the theory most easily ignored in making an application. The theory in this case is an attempt to classify decision problems in terms of the computational resources required by an abstract sequential machine. These assumptions need to be rephrased linguistically in order to apply the results sensibly. One needs to make a hypothesis that the brain is some sort of sequential computer, and that natural languages are infinite sets of strings, for example. It is worth noting that even in computer science, the presuppositions about abstract sequential machines have been challenged. Computers need not be sequential machines of potentially infinite capacity like Turing machines, but can be modeled as families of Boolean circuits or, more generally, as families of finite-capacity machines (Gurevich 1988). Incidentally, this fact suggests that connectionist models in linguistics need not be dismissed because they do not explain how infinite sets of strings can be generated. These models are quite closely related to the Boolean circuit models in computer science, and it would seem that a synthesis of ideas is possible here.

In the light of these remarks, I have decided to examine several areas of complexity theory and to include for each area an analysis of its presuppositions. I will also include for each area an example of application (or misapplication) of its results and will try to give an intuitive feeling for the relevance of the results in linguistics. (In addition to the book mentioned above, I should note Berwick's book (1985), the book by Berwick and Weinberg (1984), and Perrault's survey article (1984) as other good contributions in the same spirit.) In the concluding section I will suggest some ways in which complexity techniques may lead to the discovery of new linguistic properties, or to new ways of regarding old phenomena. As a tentative example, I will focus on a model for studying language learnability, based on techniques from complexity theory and adapted from a very interesting model of Valiant (1984). This adaptation may well require further changes, but this should be true of all formal models. They need not be frozen in the realm of abstractions but should, when necessary, be reshaped to fit empirical data and to explain new linguistic hypotheses. Doing so calls for pooling the expertise of linguists, computer scientists, and mathematicians in a truly collaborative effort.

2 Analysis of Algorithms

By an *algorithm* I mean a set of instructions in a standard form to be executed on a sequential computer. This involves the first presupposition: algorithms are generally presumed to be written in some form of imperative language. (This generally means a high-level description in a language similar to Pascal.) Each instruction takes a relatively short time to execute, so that the time required to execute a program with a given input can be obtained by a simple summation of time units. The analysis of algorithms is the study of the time and space requirements of such a program, expressed as a function of the size of the input given to the program. The second presupposition is involved here: that the input is given beforehand, so that its size is known before the program is executed. Interactive execution requires more careful modeling techniques and depends on the problem being modeled. A third presupposition is that the input is given as a string, encoding some more natural data structure. There may be more than one way to do this encoding, and the results of the analysis may depend on how this has been done.

Algorithm analysis is in many ways the area of complexity theory with the most precise results. The principal reason is that the details of an algorithm can be given exactly. The books by Knuth (1973) are classics in the field. Many algorithms with precise machine timings are presented in these books, and this style of analysis has been quite generally followed. Examples of linguistic algorithms that have been analyzed include Earley's context-free grammar parsing algorithm, presented and analyzed in Earley 1970, and Robinson's unification algorithm, given in Robinson 1965, a strong form of which is analyzed by Paterson and Wegman (1978). Variants of these algorithms are used for chart parsing and unification-based grammar formalisms (see Winograd 1983 and Shieber 1986 for overviews).

The classic paradigm of algorithm analysis is the following. Given a program, one defines the execution time of the program on a given input as the number of instructions executed, and the space requirement of the program as the maximum number of memory cells in use at any one time. If the input has size n, we try to bound these functions of the input by functions of n. That is, we consider all inputs of size n and calculate what the best and worst possibilities are over this collection. The results are expressed in O-notation, which we now review briefly.

Let f and g be functions from natural numbers to the real numbers. We say that f is $O(g)$ if and only if there is a constant K and a number n_0 such that for all $n \geq n_0$, we have $f(n) \leq Kg(n)$. For lower bounds, we say that f is $\Omega(g)$ if and only if there is a constant K and a number n_0 such that for all $n \geq n_0$, we have $f(n) \geq Kg(n)$. Finally, if f is both $O(g)$ and $\Omega(g)$, we say that f is $\Theta(g)$.[1] In the applications, $f(n)$ is the time used by an algorithm maximized over all inputs of size n. Ideally, we obtain an explicit function g such that f is $\Theta(g)$; this kind of result gives the most information about an algorithm's performance. Most algorithm developers, on the other hand, strive for a small function g such that f is $O(g)$. Paterson and Wegman show that in case of unification, restricted to first-order terms, we may take $g(n) = n$. Earley's algorithm similarly requires time at most $O(|G|^2 * n^3)$, where $|G|$ is the size of the grammar and n is the size of the input string, when implemented on a so-called random-access machine.

What are the problems we face when we wish to analyze the performance of one of these algorithms? Let us consider one problem associated with Paterson and Wegman's linear time unification algorithm. De Champeaux (1986) points out that the timing of their algorithm depends on the assumed format of the input data (thus involving our third presupposition). Paterson and Wegman assume that the terms to be unified are presented in a directed acyclic graph format, and not in the usual form as text expressions with variables. It is not clear that preprocessing into their assumed format will require only linear time.

Another problem related to, say, LISP implementations of an algorithm concerns our first presupposition. To get a good estimate of the running time of the implemented algorithm, we must ascertain that the implementation is *faithful*: elementary steps in the LISP version correspond to elementary steps in the original version, and the control structure corresponds in the two versions. This requirement is often violated, since iteration (a simple loop in the imperative version) is often replaced by a recursion in the LISP implementation, which is a differing control structure. If the implementation is not faithful in this way, then the implemented algorithm must be reanalyzed. At this point we may run afoul of the first presupposition mentioned above; the number of time steps taken by a program in an applicative language like LISP may be difficult to measure. In fact, there is no universally agreed-on standard for measuring the time performance of algorithms written in such a language. Sometimes one can count quantities like the number of CONSs, but there are still factors that complicate the analysis; these include the problems of space allocation and garbage collection in the run-time support system. None of the preceding remarks, however, should be taken to imply that the LISP version of an imperative algorithm must be less efficient than the original. The hardware of a LISP machine, for example, may support list-building primitives that work (in absolute time) an order of magnitude faster than the representations of these primitives in an imperative language.

Given these problems, it is not surprising that little specific analysis of actual implementations of linguistic algorithms has been done. However, it is almost always worthwhile to consider implementing versions of algorithms that have been shown to be efficient in both time and space, and that have imperative implementations that run with low overhead. If there are two competing imperative algorithms for the same problem, and one of these algorithms has been shown to be absolutely superior to the other (supposing, say, that one is $\Omega(n^2)$ and the other is $O(n \log n)$), then it will likely pay to implement the superior algorithm. The major exception to this rule of thumb is that in some cases the superior algorithm has only been shown to exist and has not been described directly. An example is Valiant's algorithm (1975) for context-free recognition, which reduces the context-free recognition problem to that for $n \times n$ Boolean matrix multiplication. The reduction shows that recognition, instead of taking time $O(n^3)$, need take only time $O(n^{2.48})$, according to the latest estimate for the matrix multiplication problem (Strassen 1986). However, the coefficient K introduced by the reduction, to cover overhead, is so huge that the saving in time will not be apparent until sentences of length 100,000 are processed. This is the well-known *asymptotic* problem with O-analyses.

A similar distinction between algorithms that require exponential time ($\Omega(c^n)$ for some $c > 1$) and those that are polynomial ($O(n^k)$ for some k) is usually apparent. Generally, the polynomial algorithm will run asymptotically better on any machine architecture with any implementing language. Unfortunately, there can be no proof of this fact; but it is a widely held thesis in complexity theory that there will be at most a polynomial increase in running time when an algorithm is reimplemented in a new (sequential) language on a new (sequential) machine architecture. I will discuss this matter more fully in section 3.2.

3 Complexity of Decision Problems

This area of computational complexity theory seems to hold more linguistic interest than the analysis of algorithms. It concerns the intrinsic complexity of a problem: bounds on the behavior of any possible algorithm for solving the problem. The word *algorithm* has the same meaning as in section 2. The world *problem* is taken to mean a "decision problem": for some well-defined set of finite objects, decide whether or not a given object is in the set. The first presupposition of this theory is that finite objects can be efficiently represented as strings. This leads to a natural representation of the set of objects as a *formal language*, or set of strings. The use of the word *language*, which is common in computer science, derives of course from work in early formal linguistics, when it was assumed that sentences (or nonsentences) could all be represented as strings, so that a natural language could be specified by defining which strings were grammatical. This linguistic presupposition is very easy to accept and is a major reason for the attractiveness of intrinsic complexity results. It is much easier to challenge the assumption that a particular algorithm such as unification is used by a human language processor than it is to challenge the presupposition that English or Swiss-German is a certain well-defined set of strings. However, the challenge can be made, and I will discuss some alternatives in section 4.

The formal models of syntax that have been developed since 1960 have all in a sense been responses to the challenge of defining the class of natural languages. Each formal model, when made mathematically precise, has been a method for presenting a class of grammars together with a way of associating with each grammar its corresponding language. Once these definitions are given, it becomes possible to study intrinsic complexity properties of languages in the generated class. I will call this class of languages the *weak generative capacity* of a grammar formalism, and results about the intrinsic complexity of languages in the class will be called *weak generative complexity* results.

Intrinsic complexity arguments, however, can be made for other types of decision problems. This has been done in linguistic theory principally by researchers at MIT. Berwick and Weinberg (1984) discuss the complexity of Lexical-Functional Grammar (LFG) (Kaplan and Bresnan 1982) and seem to have been among the first to have studied complexity properties other than weak generative complexity for this class of grammars. Instead of looking at the complexity of some one specific language in the weak generative capacity of LFG, they consider (although they do not express it this way) a set of pairs $\{\langle G, w \rangle\}$, where G is an LFG grammar and $w \in L(G)$, and show that this recognition problem, involving the G parameter explicitly, is intrinsically complex. This set of strings is termed by Ristad (1986a) the *universal recognition problem* for the class of grammars, and he gives a cogent argument for studying this problem rather than the full weak generative capacity. The essential idea is that when one studies the complexity of recognition of a class, one needs to consider the size of a grammar for each language, as well as the size of strings to be recognized; this is important when one is concerned with such phenomena as ease of learnability, for example. Although the term *universal recognition problem* is probably more accurate, for brevity's sake I will call a problem of this type a *parsing complexity problem*, following Barton (1985), whose work will be considered below.

I should also point out that most linguistic theories, even quite formal ones, do not regard the string as the primary data structure in natural language. Phrase structure grammars employ the tree; Relational Grammar (Perlmutter 1980) considers the relational network as primary, and unification-based grammars use the feature structure in the same way. There is a temptation to view these structures as empirically given, which should be resisted. The very fact that the structures differ from theory to theory is evidence that the structures are not part of any empirical data. This is not to say that some form of these structures is not used by the brain to represent syntactic knowledge, however. Complexity techniques can be properly used in an effort to compare formalisms using differing structures, and as part of an effort to find a common mathematical ground for the differing formalisms.

3.1 Undecidability

It makes sense to include undecidability results as part of complexity theory, because undecidable languages—those for which no algorithm will solve the membership problem—can be viewed as "infinitely complex" from the standpoint of resource bounds. As Perrault (1984) notes, and as Chomsky has argued, there is no convincing demonstration that natural languages must be decidable. I feel, however, that since we know formalisms under which it is possible to process reasonably large subsets of natural languages, then it is reasonable to reject a grammar formalism accounting for these subsets unless the formalism suggests an algorithm for processing them. Thus, type 0 phrase structure grammars, though certainly adequate to generate anything we know how to process, account for these subsets in the same way as they do undecidable sets—by simulating Turing machines directly. It seems that lexical-functional grammars, however, do not suffer so severely from this problem. The computations of a Turing machine can be simulated in a lexical-functional grammar, but only by the trick of allowing arbitrarily long sequences of applications of productions of the form $A \rightarrow B$. Such arbitrarily long derivation sequences do not normally appear in linguistically motivated grammars, and so LFG cannot be counted out so easily as type 0 grammars. Likewise, Berwick argues that Government-Binding (GB) Theory does not allow even the computational power of LFG, so it is more difficult to reject by this criterion.[2] Other theories, based more directly on processing notions, may even be impossible to reject on this ground. Marcus's parser (Marcus 1980), for example, works in time $O(n)$ and thus by definition cannot recognize undecidable languages. Whether or not such processing-based theories are adequate as cognitive models is, of course, an open question, one to which complexity theory cannot speak.

Conversely, proofs that particular natural languages are undecidable should not be prohibitions against constructing useful parsing algorithms. (I have in mind Hintikka's claim (1977) that English is not decidable, based on the contexts in which the words *any* and *every* are interchangeable.) The reason is that it may be possible to limit the difficult sentences to a tiny fraction of the normally occurring sentences. Let me illustrate with an artificial example.

Let V be an undecidable language over the one-letter alphabet $\{d\}$, and let E be some easily recognizable (say, context-free) language over an alphabet not having d as a member. Suppose further that for each length n there are $\Omega(2^n)$ strings of that length in E. Consider the language $V \cup E$. This language is undecidable since its intersection with the regular language $\{d\}^*$ is just V. However, for each n, an exponentially vanishing fraction of the strings of that length in $V \cup E$ are actually in V. Thus, a recognizer ignoring strings of d's will be correct essentially all of the time.

Finally, the difference between weak generative complexity and parsing complexity can be especially large in the case of undecidable problems. It is possible to have a class C of languages, each of which is efficiently decidable, but for which the parsing complexity problem is undecidable. For example, let C be the class of type 0 grammars that happen to generate a regular language. Then each language in the weak generative capacity of C is regular, but the parsing complexity problem is undecidable. Of course, the difficulty here is that there is no algorithm such that given a type 0 grammar, the algorithm will return a weakly equivalent regular grammar if and only if the type 0 grammar is in C. We can turn the difficulty to advantage, though, when we note that there is such a complexity gap for the case of Generalized Phrase Structure Grammar (GPSG) and related theories. In this case we can say that translations from GPSGs to equivalent context-free grammars cannot be computed efficiently. We return to this point in the next section.

3.2 NP-Completeness
The remarks I have made about undecidability apply to other kinds of intractability, to be discussed in this and the following section. I will begin by recalling some general definitions.

Let f be a function from natural numbers to the reals. Let M be a machine (for definiteness, a Turing machine) that classifies its inputs by accepting them when it halts in some designated state, and by rejecting them either when it halts in a nondesignated state or by looping forever. We say that M is f-time bounded if and only if for each input of length n that it accepts, it does so within $f(n)$ time steps. Let $L(M)$ be the set of inputs accepted by M. We say that an arbitrary language L is in the class $DTIME(f)$ if and only if there is some deterministic machine M such that M is f-time bounded and $L = L(M)$. The class $NTIME(f)$ is defined similarly; in this case M is allowed to be nondeterministic, and the definition of acceptance now refers to the existence of one possible sequence of computation steps leading to a designated accepting state. Space bounds are again treated in a similar way, and we have the classes $NSPACE(s)$ and $DSPACE(s)$ for space bounding functions s.

These definitions only become precise once a particular class of machines has been specified, and the manner of accepting fully defined. The complexity results that have been obtained so far, however, are not much affected by the choice of machine class, as long as the class of machines models the typical sequential computer. This fact was mentioned above, and it rests on the following technical notion (discussed also in Perrault 1984). We say that two classes of machines are *polynomially related* (for time complexity) if and only if there is a polynomial function $p(n)$ such that given a machine M in the first class, there is a machine N in the second such that for any x, if M accepts x in n steps, then N accepts x in $p(n)$ steps; and vice versa. It turns out that the classes of random-access machines, Turing machines, and several other sequential computer models are polynomially related. (As I have defined it, this relation is an equivalence relation on classes of machines.) A complexity result that mentions only the existence of polynomial time functions will therefore usually apply to any class of sequential machine models.

We now define the class P, the class of *polynomial-time-recognizable languages*, to be the union over all polynomial-time functions p of the classes $DTIME(p)$. Similarly, the class NP, the class of nondeterministic polynomial-time languages, is the same union of the $NTIME(p)$ classes. It follows that these classes are the same no matter which kind of machine model is used in the definition. I will refer to Turing machines implicitly in the rest of the chapter. By the hypothesis of polynomial relatedness, these machines serve as equivalents for programs written in the imperative style. However, it would be useful to define complexity measures that applied to the machine models underlying applicative and declarative languages, like LISP and Prolog, and to check that these machines are polynomially related to the usual machines. An even more psychologically interesting project would be to formalize the computational devices used in cognitive modeling (that is, various pattern-matching primitives) and to analyze complexity in the same way. In any case, we now have a new presupposition: that we are dealing with a sequential machine class polynomially related to the usual classes.

One of the most important and difficult open problems of complexity theory is the question whether or not $P = NP$. Most investigators believe that these classes are different; a proof of this result would show that many interesting decision problems known to be in the class NP cannot possibly be in the class P and therefore are *intractable*: any correct sequential decision procedure must take more than polynomially many steps on an infinite number of inputs. These problems are the so-called *NP-complete* problems. There are several differences between such problems and other problems that can be proved to be nonpolynomial, and to understand these differences, we need to examine the notions of *reduction* and *completeness*.

Informally, we say that a problem (language) L is reducible to a problem M if a method for solving M will yield a method for solving L. Our problems are decision problems, and their instances are individual strings.

Further, a method for solving a problem is an algorithm that terminates for each string with a yes-no answer depending on the string's membership in the language. One way to define a reduction of L to M is to specify a string-to-string transformation T in such a way that for any string x, x is in the language L if and only if $T(x)$ is in M. The map T must be computable by an algorithm that always terminates, and for studying polynomial-time problems, we also require that T be computable in polynomial time in the length of x. Notice that since the set of polynomial functions is closed under composition, if L is reducible to M (via some T) and if M is in P, then so is L. We now say that a language M is *complete* for a class $\mathcal{C}$ of languages if and only if (1) the language M is in $\mathcal{C}$, and (2) for any $L \in \mathcal{C}$, L is polynomial-time reducible to M. It follows that the existence of a polynomial-time algorithm for a $\mathcal{C}$-complete language would imply $\mathcal{C} \subseteq P$. Cook's major discovery (1971) was that the set of satisfiable propositional formulas is NP-complete. Karp (1972) gave the present definitions and showed that the set of NP-complete problems contained many interesting combinatorial decision problems for which no efficient algorithm had been known.

Let us now consider the meaning of these notions for linguistics. First, a grammar formalism may allow the definition of an NP-complete language. If we accept the hypothesis that a natural language should be decidable in polynomial time, then we know (assuming $P \neq NP$) that the formalism generates some nonnatural languages. As I remarked for the case of undecidability, this need not be a problem unless an NP-complete language can be generated in the same way that the natural languages (or fragments thereof) in the class can be generated. For example, I showed in Rounds 1973a that indexed grammars (Aho 1968) can generate the set of satisfiable formulas, but the uses of indexed grammars to describe natural language phenomena (Gazdar 1985) do not much resemble that example.

Next, we should notice that the two constraints that natural languages should be polynomially decidable, and also describable by one of the current grammar formalisms, are not sufficient to characterize the class of natural languages. Most of the grammar classes of current interest will generate the nonnatural language a^*. This point has been made by Berwick and others; Ristad (1986b) shows, for example, that the problem of whether a GPSG generates all of Σ^*, where Σ is the terminal vocabulary of the grammar, is undecidable, and he claims that this fact provides strong evidence that GPSGs do not characterize exactly the natural languages. I should like to comment that although this result seems to be much more negative than the mere fact that there is a GPSG generating Σ^*, it does not tell us anything directly about the weak generative capacity of GPSG, or even anything about its parsing complexity.

These last remarks bring us to consider the NP-complete parsing complexity result of Barton (1985), who shows that the language $IDPP = \{\langle G, w \rangle : G$ is an ID/LP grammar, and $w \in L(G)\}$ is NP-complete. This result is a good use of complexity techniques to show a difference between different parameterizations of linguistic decision problems. Intuitively, as Barton points out, the result shows that the claimed efficiency of context-free recognition algorithms for context-free grammars (CFGs) cannot be used if a CFG is presented in another format. In fact, we can show even more than Barton does. Recall that the language $CFPP = \{\langle G, w \rangle : G$ is a CFG, and $w \in L(G)\}$ is in P. (This follows if we use Earley's recognition algorithm as presented in Earley 1970.) Let T be *any* transformation such that if G is an ID/LP grammar, then $T(G)$ is a weakly equivalent CFG. If $P \neq NP$, then T cannot be computed in polynomial time; otherwise, T would be a polynomial-time reduction of the NP-complete language $IDPP$ to the polynomial language $CFPP$. Further, suppose that the transformation T is *honest*; this means that there is an algorithm computing $T(G)$ from G, such that the number of steps taken by the algorithm on input G is bounded above by $p(|T(G)|)$, where p is some polynomial. Then the size of $T(G)$ must grow nonpolynomially in the size of G, so that ID/LP format is exponentially more succinct than CFG format for honest transformations.[3] We will examine a few more issues concerning succinctness in section 4.1.

3.3 Provably Intractable Problems

The results of the last section depended on the conjecture $P \neq NP$. Here, I will examine some decidable problems that have been proved to be intractable; that is, there can be no polynomial-time algorithm for their solution even if $P = NP$. Such problems have in general a different flavor from the NP problems. I will try to compare the two classes intuitively at the end of the section. Let us again begin with some standard definitions and results.

We define the class of languages $EXPTIME$ to be

$$\bigcup_{c > 0} DTIME(2^{cn}).$$

There exist languages in this class that provably cannot be recognized in polynomial time. This result depends on the Hierarchy Theorem for time complexity classes, which says that if f and g are well-behaved time bounds and the ratio $f(n)/(g(n)\log g(n))$ grows without bounds as n grows without bound, then there will be languages in $DTIME(f)$ but not in $DTIME(g)$. (See Hopcroft and Ullman 1979:299 for a proof.) We apply this theorem to the functions $f(n) = 2^n$, and $g(n) = 2^{\sqrt{n}}$. We obtain a language L not recognizable in time $g(n)$, and therefore not in polynomial time, because every polynomial is eventually dominated by $g(n)$. As a consequence, any language that is $EXPTIME$-complete with respect to polynomial-time reductions cannot be recognized in polynomial time, because the language L reduces to the complete language. There are a large number of known exponential-time-complete languages, representing various interesting decision problems. None of these languages seems remotely like any natural language in the weak sense. For example, the problem of determining the existence of a winning strategy in a certain kind of combinatorial game is shown in Stockmeyer and Chandra 1978 to be a complete problem of this type.

Nevertheless, there do exist exponentially difficult problems related to grammar formalisms. Perhaps the most interesting is the parsing complexity problem for GPSGs (Ristad 1986a). In this case, every language in $DTIME(2^{p(n)})$, where $p(n)$ is any polynomial, will reduce to this problem. This strengthens Barton's parsing complexity result to the full class of GPSGs and begins to show that there can be a real gap between weak generative complexity and parsing complexity. It would be interesting to learn just how wide this gap may become. If it could be shown that there was a double exponential gap (that is, the parsing complexity problem was complete for $DTIME(2^{2^n})$), then it would follow that any translation to a CFG could not be computed in polynomial space. If, however, there were a transformation from a GPSG to a CFG requiring at most exponential time, then reduction (in exponential time) to the polynomial-time CFG parsing complexity problem would show that the GPSG parsing complexity problem is in the $2^{p(n)}$ complexity class mentioned above, and therefore complete for this class.

I have also found some results that characterize the weak generative complexity of some formalisms related to theories of natural language syntax. The earliest of these concerns the transformational formalism; I showed in Rounds 1973b that transformational grammars, with a constraint on the transformational cycle disallowing a growth in the terminal string length, generate exactly the class $EXPTIME$. The same result holds for a variant of definite clause grammars (Pereira and Warren 1980), called CLFP (Rounds 1988). In this latter formalism, grammars are expressed using predicates over strings. Thus, the rule $S \rightarrow NP\ VP$ would be expressed as

$$S(x) \Leftrightarrow \exists yz(NP(y) \wedge VP(z) \wedge x = yz),$$

where x, y, and z range over strings. In addition, the range of the quantifiers is suitably bounded, to make the recognition problem decidable. A grammar is thus a logical formula, and formulas are satisfied by strings. Each formula defines a language; the theorem states that the class of languages defined by CLFP formulae is exactly $EXPTIME$. (There is another variant, called ILFP, which describes exactly polynomial time.)

It is tempting, given characterizations of this kind, to assume that the general formalism is somehow correct for the purpose of syntactic modeling. However, the LFP grammars are at this point not adequate for linguistic purposes, because they do not assign any structural information whatsoever to generated strings. In fact, the CLFP grammars are in a general sense very much like arbitrary Turing machines, which compute by continually passing over their tapes and rewriting previous tape contents. Most grammar formalisms do not require this "destructive rewriting" capability of Turing machines in order to implement parsing algorithms.

Most exponential-time-complete languages, and also the class of languages complete for polynomial space, seem to share the property that arbitrary Turing machine computations are required to test membership. This intuitive property distinguishes these problems from problems in NP, many of which require some kind of structure (a "witness") to be guessed nondeterministically and then verified to check that the witness does confirm membership of the string in the language. For example, a witness for membership of a string in a given context-free language is just a derivation tree whose yield is that string. The size of a derivation tree for a string need never be more than linear in the length of the string, and checking that its yield is the given string can be done efficiently. This leads us to speculate that if complexity considerations are to be used at all to evaluate the descriptive adequacy of grammar formalisms, then the weak generative capacity of a class of grammars should be within the class NP. Other processing reasons for requiring this property are that very often, efficient average-case algorithms exist even for NP-complete problems, and that algorithms exist for such problems that are not always correct, but are worst-case polynomial and work correctly on a large fraction of the interesting instances of a problem. Finally, there are random algorithms, which use coin tossing to choose steps, that solve interesting problems in NP correctly with high probability and that work in polynomial time. An example is Rabin's random algorithm (1979) for determining whether or not a number is prime. To my knowledge, such techniques have not been seriously tried in computational linguistics. It may well be, for example, that the parsing complexity problem for ID/LP grammars can be solved efficiently on the average. This would require *not* first translating the given grammar into phrase structure form, since the standard translation very often requires exponential time.

4 New Complexity Paradigms in Formal Linguistics

We have seen how standard complexity notions relate to methodological questions in computational linguistics. In this section I would like to speculate on some different notions and their possible relevance to linguistic modeling.

4.1 Succinctness

Linguistic theory and scientific methodology in general prefer short or simple explanations for empirical observations. The linguistic literature is replete with examples in which complicated combinations of rules have been rejected in favor of more general or simpler rules explaining observed patterns. A precise account of the notion of succinctness would be of help in selecting between competing theories or rules. I do not believe that any of the general accounts of this notion have immediate application to linguistic modeling, but the techniques that have been used may well be adaptable for linguistic purposes. Berwick (1985:sec. 5.1) discusses, for example, a potential adaptation of Chaitin-Kolmogorov-Solomonoff (CKS) complexity theory (Chaitin 1974; Kolmogorov 1968; Solomonoff 1964) to account for the complexity of language acquisition.

Two types of succinctness results seem to be potentially useful for our purpose. One is the CKS theory mentioned above, discovered independently by each of the three authors, which is most accessible in Chaitin's work (see Chaitin 1974, for example). The other is a collection of results that measure the size of specific automaton or grammar models necessary for various language recognition tasks. This work is exemplified in an early paper by Meyer and Fischer (1971), which considers trade-offs between pushdown automata, context-free grammars, and finite automata for context-free and regular language recognition. I will start by summarizing some of the basic CKS theory, using Chaitin's definitions. (These are also recalled by Berwick in his book.)

A *computer* is a computable partial function from strings to strings. (It helps to identify a computer with a Turing machine computing the function.) Let s be a string representing some kind of empirical data. We say that a string p is an *explanation* of the string s if $C(p) = s$. In this formulation, therefore, the string p is a kind of recipe for recreating the bits of s, and the computer C is viewed as a general-purpose calculating device that is not dependent on any theory-specific hypotheses. In practice, the string s may not be just one observation, but a concatenation of many observations, so that the explanation p is a program for reproducing these observations. In any case, we define the *complexity* of the string s with respect to C as

$$I_C(s) = \min_{C(p)=s} |p|,$$

where $|p|$ is the length of the string p. If no p makes $C(p) = s$, then $I_C(s) = \infty$.

Now we remove all dependence on the computer C. In essence, this is the process of passing to a universal Turing machine. We say that a computer U is *universal*, if for any computer C and any s, we have

$$I_U(s) \le I_C(s) + c,$$

where c is a constant depending only on the computer C. Universal computers are known to exist; they are essentially the universal Turing machines. We fix one such universal computer U. Then the *complexity* $I(s)$ of a string s is just $I_U(s)$. Thus, the complexity of a string s is essentially the length of its minimum verifiable description.

Chaitin uses this definition to explain the notion of randomness or patternlessness in a finite string. He defines a string to be *random* if its complexity is essentially its own length; no explanation or description of the string is shorter than listing the string itself. In fact, let c be the constant associated with the computer C such that $C(p) = p$. Then all strings of length n have complexity $\le n + c$. It is easy to show that a great majority of strings of length n have complexity greater than $n - c$. Imagine that we work with binary strings. There are exactly 2^{n-c} strings of length $n - c$, and all strings of length n, of which there are 2^n, have complexity less than $n + c$. The fraction of the strings of length n or less with complexity less than $n - c$, of the total number of length n strings, is thus 2^{-c}. If, say, $c = 10$ (a conservative estimate), then at least 99.9 percent of the strings of length n are random, with complexity greater than $n - 10$.

These definitions are very general and may not give us exactly the results we are looking for on the succinctness properties of real grammars. It turns out, for example, that in CKS's theory, the complexity of a string is not calculable; assuming that a formal system has at most k bits of axioms, it will be impossible to prove that a particular string has complexity greater than $k + c$ (Chaitin 1974, theorem 2). Since a calculation procedure can be viewed as a proof procedure (the history of the calculation being the proof that the output is correct), we see that only a small number of strings can have their complexity calculated by any one fixed procedure.

I believe, however, that the methods of this theory can be adapted to studying succinctness within linguistics. Berwick (1985: chap. 5ff.) has suggested exactly this approach in his proposals for a theory of acquisition complexity. He suggests that to adapt CKS's definitions to the language acquisition problem, one needs to imagine a program p, which is supplied with a sequence of inputs $\langle x_i \rangle$, each representing an instance of membership in some language L. Then the output $C(p, x_i)$ can be thought of as the ith approximation to a grammar for the given language, interpreted on computer C. One is then free to demand that p be as small as possible, or that p use the fewest number of inputs x in order to eventually fix a grammar G for the language L, or some combination of both of these requirements. Berwick gives no general results following from such assumptions, but there certainly should be some connection to CKS's results.

Another approach that seems worth trying is one that particularizes CKS's definitions to specific grammar classes. We can imagine that descriptions *are* just grammars, denoted by g instead of p. The complexity of a language L with respect to a class of grammars $\mathscr{G}$ will be the length of the shortest grammar $g \in \mathscr{G}$ such that $L(g) = L$. In this case, the computer C will be a particular way of enumerating $L(G)$. A way of connecting this idea to Berwick's would then be to consider the language L presented in stages, by the sequence $x_1 \ldots x_n$. Instead of requiring that $L(g) = L$, we could hypothesize a grammar g_n for each stage and require only that $\{x_1, \ldots, x_n\} \subseteq L(g_n)$.

Yet another variation on this definition, and one that may still give more specific information, is to consider the grammatical complexity of *finite languages*. This complexity is defined just as above, but the languages L are required to be finite. Then we may present a given language L as a sequence of its sublanguages $L(n)$, where the strings in $L(n)$ have length at most n. Suppose that in addition, we are dealing with a family of grammars $\mathscr{G}$ such that for grammar g in the family and any finite language L, it is possible to decide whether or not g generates L and also to effectively find *some* grammar in the family generating L, if there is one. Then the grammatical complexity of a finite language will be bounded by a calculable function, and if an infinite language L is decidable, then there will be a way to estimate its complexity by looking at its initial segments of length n.

Now most generative grammar definitions allow exhaustive enumeration of a finite set. Fix the vocabulary size, say to 2 for convenience. Then there will be a $2^{O(n)}$ upper bound for grammatical complexity measured this way for such a grammar class, because we can always list all 2^n strings if necessary. We should require more than this; the ability to deal with strings of length n should be acquired in time polynomial in n. This observation can be used to rule out certain grammar classes as being inadequate to generate even finite languages. Rounds, Manaster-Ramer, and Friedman (1987) show that the finite language $L_n = \{xx : |x| = n\}$ cannot be generated by a context-free grammar G_n with bounded production length unless it has exponentially (in n) many nonterminal symbols, and therefore the size of G_n must be exponential.

For the problem of language learnability, we need to model something other than grammatical complexity, as Berwick has noted in his discussions of size complexity. A possible attack on this problem is described next.

4.2 Dynamic Languages and Learnability

We have seen that studying finite languages can lead to useful criteria of grammatical adequacy. In this section I propose that, in fact, we can view a formal language as not just an infinite set of strings, but as an infinite family of finite sets of strings. This idea, proposed by Rounds, Manaster-Ramer, and Friedman (1987) and also considered by Savitch (1987), corresponds to a notion of Gurevich (1988), who is interested in modeling sequential computers not as infinite-capacity machines but as families of finite-capacity machines. Each element of the family corresponds to putting a resource bound on the memory of an unbounded machine. We therefore define a *dynamic language* to be a nondecreasing sequence $L(m)$ of finite languages. We intend that such a family represent a sort of ideal performance model, in that the language $L(m)$ is the set of sentences that are possible to acquire by stage m in some time sequence. (This definition is very tentative, and it may be that some variation is more workable.) One way to get such a family, of course, is to take the length n strings of an infinite language, but other possibilities suggest themselves—for example, we could model the process of lexical change by increasing the terminal vocabulary at each stage.

Now, I wish to combine this idea with a definition of grammar learnability, based on complexity theory. To define learnability, I adapt a notion due to Valiant (1984). In this paper, Valiant proposes that learning machines consist of a *learning protocol* and a *deduction procedure*. The learning protocol specifies the manner in which information is obtained from external sources, and the deduction procedure is a way of synthesizing the cognitive mechanism to be learned—in our case, a grammar. There are two key aspects of Valiant's model. One is that the deduction procedure works in polynomial time so that learning is feasible. The second is that the deduction procedure makes use of probabilistic techniques. A grammar synthesized by the procedure is said to be correct if it never generates sentences not generated by the target grammar; it may *not* generate some of the sentences that *are* generated by the target grammar, provided this happens on a vanishingly small fraction of the probability space of positive examples. Now the deduction procedure itself may not actually synthesize a correct grammar, but again it will do so with high likelihood. The reason that the deduction procedure may fail is that it calls on a probabilistic source of positive examples, and the sequence of calls may (with low probability) cause the deduction procedure to synthesize an unacceptable grammar. The input space of positive examples is therefore required to have a probability distribution on it, say $D(w)$, such that if a string w is returned on a call to an EXAMPLES procedure, then this happens with probability $D(w)$. Here is where the concept of a finite language is important; we can consider just a finite language $L(n)$ and hypothesize a discrete, finite probability distribution on this language. The deduction procedure should work as described here, no matter what this distribution actually is. Valiant shows that certain classes of Boolean functions are learnable under these criteria, and he does not consider grammar learnability. In making an adaptation of his model, I do not show that any particular classes of grammars of languages are learnable, but I do show that the question of whether or not a particular grammar-learning algorithm works correctly is now well posed and capable of a theoretical answer. Particular results will have to await further research.

Let us proceed with a few definitions. We say that a class of grammars $\mathscr{G}$ is *learnable* if there is an algorithm A depending on an input parameter n, and using a standard learning protocol (to be described below), such that:

1. A runs in time polynomial in n.
2. For all grammars g such that $L(g)$ contains at most length n strings, and all probability distributions D on $L(g)$, the algorithm will produce, with probability at least $1 - 1/n$, a grammar $h \in \mathscr{G}$ such that (1) $L(h) \subseteq L(g)$, and (2) the sum of the values $D(w)$, over $w \in L(g) - L(h)$, is at most $1/n$.

Now we must describe the learning protocol. The algorithm A is supplied initially with a value of n. In addition to ordinary computational steps, the algorithm may call either of the two following procedures:

1. A procedure EXAMPLES, with no arguments, which will return a string $w \in L(g)$, with probability $D(w)$.
2. A procedure ORACLE(w), which will return "yes" or "no" depending on whether or not $w \in L(g)$.

Each run of the algorithm A on a particular n will query these two procedures, which will return answers depending on just one grammar $g \in \mathscr{G}$, and with a specific distribution D. The oracles thus simulate a teacher of the grammar g, and the run of the algorithm a learning session.

Now we may say what it means for a class of dynamic languages to be learnable via a particular class of grammars. First let us rephrase the learnability definitions somewhat. If $g \in \mathscr{G}$ is a grammar generating a finite language $L(g)$, and A is an algorithm invoking the above protocol, then we say that A can learn g if there is a polynomial $p(n)$, not depending on g, such that for any probability distribution D on $L(g)$, the algorithm will produce, with probability at least $1 - 1/n$, a grammar $h \in \mathscr{G}$ such that $L(h) \subseteq L(g)$; the sum of the values $D(w)$, over $w \in L(g) - L(h)$, is at most $1/n$; and further, A runs in time $p(n)$, where n is the length of the longest string in $L(g)$. Now let $\mathscr{L}$ be a class of dynamic languages and $L = \langle L(m) \rangle$ be a dynamic language in $\mathscr{L}$. Then $\mathscr{L}$ is *learnable via* $\mathscr{G}$ if there is an algorithm

A depending only on $\mathcal{L}$ and $\mathcal{G}$ such that for any $L \in \mathcal{L}$, and any *m*, there is a grammar $g \in \mathcal{G}$ such that $L(g) = L(m)$ and *A* can learn *g*.

An obvious question: Can the class of context-free grammars be learned under this definition? I do not wish at this point to consider such questions, or to compare the definitions with others in the literature; this would turn the chapter into a work on learnability theory. (For a survey of relevant results, see Savitch 1987.) In fact, the definition may still be unworkable because its conditions are unrealistic or even unsatisfiable. What I hope to show by rephrasing Valiant's work is that productive application of techniques from complexity theory is possible, by adapting them to linguistic purposes. Once a model has been carefully proposed, we can study its consequences with some degree of rigor, and we may find ourselves asking different questions than we had thought to ask before. I hope also that putting forth this definition, even with no results following from it, will encourage readers to modify the definition to their own taste and to ask their own questions.

Notes

1. The term *O-notation* usually includes Ω- and Θ-notations, by convention.
2. Berwick does not argue, however, that complexity is a valid criterion by which to judge the empirical adequacy of a linguistic theory.
3. The question of whether or not *any* transformation must output an exponentially bigger CFG has been answered affirmatively; see Moshier and Rounds 1987.

References

Aho, A. V. 1968. Indexed grammars: An extension of the context-free grammars. *Journal of the ACM* 15:641–671.

Barton, G. E., Jr. 1985. The computational difficulty of ID/LP parsing. In *Proc. 23rd Ann. Meeting of ACL*, 76–81.

Barton, G. E., Jr. 1986. Computational complexity of two-level morphology. In *Proc. 24th Ann. Meeting of ACL*, 53–59.

Barton, G. E., Jr., R. C. Berwick, and E. S. Ristad. 1987. *Computational complexity and natural language*. MIT Press, Cambridge, Mass.

Berwick, R. 1985. *The acquisition of syntactic knowledge*. MIT Press, Cambridge, Mass.

Berwick, R., and A. Weinberg. 1984. *The grammatical basis of linguistic performance*. MIT Press, Cambridge, Mass.

Chaitin, G. J. 1974. Information-theoretic computational complexity. *IEEE Trans. on Information Theory* IT-20:10–15.

de Champeaux, D. 1986. About the Paterson-Wegman linear unification algorithm. *J. Comput. Sys. Sci.* 32:79–90.

Chomsky, N. 1965. *Aspects of the theory of syntax*. MIT Press, Cambridge, Mass.

Cook, S. A. 1971. The complexity of theorem-proving procedures. In *Proc. 3rd ACM Symp. on Theory of Computing*, 151–158.

Earley, J. 1970. An efficient context-free parsing algorithm. *Comm. ACM* 13:94–102.

Gazdar, G. 1985. Applicability of indexed grammars to natural languages. Technical report CSLI-85-34, Center for the Study of Language and Information, Stanford University.

Gazdar, G., E. Klein, G. Pullum, and I. Sag. 1985. *Generalized Phrase Structure Grammar.* Harvard University Press, Cambridge, Mass.

Gurevich, Y. 1988. Logic and the challenge of computer science. In E. Boerger (ed.) *Trends in theoretical computer science.* Computer Science Press, Rockville, Md.

Hintikka, J. K. K. 1977. Quantifiers in natural language: Some logical problems. *Linguistics and Philosophy* 2:153–172.

Hopcroft, J., and J. Ullman. 1979. *Introduction to automata theory, languages, and computation.* Addison-Wesley, Reading, Mass.

Kaplan, R., and J. Bresnan. 1982. Lexical-Functional Grammar: A formal system for grammatical representation. In J. Bresnan (ed.) *The mental representation of grammatical relations.* MIT Press, Cambridge, Mass.

Karp, R. M. 1972. Reducibility among combinatorial problems. In R. E. Miller and J. W. Thatcher (eds.) *Complexity of computer computations.* Plenum, New York.

Knuth, D. E. 1973. *The art of computer programming*, vols. 1–3. Addison-Wesley, Reading, Mass.

Kolmogorov, A. N. 1968. The logical basis for information theory and probability theory. *IEEE Trans. on Information Theory* IT-14:662–664.

Marcus, M. 1980. *A theory of syntactic recognition for natural language.* MIT Press, Cambridge, Mass.

Meyer, A., and M. Fischer. 1971. Economy of description by automata, grammars, and formal systems. In *Proc. 12th Ann. IEEE Symp. on Switching and Automata Theory,* 188–191.

Moshier, M. D., and W. Rounds. 1987. On the succinctness properties of unordered context-free grammars. In *Proc. 25th Ann. Meeting of ACL,* 112–116.

Paterson, M., and M. Wegman. 1978. Linear unification. *J. Comput. Sys. Sci.* 16:158–167.

Pereira, F. C. N., and D. Warren. 1980. Definite clause grammars for language analysis: A survey of the formalism and a comparison with augmented transition networks. *Artificial Intelligence* 13:231–278.

Perlmutter, D. M. 1980. Relational Grammar. In E. A. Moravcsik and J. R. Wirth (eds.) *Syntax and semantics 13: Current approaches to syntax.* Academic Press, New York.

Perrault, C. R. 1984. On the mathematical properties of linguistic theories. *Computational Linguistics* 10(3, 4):165–176.

Peters, S., and R. Ritchie. 1973. On the generative power of transformational grammars. *Information Sciences* 6:49–84.

Pinker, S. 1979. Formal models of language learning. *Cognition* 7:217–283.

Rabin, M. O. 1979. Probabilistic algorithms. In J. Traub (ed.) *Algorithms and complexity: New directions and recent results.* Academic Press, New York.

Ristad, E. S. 1986a. Computational complexity of current GPSG theory. In *Proc. 24th Ann. Meeting of ACL,* 30–39.

Ristad, E. S. 1986b. Defining natural language grammars in GPSG. In *Proc. 24th Ann. Meeting of ACL,* 40–44.

Robinson, J. A. 1965. A machine-oriented logic based on the resolution principle. *Journal of the ACM* 12(1):23–41.

Rounds, W. 1973a. Complexity of recognition in intermediate-level languages. In *Proc. 14th Ann. IEEE Symp. on Switching and Automata Theory,* 145–158.

Rounds, W. 1973b. A grammatical characterization of the exponential-time languages. In *Proc. 11th Ann. IEEE Symp. on Foundations of Computer Science,* 135–143.

Rounds, W. 1988. LFP: A logic for linguistic descriptions and an analysis of its complexity. *Computational Linguistics* 14.4:1–9.

Rounds, W., A. Manaster-Ramer, and J. Friedman. 1987. Finding formal languages a home in natural language theory. In A. Manaster-Ramer (ed.) *Mathematics of language*. John Benjamins, Amsterdam.

Savitch, W. 1987. Theories of language learnability. In A. Manaster-Ramer (ed.) *Mathematics of language*. John Benjamins, Amsterdam.

Shieber, S. M. 1986. *Introduction to unification-based approaches to grammar*. University of Chicago Press, Chicago.

Solomonoff, R. 1964. A formal theory of inductive inference. *Infor. Control* 7:224–254.

Stockmeyer, L., and A. Chandra. 1978. Provably difficult combinatorial games. IBM Research Report RC-6957, T. J. Watson Res. Ctr., Yorktown Heights, N.Y.

Strassen, V. 1986. The asymptotic spectrum of tensors and the exponent of matrix multiplication. In *Proc. 27th Ann. IEEE Symp. on Foundations of Computer Science*, 49–54.

Valiant, L. 1975. General context-free recognition in less than cubic time. *J. Computer. Sys. Sci.* 10:308–315.

Valiant, L. 1984. A theory of the learnable. In *Proc. 16th Ann. ACM Symp. on Theory of Computation*, 436–445.

Winograd, T. 1983. *Language as a cognitive process, vol. 1: Syntax*. Addison-Wesley, Reading, Mass.

Chapter 2

The Convergence of Mildly Context-Sensitive Grammar Formalisms

Aravind K. Joshi, K. Vijay-Shanker, and David Weir

1 Introduction

Since the late 1970s there has been vigorous activity in constructing highly constrained grammatical systems by eliminating the transformational component either totally or partially. This was caused by increasing recognition that the entire range of dependencies that transformational grammars in their various incarnations have tried to account for can be captured satisfactorily by classes of grammars that are *nontransformational* and at the same time highly constrained in terms of the classes of grammars and languages they define. Peters and Ritchie (1972) showed that context-sensitive grammars (CSGs)—if used for analysis (and not for generation), thus providing more descriptive power than context-free grammars (CFGs) —have the same weak generative capacity as CFGs. This result was generalized by Joshi and Levy (1977) to Boolean combinations of contextual predicates and domination predicates.

In the early 1980s Gazdar (1982) proposed a grammatical formalism (which later became the Generalized Phrase Structure Grammar (GPSG) formalism; see Gazdar et al. 1985) whose weak generative capacity is the same as that of the CFGs, but which is adequate to describe various syntactic phenomena previously described in transformational terms. Gazdar was careful to note that his results did not mean that syntactic phenomena that required formal power beyond CFG did not exist. Rather, his claim was that, with respect to the range of phenomena known at that time, CFGs seemed to be quite adequate. Later, some clear examples of natural language phenomena were discovered that required formal power beyond CFG (see, for example, Shieber 1985 and Culy 1985, for an argument from

This chapter is a revised version of a paper presented by the first author at the conference on "The Processing of Linguistic Structure" sponsored by the System Development Foundation held at Santa Cruz, CA, January 1987. We want to thank Jean Gallier, Tony Kroch, Mitch Marcus, Remo Pareschi, Yves Schabes, Mark Steedman, Ramesh Subrahmanyam, and Bonnie Webber for valuable discussion about several aspects of this chapter. This work was partially supported by NSF grant IRI84-10413 A02, US Army grant DAA6-29-84K-0061, DARPA grant N0014-85-K0018, and Advanced Technology Center (PA) grant #309.

weak generative capacity, and Bresnan et al. 1982, for an argument from strong generative capacity). Hence, the question of how much power beyond CFG is necessary to describe these phenomena became important.

Pollard (1984) proposed an extension of CFG, called head grammars (HGs), which introduced some wrapping operations beyond the concatenation operation in CFG. Roach (1987) investigated some formal properties of HGs. HGs, like CFGs, are string-generating systems.

Joshi, Levy, and Takahashi (1975) introduced a grammatical formalism called tree-adjoining grammars (TAGs), which are tree-generating systems, and investigated some of their formal properties. Joshi (1985) showed how TAGs factor recursion and the domain of dependencies in a novel way, leading to "localization" of dependencies, their long-distance behavior following from the operation of composition, called "adjunction." TAGs have more power than CFGs, and this extra power is a corollary of factorization of recursion and the domain of dependencies. This extra power appeared to be adequate for the various phenomena requiring more formal power than CFG. The linguistic significance of TAGs has been discussed by Joshi (1985), Kroch and Joshi (1985, 1986), Kroch (1986), and Kroch and Santorini (to appear). Based on the formal properties of TAGs, Joshi (1985) proposed that the class of grammars that is necessary for describing natural languages might be characterized as the class of *mildly context-sensitive grammars* (MCSG; MCSL for the corresponding languages) possessing at least the following properties: (1) context-free languages (CFLs) are properly contained in MCSL; (2) languages in MCSL can be parsed in polynomial time; (3) MCSGs capture only certain kinds of dependencies, such as nested dependencies and certain limited kinds of crossing dependencies (for example, in subordinate clause constructions in Dutch or some variations of them, but perhaps not in the so-called MIX (or Bach) language, which consists of equal numbers of a's, b's, and c's in any order); and (4) languages in MCSL have the constant growth property. This last property means that if the strings of a language are arranged in increasing order of length, then two consecutive lengths do not differ by arbitrarily large amounts. In fact, any given length can be described as a linear combination of a finite set of fixed lengths. This property is slightly weaker than the property of semilinearity. It is intended to be an approximate characterization of the linguistic intuition that sentences of a natural language are built from a finite set of clauses of bounded structure using certain simple linear operations. The characterization of this intuition by the constant growth property is approximate because it refers to the growth of strings and not to the growth of structures.

It should be noted that these properties do not precisely define MCSG but rather give only a rough characterization, because the properties are only necessary conditions, and because some of the properties are properties of structural descriptions rather than of the languages and therefore are difficult to characterize precisely. This characterization of MCSG, obviously motivated by the formal properties of TAGs, would have remained only a passing remark were it not for some subsequent developments.

In response to a talk by Geoffrey Pullum at COLING 84, Joshi pointed out that all the known formal properties of HGs appeared to be exactly the same as those of TAGs. Later it was shown that with a slight modification of HGs (which is necessary because the wrapping operations are undefined for null strings), HGs are equivalent to TAGs (Vijay-Shanker, Weir, and Joshi 1986; Weir, Vijay-Shanker, and Joshi 1986).

Since then, two other formalisms have also been shown to be equivalent to TAGs. These are linear indexed grammars (LIGs) (Gazdar 1985) and combinatorial categorial grammars (CCGs) (as developed in Steedman 1987, 1990). Thus, four quite different formalisms have been shown to be equivalent and thus belong to the class of MCSGs. These formalisms are different from each other in the sense that the formal objects and operations they employ are quite distinct and in the sense that they are motivated by attempts to capture different aspects of language structure. Each of these formalisms has a domain of locality that is larger than that specifiable in a CFG. By a domain of locality we mean the elementary structures of a formalism over which dependencies such as agreement, subcategorization, and filler-gap relations can be specified. However, it is not the case that each one of these formalisms extends the domain of locality to the same extent. TAGs extend the domain of locality far enough that recursion is factored away from the domain of dependencies.

When two formalisms based on apparently completely different ideas turn out to be equivalent, there is a possibility that we are getting a handle on some fundamental properties of the objects that these formalisms were designed to describe. When more than two distinct formalisms turn out to be equivalent, the possibility is even greater. In fact, a deeper understanding of the relationships between these formalisms is obtained if we look at the derivation structures (related to structural descriptions) provided by each formalism. A first attempt to capture the closeness of some of these formalisms at the level of derivation structures resulted in the linear context-free rewriting systems (LCFRSs) described in section 6.

The rest of the chapter is organized as follows. In section 2 we present an introduction to TAGs, including some simple examples. We discuss TAGs in more detail than the other formalisms because the theory of TAGs has played a key role in our investigations of the relationships between different grammatical formalisms. In fact, most of the equivalences described in this chapter have been established via TAGs. In section

2 we also describe an extension of TAGs, called multicomponent TAGs (MCTAGs), first discussed by Joshi, Levy, and Takahashi (1975) and later defined precisely by Weir (1988). MCTAGs also belong to the class of MCSGs and are in fact equivalent to LCFRSs.

In section 3 we briefly describe HGs and show their equivalence to TAGs. In section 4 we show the equivalence of LIGs to TAGs, and in section 5 the equivalence of CCGs to LIGs and thereby to TAGs and HGs. In section 6 we present LCFRSs.

In section 7 we briefly present feature-structure-based TAGs (FTAGs), where adjunction becomes function application and unification. FTAGs, in general, are unconstrained; however, if the feature structures associated with each node in an elementary tree are bounded, then this restricted FTAG (RFTAG) is equivalent to TAG. This restriction on feature structures is similar to that in GPSG. However, since TAGs have an extended domain of locality, RFTAGs (equivalent to TAGs) are more powerful than GPSGs (equivalent to CFGs).

In section 8 we consider a variant of TAGs, the lexicalized TAGs (LTAGs). Although adjunction can simulate substitution, by adding the operation of substitution explicitly, we obtain LTAGs. Such a lexicalization is implicit in TAGs in the sense that all the elementary trees need not be explicitly stated. However, the framework of LTAGs brings this out explicitly. LTAGs are equivalent to TAGs. The relationship between TAGs and CCGs also becomes clear in the framework of LTAGs.

Finally, in section 9 we consider a generalization of TAGs, called TAG(LD/LP), which decouples (local) domination from linear precedence and allows a treatment of complex word-order patterns including those that exhibit long-distance behavior similar to the filler-gap dependencies, but different in the sense that "movement" is not to a grammatically defined position. The languages of TAGs are obviously contained in TAGs(LD/LP). It is not known yet whether the containment is proper.

Figure 2.1 summarizes all these relationships. The nodes are labeled by the grammar formalisms. The containments shown are, of course, with respect to the corresponding languages. Two formalisms outside of MCSG are also shown in the figure.

We present our results here informally, giving examples to illustrate the ideas in the proofs. We leave more detailed proofs with full technical details to future work.

2   Tree-Adjoining Grammar Formalism

A *tree-adjoining grammar* (*TAG*) $G = (I, A)$, where I and A are finite sets of *elementary trees*. The trees in I will be called the *initial trees* and the trees in A, the auxiliary trees. A tree α is an initial tree if it is of the form in (1):

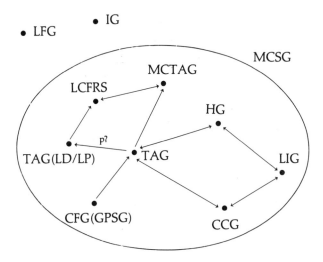

[The containments are with respect to the languages.]

CCG: Combinatory categorial grammars
CFG(GPSG): Context-free grammars (generalized phrase structure grammars)
HG: Head grammars
IG: Indexed grammars
LCFRS: Linear context-free rewriting systems
LFG: Lexical-functional grammars
LIG: Linear indexed grammars
MCTAG: Multicomponent TAGs
TAG: Tree-adjoining grammars
TAG(LD/LP): TAGs (local domination/linear precedence)

Figure 2.1
Mildly context-sensitive grammar formalisms (MCSG)

(1) α =   S

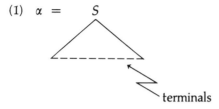

terminals

That is, the root node of α is labeled S and the frontier nodes are all terminals. A tree β is an auxiliary tree if it is of the form in (2):

(2)   β =   X

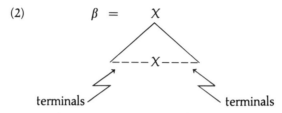

terminals   terminals

That is, the root node of β is labeled X, where X is a nonterminal, and the frontier nodes are all terminals except one, which is also labeled X. The frontier node labeled X will be called the *foot node* of β. The internal nodes are nonterminals. The initial and the auxiliary trees are not constrained in any other manner. The idea, however, is that both the initial and the auxiliary trees will be *minimal* in some sense. An initial tree will correspond to a minimal sentential tree (that is, without recursing on any nonterminal), and an auxiliary tree, with root and foot node labeled X, will correspond to a minimal recursive structure that must be brought into the derivation, if one recurses on X.

We will now define a composition operation called *adjunction*, which composes an auxiliary tree β with a tree γ. Let γ be a tree containing a node n bearing the label X and let β be an auxiliary tree whose root node is also labeled X. (Note that β must have, by definition, one (and only one) frontier node labeled X.) Then the adjunction of β to γ at node n will be the tree γ' that results when the following operations are carried out:

1. The subtree of γ dominated by n, call it t, is excised.
2. The auxiliary tree β is attached at n and its root node is identified with n.
3. The subtree t is attached to the foot node of β and the root node n of t is identified with the foot node of β.

Figure 2.2 illustrates this operation.

The intuition underlying the adjunction operation is a simple one, but the operation is distinct from other operations on trees that have been discussed in the literature. In particular, we want to emphasize that adjunction is not a substitution operation in the usual sense.

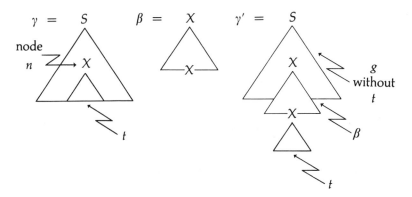

Figure 2.2
Adjunction

Adjunction can, however, simulate substitution. A variant of TAG (called lexicalized TAG) that explicitly uses both adjunction and substitution is discussed in section 8. Lexicalized TAGs are equivalent to TAGs. For the rest of the chapter we will only consider adjunction as defined above.

The definition of adjunction allows more complex constraints to be placed on adjoining. Associated with each node is a *selective adjunction (SA)* constraint specifying the subset of auxiliary trees that can be adjoined at this node. Trees can be included in the SA constraint associated with a particular node only if their root and foot are labeled with the same nonterminal that labels the node. A mechanism is provided for ensuring that adjunction is performed at a node. This is done by associating an *obligatory adjunction (OA)* constraint with that node.

We should note that the SA and OA constraints are more than mere notational convenience, since they increase the generative power of the formalism. If the SA constraint specifies an empty subset of trees, then adjunction cannot be performed at this node—we call this constraint the *null adjunction (NA)* constraint.

(In section 7 we will describe a feature-structure-based TAG (FTAG). In this framework, adjunction becomes function application and unification, and the constraints described above are implicit in the feature structures and the success or failure of unification during composition. A restricted version of FTAG, RFTAG, also described in section 7, is equivalent to TAG. For the rest of the chapter we will consider the constraints as described above.)

Let us now define two auxiliary notions, the tree set of a TAG and the string language of a TAG. Suppose $G = (I, A)$ is a TAG with a finite set of initial trees, a finite set of auxiliary trees, and the adjunction operation, as above. Then we define the *tree set* of a TAG G, $T(G)$, to be the set of all trees derived in G starting from initial trees in I. We further define the *string language* (or *language*) of G to be the set of all terminal strings of the trees in $T(G)$. The relationship between TAGs, CFGs, and the corresponding string languages can then be summarized in the following theorems (Joshi, Levy, and Takahashi 1975; Joshi 1985):

1. For every CFG, G', there is a TAG, G, which is both weakly and strongly equivalent to G'. In other words, $L(G) = L(G')$ and $T(G) = T(G')$.

2. There exists a nonempty set of TAGs G_1 such that for every $G \in G_1$, $L(G)$ is context free but there is no CFG G' such that $T(G') = T(G)$. That is, TAGs are capable of providing structural descriptions for context-free languages that are not obtainable by a CFG.

3. There exists a nonempty set of TAGs G_2 such that for every $G \in G_2$, $L(G)$ is strictly context sensitive. That is, there is no CFG G' such that $L(G) = L(G')$ (or, in other words, TAGs are strictly more powerful than CFGs).

4. There exist context-sensitive languages for which there are no equivalent TAGs. That is, TAGs are properly contained in context-sensitive languages.

5. TAGs are semilinear and hence have the constant growth property.

6. TAGs can capture only certain limited kinds of crossed dependencies. This follows from the nature of the automaton that corresponds to a TAG, called an *embedded pushdown automaton (EPDA)*, which is a generalization of the *pushdown automaton (PDA)*.

7. TAGs can be parsed in polynomial time—in fact, with a time based Kn^6, where n is the length of the string and K is a constant depending on the grammar.

2.1 Some Examples of Formal Languages

EXAMPLE 1   Let $G = (I, A)$ be a TAG with local constraints where

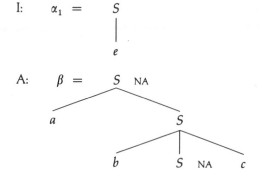

There are no constraints in α_1. In β no auxiliary trees can be adjoined at either the root node or the foot node; the center S node has no constraints. Starting with α_1 and adjoining β to α_1 at the root node, we obtain

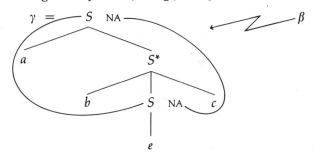

Adjoining β to the center S node (the only node at which adjunction can occur), we have

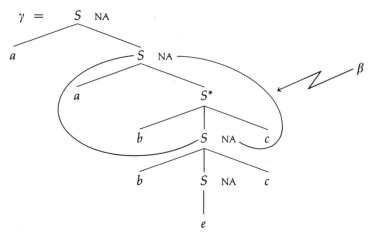

It is easy to see that G generates the string language

$L = \{a^n b^n e c^n | n \geq 0\}$.

EXAMPLE 2   Let G' be a TAG similar to G in example 1, except that in G' there are no constraints in β. G' generates

$L = \{wec^n | n \geq 0,\ \#a\text{'s in } w = \#b\text{'s in } w = n,$
$\qquad\qquad \text{and for any proper initial string } u$
$\qquad\qquad \text{of } w,\ \#a\text{'s in } u \geq \#b\text{'s in } u\}$.

This language is closely related to the context-sensitive language discussed by Higginbotham (1984), which can also be shown to be a TAG language.

EXAMPLE 3   Let $G = (I, A)$ be a TAG with local constraints, where

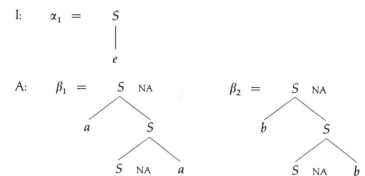

I: $\alpha_1 =$ S
                      |
                      e

A: $\beta_1 =$ ... $\beta_2 =$ ...

G generates the language

$$L = \{wew \mid w \in \{a, b\}^*\}.$$

EXAMPLE 4   Let G' be a TAG that is the same as G in example 3 but without any local constraints. The corresponding language is

$$L = \{wew' \mid w, w' \in \{a, b\}^*, |w| = |w'|$$
$$\#a\text{'s in } w = \#a\text{'s in } w', \#b\text{'s}$$
$$\text{in } w = \#b\text{'s in } w' = n\}.$$

This language is related to the Swiss-German example discussed by Shieber (1985).

EXAMPLE 5   Let $G = (I, A)$ be a TAG with local constraints, where

I: $\alpha_1 =$ S
                      |
                      e

A: $\beta =$ S   NA
              / | \
             a   S   d
                 / | \
                b S NA c

G generates

$$L = \{a^n b^n e c^n d^n \mid n \geq 1\}.$$

Note that it can be shown that languages

$$L^1 = \{a^n b^n c^n d^n e^n \mid n \geq 1\}$$

and

$$L^2 = \{www \mid w \in \{a, b\}^*\}$$

cannot be generated by TAGs either with or without local constraints (Joshi 1985). Other languages such as $L' = \{a^{n^2} \mid n \geq 1\}$ also cannot be generated by TAGs. This is because the strings of a TAG have the constant growth property.

2.2 Derivation in a TAG

We will not describe formally the notion of derivation in a TAG; however, the informal discussion to follow will make the notion of derivation in TAG precise enough for our purpose. Adjunction is an operation defined on an elementary tree, say γ, an auxiliary tree, say β, and a node (that is, an address) in γ, say n. Thus, every instance of adjunction is of the form "β is adjoined to γ at n," and this adjunction is always and only subject to the local constraints associated with n. Although we very often speak of adjoining a tree to a node in a complex structure, we do so only for convenience. Strictly speaking, adjunction is always at a node in an elementary tree; therefore, it is more precise to talk about adjoining at an address in an elementary tree. More than one auxiliary tree can be adjoined to an elementary tree as long as each tree is adjoined at a distinct node. After these auxiliary trees are adjoined to the elementary tree, only nodes in the auxiliary trees are available for further adjunction. This precision in the definition of adjunction will be necessary when we define multi-component adjunction in section 2.3.

Now suppose that α is an initial tree and that β_1, β_2, ... are auxiliary trees in a TAG, G. Then the derivation structure corresponding to the generation of a particular string in $L(G)$ might look as follows:

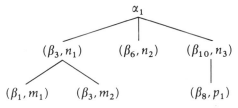

α_1 is an initial tree. β_3, β_6, and β_{10} are adjoined at nodes n_1, n_2, and n_3 respectively in α_1, where n_1, n_2, and n_3 are all distinct nodes. β_1 and β_3 are adjoined to β_3 at nodes m_1 and m_2 respectively. Again, m_1 and m_2 are distinct. β_6 has no further adjunctions, but β_8 is adjoined to β_{10} at node p_1. Note that the derivation structure implicitly characterizes the "surface" tree that is generated by it. (See section 7 for the relationship of TAG and the unification formalism.) In this way the derivation structure can be seen as the basic formal object constructed in the course of deriving a sentence.

Associated with it will be two mappings, one to a surface syntactic tree and the other to a semantic interpretation, as below. (We are not concerned with semantic interpretation in this chapter.)

surface tree ← derivation structure → semantic interpretation

In a CFG the derivation structure is the same as the surface structure. In a TAG this is not the case. Several of the formalisms that we have shown to be equivalent are comparable at the level of the derivation structures. Based on this observation, in section 6 we discuss a framework called the linear context-free rewriting system (LCFRS), which captures the commonality at the level of derivation structures.

2.3 Multicomponent TAGs

In Joshi, Levy, and Takahashi 1975 a version of the adjunction operation is introduced under which, instead of a single auxiliary tree, a set of such trees is adjoined to a given elementary tree. This extension of TAG is known as *multicomponent TAG (MCTAG)*. We define the adjunction of such a set as the simultaneous adjunction of each of its component trees to a distinct node (address) in an elementary tree. This adjunction can, of course, take place only if the local constraints associated with each affected node of the elementary tree are satisfied. Consider, for example, the following grammar $G = (I, A)$:

β_1 is an auxiliary set consisting of the two trees β_{11} and β_{12}. Here is a sample derivation in G:

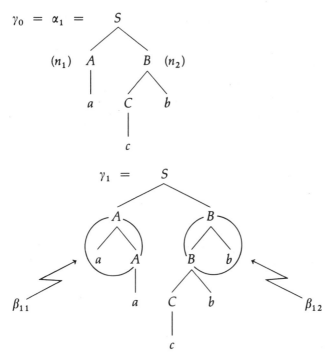

γ_1, it should be clear, is obtained by adjunction of the components β_{11} and β_{12} of the auxiliary set β_1 to γ_0 at the nodes n_1 and n_2 respectively. In the current example, the set β_1 has two component trees and β_2 has only one component. If every auxiliary tree set of a TAG has only one component, we have a TAG as defined earlier. It can be shown that the number of components in the auxiliary sets does not make any difference to the generative capacity; in other words, both the weak and strong (with respect to tree sets generated and not, of course, with respect to the derivation structures) generative capacities of MCTAGs are the same as those for TAGs where each auxiliary set has exactly one component. On the other hand, derived auxiliary sets can be defined by adjoining an auxiliary set, say β_1, to another auxiliary set, say β_2, as follows. Each component of β_1 is adjoined to one (and exactly one) component of β_2, and all adjunctions are at distinct nodes. Note that since it is not required that each component of β_1 adjoin to the same component of β_2, one component may adjoin to one component and another component to a different component of β_2; that is, adjunctions of components are not to the same component (elementary tree) of β_1, but they are all adjunctions to the *same auxiliary set*. Thus, *locality* of adjunction can be defined in two ways: (1) by requiring that all components of an auxiliary set adjoin to the *same elementary tree*, (2) by requiring that all components of an auxiliary set adjoin to the *same auxiliary*

set, not necessarily to the same elementary tree. The first type of locality does not add to the generative capacity of the MCTAG. The second type of locality does add to the weak generative capacity of the MCTAG; however, the resulting class of languages still falls within the class of "mildly context-sensitive" languages. With the second type of locality an MCTAG can be defined for the language $L' = \{a^n b^n | n \geq 1\}$ such that the a's all hang from one path from the root node S and the b's all hang from another path from the root node. Such a structural description cannot be provided by TAGs, where each auxiliary set has exactly one component (see also Joshi 1985). For further details of MCTAGs, see Weir 1988. Weir (1988) has also shown that MCTAGs (with the second definition of locality) are equivalent to LCFRSs (see section 6).

2.4 *Some Linguistic Examples*

EXAMPLE 6   Starting with the initial tree $\gamma_1 = \alpha_1$ and then adjoining β_6 at the indicated node (marked by *) in α_1, we obtain γ_2.

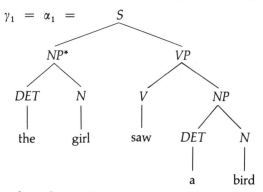

the girl saw a bird

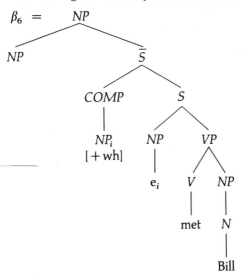

$$\beta_6 =$$

NP who met Bill

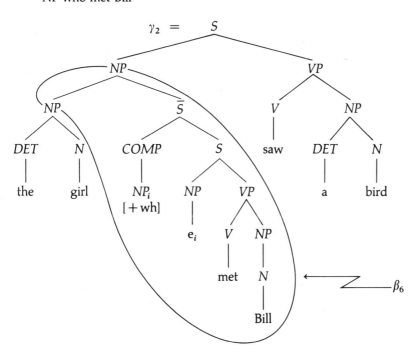

$$\gamma_2 =$$

The girl who met Bill saw a bird.

EXAMPLE 7   Starting with the initial tree $\gamma_1 = \alpha_6$ and adjoining β_1 at the indicated node in α_6, we obtain γ_2.

$\gamma_1 = \alpha_6 =$

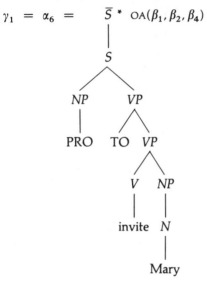

PRO to invite Mary

$\beta_1 =$

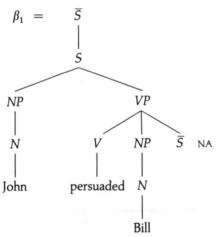

John persuaded Bill $\overline{S}$

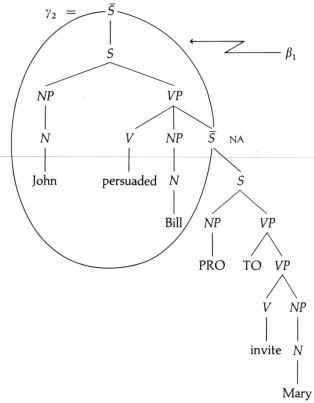

John persuaded Bill PRO to invite Mary.

Since the initial tree α_6 is not a root sentence, it must undergo an adjunction at its root node, for example, by the auxiliary tree β_1 as shown above. Thus, for α_6 we have specified a local constraint OA(β_1, β_2, β_4) for the root node, indicating that α_6 must undergo an adjunction at the root node by an auxiliary tree β_1.

EXAMPLE 8   Starting with the initial tree $\gamma_1 = \alpha_8$ and adjoining β_4 to α_8 at the indicated node in α_8, we obtain γ_2.

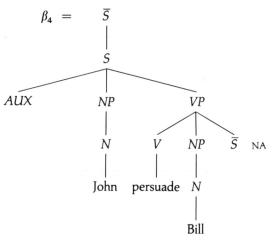

who PRO to invite

did John persuade Bill $\bar{S}$

$\gamma_2 =$

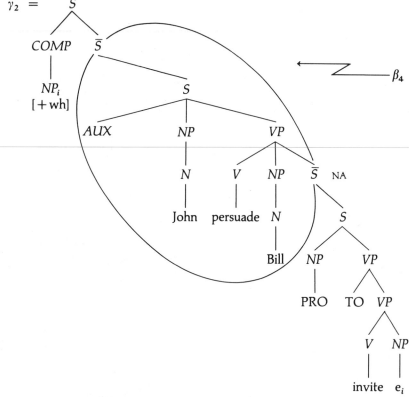

Who did John persuade Bill PRO to invite?

Note that the link in γ_1 is *preserved* in γ_2; it is *stretched*, resulting in a so-called unbounded dependency. Also note that, as in previous examples, α_8 is an initial tree that cannot serve as a root sentence and the obligatory adjunction possibilities are as indicated. Again the local constraint (NA) at the foot node of β_4 prevents further adjunction at this node in γ_2.

3 Head Grammars: Head Wrapping and Tree Adjunction

In this section we will briefly describe *head grammars* (HGs) (Pollard 1984) and relate them to TAGs. (For further details, see Weir, Vijay-Shanker, and Joshi 1986; Vijay-Shanker, Weir, and Joshi 1986). HGs are not to be confused with head-driven phrase structure grammars (HPSGs) (Pollard 1985).

3.1 Head Grammars
Head grammars are string-rewriting systems like CFGs, but differ from them in that each HG string has a distinguished symbol corresponding to the

head of the string. These are therefore called *headed strings*. The formalism allows not only concatenation of headed strings but also so-called *head-wrapping* operations, which split a string on one side of the head and place another string between the two substrings. When we wish to explicitly mention the head, we use the notation $w_1 \bar{a} w_2$; alternatively, we simply denote a headed string by $\bar{w}$. Productions in an HG are of the form $A \rightarrow f(\alpha_1, \ldots, \alpha_n)$ or $A \rightarrow \alpha_1$, where A is a nonterminal, α_i is either a nonterminal or a headed string, and f is either a concatenation or a head-wrapping operation. Roach (1987) has shown that there is a normal form for HGs that uses only the following operations:

$$LC1(u_1 \bar{a}_1 u_2, v_1 \bar{a}_2 v_2) = u_1 \bar{a}_1 u_2 v_1 a_2 v_2$$

$$LC2(u_1 \bar{a}_1 u_2, v_1 \bar{a}_2 v_2) = u_1 a_1 u_2 v_1 \bar{a}_2 v_2$$

$$LL1(u_1 \bar{a}_1 u_2, v_1 \bar{a}_2 v_2) = u_1 \bar{a}_1 v_1 a_2 v_2 u_2$$

$$LL2(u_1 \bar{a}_1 u_2, v_1 \bar{a}_2 v_2) = u_1 a_1 v_1 \bar{a}_2 v_2 u_2$$

$$LR1(u_1 \bar{a}_1 u_2, v_1 \bar{a}_2 v_2) = u_1 v_1 a_2 v_2 \bar{a}_1 u_2$$

$$LR2(u_1 \bar{a}_1 u_2, v_1 \bar{a}_2 v_2) = u_1 v_1 \bar{a}_2 v_2 a_1 u_2.$$

$LC1$ concatenates the two strings; the head of the resulting string comes from the first string. Similarly for $LC2$. $LL1$ inserts the second string into the first string to the right of the head of the first string; that is, the head of the first string is to the left. The head of the resultant string is the head of the first string. Similarly for $LL2$, $LR1$, and $LR2$.

Pollard's definition of headed strings includes the headed empty string $\bar{\lambda}$. However, the term $fi(\bar{w}_1, \ldots, \bar{w}_i, \ldots, \bar{w}_n)$ is undefined when $\bar{w}_i = \bar{\lambda}$. This nonuniformity has led to difficulties in proving certain formal properties of HGs (Roach 1987). This difficulty can be removed by formulating HGs as follows.

Instead of headed strings, we will use so-called *split strings*. Unlike a headed string, which has a distinguished symbol, a split string has a distinguished *position* about which it may be split. There are three operations on split strings: W, $C1$, and $C2$. The operations $C1$ and $C2$ correspond to the operations $LC1$ and $LC2$ in HGs. They are defined as follows:

$$C1(w_1 \uparrow w_2, u_1 \uparrow u_2) = w_1 \uparrow w_2 u_1 u_2$$

$$C2(w_1 \uparrow w_2, u_1 \uparrow u_2) = w_1 w_2 u_1 \uparrow u_2.$$

Since the split point is not a symbol (which can be split either to its left or to its right) but a position between strings, separate left and right wrapping operations are not needed. The wrapping operation, W, is defined as follows:

$$W(w_1 \uparrow w_2, u_1 \uparrow u_2) = w_1 u_1 \uparrow u_2 w_2.$$

It can be shown that this reformulation is equivalent to HG. We will use this reformulation in our further discussion.

3.2 Wrapping and Adjunction

The weak equivalence of HGs and TAGs is a consequence of the similarities between the operations of wrapping and adjunction. It is the roles played by the split point and the foot node that underlie this relationship. When a tree is used for adjunction, its foot node determines where the excised subtree is reinserted. The strings in the frontier to the left and right of the foot node appear on the left and right of the frontier of the excised subtree. As shown in figure 2.3, the foot node can be thought of as a position in the frontier of a tree, determining how the string in the frontier is split.

Adjunction, in this case, corresponds to wrapping $w_1 \uparrow w_2$ around the split string $v_1 \uparrow v_2$. Thus, the split point and the foot node perform the same role. The proof showing the equivalence of TAGs and HGs is based on this correspondence.

3.3 Inclusion of TAL in HL

We will briefly present a scheme for transforming a given TAG to an equivalent HG. We associate with each auxiliary tree a set of productions such that each tree generated from this elementary tree with frontier $w_1 X w_2$ has an associated derivation in the HG, using these productions, of the split string $w_1 \uparrow w_2$. The use of this tree for adjunction at some node labeled X can be mimicked with a single additional production that uses the wrapping operation.

For each elementary tree we return a sequence of productions capturing the structure of the tree in the following way. We use nonterminals that are named by the nodes of elementary trees rather than the labels of the nodes.

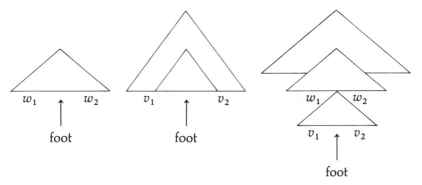

Figure 2.3
Wrapping and adjunction

For each node η in an elementary tree, we have two nonterminal nodes X_η and Y_η allowing for the possibility that an adjunction occurs at η: X_η derives the strings appearing on the frontier of trees derived from the subtree rooted at η; Y_η derives the concatenation of the strings derived under each daughter of η. If η has daughters $\eta_1, \ldots, \eta_k$, then we have the production

$$Y_\eta \rightarrow Ci(X_{\eta_1}, \ldots, X_{\eta_k}),$$

where the node η_i dominates the foot node (by convention, we let $i = 1$ if η does not dominate the foot node). Adjunction at η is simulated by use of the production

$$X_\eta \rightarrow W(X_\mu, Y_\eta),$$

where μ is the root of some auxiliary tree that can be adjoined at η. If adjunction is optional at η, then we include the production

$$X_\eta \rightarrow Y_\eta.$$

Notice that when η has an NA or OA constraint, we omit the second or third of the above productions, respectively.

We illustrate the construction with an example showing a single auxiliary tree and the corresponding HG productions. In this example, μ_1, $\mu_2, \ldots, \mu_n$ are the root nodes of the trees that can be adjoined at η_2 in β.

β:

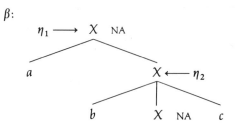

HG productions corresponding to β are

$$X_{\eta_1} \rightarrow Y_{\eta_1},$$
$$Y_{\eta_1} \rightarrow C2(a, X_{\eta_2}),$$
$$X_{\eta_2} \rightarrow W(X_{\mu_1}, Y_{\eta_2}),$$
$$X_{\eta_2} \rightarrow W(X_{\mu_n}, Y_{\eta_2}),$$
$$X_{\eta_2} \rightarrow Y_{\eta_2},$$
$$Y_{\eta_1} \rightarrow C2(b, X_{\eta_3}c),$$
$$X_{\eta_3} \rightarrow Y_{\eta_3},$$
$$Y_{\eta_3} \rightarrow \lambda.$$

3.4 Inclusion of HL in TAL

In this construction, we use elementary trees to simulate directly the use of productions in HG to rewrite nonterminals. Generation of a derivation tree in string-rewriting systems involves the substitution of nonterminal nodes, appearing in the frontier of the unfinished derivation tree, by trees corresponding to productions for that nonterminal. From the point of view of the string languages obtained, tree adjunction can be used to simulate substitution, as illustrated in the following example.

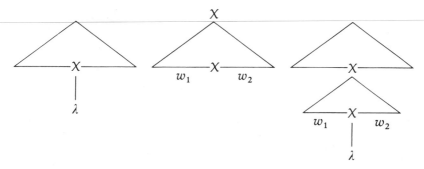

Notice that although the node where adjunction occurs does not appear in the frontier of the tree, the presence of the node labeled by the empty string does not affect the string language.

For each production in the HG we have an auxiliary tree. A production in an HG can use one of the three operations $C1$, $C2$, and W. Correspondingly, we have the following three types of trees.

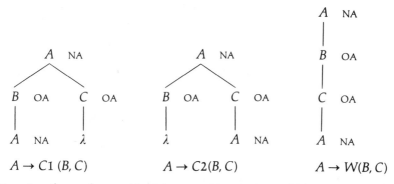

$$A \to C1\,(B, C) \qquad A \to C2(B, C) \qquad A \to W(B, C)$$

Drawing the analogy with string-rewriting systems: NA constraints at each root node ensure that a nonterminal is rewritten only once; NA constraints at the foot node ensure that, like the nodes labeled by λ, they do not contribute to the strings derived; and OA constraints ensure that every nonterminal introduced is rewritten at least once.

The two trees mimicking the concatenation operations differ only in the position of their foot node. This node is positioned in order to satisfy the following requirement: for every derivation in the HG there must be a derived tree in the TAG for the same string, in which the foot is positioned at the split point.

The tree associated with the wrapping operation is quite different. The foot node appears below the two nodes to be expanded because the wrapping operation of HGs corresponds to the $LL1$ operation of HGs in which the head (split point) of the second argument becomes the new head (split point). Placement of the nonterminal that is to be wrapped above the other nonterminal achieves the desired effect, as described earlier.

Though straightforward, this construction does not capture the linguistic motivation underlying TAGs. The auxiliary trees directly reflect the use of the concatenation and the wrapping operations. Elementary trees for natural languages are constrained to capture meaningful linguistic structures. In the TAGs generated in the above construction, the elementary trees are incomplete in this respect, as reflected by the extensive use of the OA constraints. Since HGs do not explicitly give minimal linguistic structures in the sense of TAG, it is not surprising that such a direct mapping from HGs to TAGs does not recover this information.

3.5 Notational Differences between TAGs and HGs

TAGs and HGs are notationally very different, and this has a number of consequences that influence the way in which the formalisms can be used to express various aspects of language structure. The principal differences derive from the fact that TAGs are a tree-rewriting system, whereas HGs manipulate strings or pairs of strings.

In order to be linguistically meaningful, the elementary trees in a TAG must conform to certain constraints that are not explicitly specified in the definition of the formalism. In particular, each elementary tree must constitute a *minimal linguistic structure* elaborated up to preterminal (terminal) symbols and containing a head and all its complements or a modifier. Initial trees have essentially the structure of simple sentences; auxiliary trees correspond to minimal recursive constructions and generally constitute structures that act as modifiers of the category appearing at their root and foot nodes.

A hypothesis that underlies the linguistic intuitions of TAGs is that all dependencies are captured within elementary trees. This is based on the assumption that elementary trees are the appropriate domain upon which to define dependencies, rather than, for example, productions in a CFG. Since in string-rewriting systems dependent lexical items cannot always appear in the same production, the formalism does not prevent the possibility that it may be necessary to perform an unbounded amount of computation in order to check that two dependent lexical items agree in certain features. However, since in TAGs dependencies are captured by bounded structures, we expect that the complexity of this computation does not depend on the derivation. Features such as agreement may be checked within the elementary trees (instantiated up to lexical items) without need to percolate information up the derivation tree in an unbounded way. Some checking is necessary between an elementary tree and an auxiliary tree adjoined to it at some node, but this checking is still local and bounded. Similarly, elementary trees, being minimal linguistic structures, capture all of the subcategorization information.

TAGs have only one operation of composition, namely, adjunction. HGs have concatenation and a variety of types of wrapping. Further, TAGs differ from HGs in that they generate phrase structure trees. As a result, the elementary trees must conform to certain constraints such as left-to-right ordering and dominance relations. Unlike other string-rewriting systems that use only the operation of concatenation, HGs do not associate a phrase structure tree with a derivation: wrapping, unlike concatenation, does not preserve the word order of its arguments.

It is still possible to associate a phrase structure with a derivation in HGs that indicates the constituents, and we use this structure when comparing the analyses made by the two systems. These trees are not really phrase structure trees but rather trees with annotations that indicate how the constituents will be wrapped (or concatenated). It is thus a derivation structure, recording the history of the derivation. The following example illustrates how a constituent analysis is produced by a derivation in an HG, corresponding to the order *John Mary saw swim* as required in a Dutch subordinate clause.

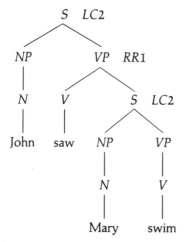

Although a TAG generates trees (phrase structure trees), these trees are not the derivation trees. For a tree γ generated in a TAG, G, there is a derivation structure associated with γ. Because TAG and HG are different systems, it is not possible to directly compare them with respect to their "strong" generative capacities. (In Weir, Vijay-Shanker, and Joshi 1986 we discuss a few linguistic examples comparing the structural descriptions provided by HG and TAG.) HG and TAG are comparable at the level of the derivation structures they produce. This aspect will be discussed in section 6.

4 Linear Indexed Grammars

Indexed grammars (IGs) were introduced by Aho (1968) as a generalization of CFG, and their mathematical properties have been investigated extensively. The class of indexed languages (ILs) is properly contained in the class of context-sensitive languages (CSLs) and properly contains CFLs. IGs IGs were not introduced as grammatical formalisms for natural language; however, because IGs are more powerful than CFGs and because recent investigations have shown that additional power beyond that of CFGs is required, IGs have received attention from linguists. Gazdar (1985) discusses the relevance of IGs to natural language. The class of ILs as a whole is clearly larger than the class of so-called mildly context-sensitive languages (MCSLs), simply because ILs, in general, do not have the constant growth property, because not all ILs are semilinear. For example, $L = \{a^{n^2} | n > 1\}$, $L = \{a^{2^n} | n \geq 1\}$ are ILs, but are not semilinear.

IGs are defined as follows. (We will adopt the notation used in Gazdar 1985, which is essentially the same notation used in Hopcroft and Ullman 1979.) Let $A, B, C, \ldots$ be the nonterminals; $a, b, c, \ldots$ the terminals; $W, W_1, W_2, \ldots$ strings of terminals and nonterminals; $i, j, k, \ldots$ indices; $[\ ], [..], [i..]$ stacks of indices, where $[\ ]$ denotes an empty stack, $[..]$ a possibly empty stack, and $[i..]$ a stack whose topmost index is i. The productions are as follows:

1. $A[..] \rightarrow W[..]$
2. $A[..] \rightarrow B[i..]$
3. $A[i..] \rightarrow W[..]$

$W[..]$ is a shorthand for, for example, $A_1[..] \ldots A_n[..]$; in other words, it stands for a right-hand side in which each *nonterminal* in W has $[..]$ associated with it.

Rule 1 copies the stack on A to all the nonterminal daughters. It is assumed by convention that no stacks are associated with the terminals. Rule 2 pushes an index i on the stack passed from A to a unique nonterminal daughter. Rule 3 pops an index i and then copies the stack on A to all the nonterminal daughters. Gazdar (1985) includes some additional rules, albeit redundantly. These are

4. $A[..] \rightarrow W_1[\ ]B[..]W_2[\ ]$
5. $A[..] \rightarrow W_1[\ ]B[i..]W_2[\ ]$
6. $A[i..] \rightarrow W_1[\ ]B[..]W_2[\ ]$

Rule 4 copies the stack on A to exactly one nonterminal daughter. Rules 5 and 6 push and pop an index on the stack of a designated daughter.

An IG that has only rules of the form 4, 5, and 6 will be called a *linear indexed grammar* (LIG). It can be shown that LIGs and TAGs, and therefore HGs, are weakly equivalent (Vijay-Shanker 1987). We will briefly illustrate the relationship between LIG and TAG by means of an example.

Let G be an LIG as follows:

1. $S[..] \rightarrow aA[a..]$
2. $S[..] \rightarrow aB[a..]$
3. $A[..] \rightarrow aA[a..]$
4. $A[..] \rightarrow aB[a..]$
5. $B[a..] \rightarrow bB[..]c$
6. $B[\ ] \rightarrow e$

Let $w_1 = abec$. The derivation of w_1 is given in (3).

(3)

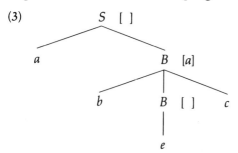

Let $w_2 = aabbecc$. The derivation of w_2 is given in (4).

(4)

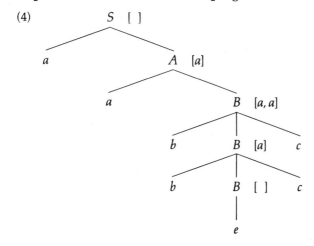

Comparing (3) and (4), one can see that $(n - 1)$ applications of rule 3, one application of rule 4, then n applications of rule 5 allows us to add n *a*'s, n *b*'s, and n *c*'s in the right order.

Note that (3) is a minimal derivation in G. We now take (3) to be an elementary tree (initial tree), say α, of a TAG G', as shown in (5).

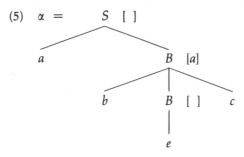

There is no need to keep the stacks that are associated with the non-terminals in α. Thus, we can have (6).

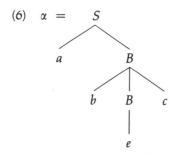

If we now introduce an auxiliary tree, say β, as in (7),

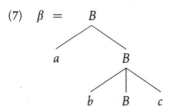

which introduces one *a*, one *b*, and one *c*, in the right order, we can simulate the effect of applying rules 3, 4, and 5 in LIG, assuming β is adjoined only to the node B that is the sibling of *a*. β should not be adjoined to the node B that dominates *e* in α. Similarly in β, since β can be adjoined to β itself, we want this adjunction to take place only to the interior B node of β, and not to the root and foot nodes of β. We can achieve this by placing the NA constraint at the appropriate nodes. Hence, the equivalent TAG, G', is

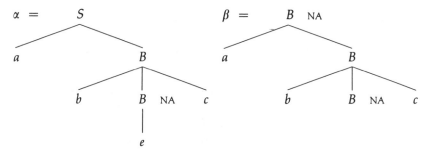

The operation of adjunction indirectly pairs the pushes and pops of indices in just the right way. Also, this information is implicitly communicated from the root of an auxiliary tree to its foot, along its spine (that is, along the path from the root to the foot). This corresponds roughly to the LIG constraint that the stack passes on from the left-hand side of a rule only to a designated daughter.

The equivalence of LIG and TAG thus explains a conjecture made by Bill Marsh (referred to in Gazdar 1985) that the languages $L_1 = \{a^n b^n c^n d^n e^n | n \geq 1\}$ and $L_2 = \{www | w \in \{0, 1\}^*\}$ cannot be generated by LIG.

One variant of MCTAGs is more powerful than TAGs both weakly and strongly (as described in section 2.3). For example, MCTAGs can generate, for each $k \geq 1$, $L_3 = \{a_1^n, a_2^n, \ldots, a_k^n | n \geq 1\}$ and can also generate the double-spined structural descriptions for $L_4 = \{a^n b^n | n \geq 1\}$, that is, structural descriptions of the form

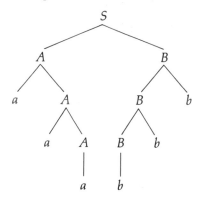

LIGs are inadequate for this purpose, because they do not permit branching stacks. MCTAGs are capable of achieving some of the effects permitted by branching stacks; however, since they still maintain the constant growth property, they are more constrained. Whether there is any appropriate extension of LIG that permits branching stacks without leading to the full power of IG is not known at present. Finding a subset of IG that is exactly or nearly equivalent to MCTAG is a challenging open problem.

Note that although the equivalence of LIG and TAG has been established, there are some key differences between them. If we consider the example described above, it is immediately clear that the "dependent" a, b, and c are always in the same elementary tree. This is only implicit in LIG. The dependency can only be inferred by examining the state of the stacks at the various stages of the derivation. This is due to the fact that TAGs factor recursion and dependency, whereas string-rewriting systems, of which LIG is an example, do not do so.

5 Combinatory Categorial Grammars

In this section we examine *combinatory categorial grammars* (*CCGs*), an extension of classical categorial grammars (Ajdukiewicz 1935) developed by Steedman and his collaborators (Ades and Steedman 1982; Steedman 1985, 1987, 1990). Classical categorial grammars are known to be weakly equivalent to CFGs (Bar-Hillel, Gaifman, and Shamir 1964), and the main result in this section is that under a certain definition (which corresponds to Steedman's recent work) CCGs are weakly equivalent to TAGs, HGs, and LIGs. We show this by showing that combinatory categorial languages (CCLs) are included in linear indexed languages (LILs) and that tree-adjoining languages (TALs) are included in CCLs (Weir and Joshi 1988).

On the basis of their weak equivalence with TAGs and HGs, it appears that CCGs should be classified as a mildly context-sensitive grammar formalism. The derivation tree sets traditionally associated with CCGs have context-free path sets; they are similar to those of LIGs and therefore differ from those of LCFRSs. This does not, however, rule out the possibility that there may be alternative ways of representing the derivation of CCGs that will allow them to be classified as LCFRSs.

The complexity of TAL recognition is $O(n^6)$. Thus, a corollary of our result is that this is also a property of CCLs. Although previous work has been done on the parsing of CCGs (Pareschi and Steedman 1987; Wittenburg 1986), no specific upper bound on recognition has been previously suggested.

5.1 Definition of CCGs

As defined here, CCG is the most recent version of a system that has evolved in a number of papers by Steedman (1985, 1987, 1990). In this section we first define CCGs and then show that the class of string languages generated by CCGs is equal to the languages generated by TAGs (and LIGs).

DEFINITION 1   A CCG, G, is denoted by (V_T, V_N, S, f, R) where

V_T is a finite set of terminals (lexical items),
V_N is a finite set of nonterminals (atomic categories),
S is a distinguished member of V_N,
f is a function that maps elements of $V_T \cup \{\epsilon\}$ to finite subsets of $C(V_N)$ is the set of categories,[1] where

$V_N \subseteq C(V_N)$ and if $c_1, c_2 \in C(V_N)$ then $(c_1/c_2) \in C(V_N)$ and $(c_1 \backslash c_2) \in C(V_N)$,

R is a finite set of combinatory rules as defined below.

There are four types of combinatory rules, which involve variables x, y, z over $C(V_N)$, and each $|_i \in \{\backslash, /\}$:

1. Forward application:
   $$(x/y) \quad y \rightarrow x$$
2. Backward application:
   $$y \quad (x\backslash y) \rightarrow x$$
3. Generalized forward composition for some $n \geq 1$:
   $$(x/y) \quad (\ldots(y|_1 z_1)|_2 \ldots|_n z_n) \rightarrow (\ldots(x|_1 z_1)|_2 \ldots|_n z_n)$$
4. Generalized backward composition for some $n \geq 1$:
   $$(\ldots(y|_1 z_1)|_2 \ldots|_n z_n) \quad (x\backslash y) \rightarrow (\ldots(x|_1 z_1)|_2 \ldots|_n z_n)$$

Restrictions can be associated with the use of the combinatory rules in R. These restrictions take the form of constraints on the instantiations of variables in the rules. These can be constrained in two ways:

1. The initial nonterminal of the category to which x is instantiated can be restricted.
2. The entire category to which y is instantiated can be restricted.

Derivations in a CCG involve the use of the combinatory rules in R. Let the *derives* relation be defined as follows:

$$\alpha c \beta \underset{G}{\Rightarrow} \alpha c_1 c_2 \beta,$$

if R contains a combinatory rule that has $c_1 c_2 \rightarrow c$ as an instance, and α and β are (possibly empty) strings of categories. The string language, $L(G)$, generated by a CCG, G, is defined as follows:

$$\{a_1 \ldots a_n | S \underset{G}{\overset{*}{\Rightarrow}} c_1 \ldots c_n, c_i \in f(a_i), a_i \in V_T \cup \{\epsilon\}, 1 \leq i \leq n\}.$$

Although there is no type-raising rule, its effect can be achieved to a limited extent since f can assign type-raised categories to lexical items. This is the scheme employed in Steedman's recent work.

5.2 Weak Generative Capacity

In this section we show that CCGs are weakly equivalent to TAGs, HGs, and LIGs. We do this by showing the inclusion of CCLs in LILs and the inclusion of TALs in CCLs. We have already seen that TAG and LIG are equivalent (and TAG and HG are equivalent) (Weir, Vijay-Shanker, and Joshi 1986). Thus, the two inclusions shown below imply the weak equivalence of all four systems (TAG, HG, LIG, and CCG).

5.2.1 CCLs ⊆ LILs

We describe how to construct an LIG, G', from an arbitrary CCG, G, such that G and G' are equivalent. Let us assume that categories are written without parentheses, unless they are needed to override the left associativity of the slashes.

A category c is *minimally parenthesized* if and only if one of the following holds:

$c = A$ for $A \in V_N$;
$c = (A|_1 c_1 |_2 \ldots |_n c_n)$, for $n \geq 1$, where $A \in V_N$ and each c_i is minimally parenthesized.

It will be useful to be able to refer to the *components* of a category c. We first define the immediate components of c:

When $c = A$, the immediate component is A,
When $c = (A|_1 c_1 |_2 \ldots |_n c_n)$, the immediate components are A, c_1, $\ldots$, c_n.

The components of a category c are its immediate components together with the components of its immediate components. The immediate components are the category's arguments. Thus, $c = (A|_1 c_1 |_2 \ldots |_n c_n)$ is a category that takes n arguments of category $c_1, \ldots, c_n$ to give the *target* category A.

Although in CCGs there is no bound on the number of categories that are derivable during a derivation (categories resulting from the use of a combinatory rule), there is a bound on the number of *components* that derivable categories may have. This would no longer hold if unrestricted type raising were allowed during a derivation.

Let the set $D_C(G)$ be defined as follows:

$c \in D_C(G)$ if c is a component of c' where
$c' \in f(a)$ for some $a \in V_T \cup \{\epsilon\}$.

Clearly for any CCG, G, $D_C(G)$ is a finite set. $D_C(G)$ contains the set of all *derivable* components; that is, for every category c that can appear in a sentential form of a derivation in some CCG, G, each component of c is in $D_C(G)$. This can be shown, since, for each combinatory rule, if it holds of the categories on the left of the rule, then it will hold of the category on the right. The number of derivable *categories* is unbounded because they can have an unbounded number of immediate components.

Each of the combinatory rules in a CCG can be viewed as a statement about how a pair of categories can be combined. For the sake of this discussion, let us name the members of the pair according to their role in the rule:

> The first of the pair in forward rules and the second of the pair in backward rules will be named the *primary* category. The second of the pair in forward rules and the first of the pair in backward rules will be named the *secondary* category.

As a result of the form that combinatory rules can take in a CCG, they have the following property. When a combinatory rule is used, there is a bound on the number of immediate components that the secondary categories of that rule may have. Thus, because immediate constituents must belong to $D_C(G)$ (a finite set), there is a bound on the number of categories that can fill the role of secondary categories in the use of a combinatory rule. Thus, there is a bound on the number of instantiations of the variables y and z_i in the combinatory rules in section 5.1. The only variable that can be instantiated to an unbounded number of categories is x. Thus, by enumerating each of the finite number of variable bindings for y and each z_i, the number of combinatory rules in R (while remaining finite) can be increased in such a way that only x is needed. Notice that x will appear only once on each side of the rules (in other words, they are linear).

We are now in a position to describe how to represent each of the combinatory rules by a production in the LIGs, G'. In the combinatory rules, categories can be viewed as stacks since symbols need only be added and removed from the right. The secondary category of each rule will be a ground category: either A or $(A|_1 c_1|_2 \ldots |_n c_n)$, for some $n \geq 1$. These can be represented in an LIG as $A[\ ]$ and $A[|_1 c_1|_2 \ldots |_n c_n]$ respectively. The primary category in a combinatory rule will be unspecified except for the identity of its leftmost and rightmost immediate components. If its leftmost component is a nonterminal, A, and its rightmost component is a member of $D_C(G)$, c, this can be represented in an LIG by $A[..c]$.

In addition to mapping combinatory rules onto productions, we must include productions in G' for the mappings from lexical items:

> If $A \in f(a)$, where $a \in V_T \cup \{\epsilon\}$, then $A[\ ] \to a \in P$.
> If $(A|_1 c_1|_2 \ldots |_n c_n) \in f(a)$, where $a \in V_T \cup \{\epsilon\}$, then
> $A[|_1 c_1|_2 \ldots |_n c_n] \to a \in P$.

We now illustrate this construction by giving an LIG from a CCG that generates the language

$$\{a^n b^n c^n d^n | n \geq 0\}.$$

EXAMPLE 9   Let a CCG be defined as follows, where we have omitted unnecessary parentheses:

$A \in f(a)$ $B \in f(b)$ $C \in f(c)$ $D \in f(d)$

$S/S_1 \in f(\epsilon)$ $S_1 \in f(\epsilon)$ $S_1 \backslash A/D/S_1 \backslash B/C \in f(\epsilon)$

The following combinatory rules are permitted:

· Forward application involving x/y and y either when x begins with S_1 and y is C, or when x begins with S and y is S_1 or D.
· Backward application involving y and $x \backslash y$ when x begins with S and y is A or B.
· Forward composition involving x/y and $y \backslash z_1 /z_2 /z_3 \backslash z_4$ when x begins with S and y is S_1.

The productions of the LIG that would be constructed from this CCG are as follows. The first seven rules result from the definition of f. (In the notation for stacks below, the top of the stack appears to the right. In section 4, in the notation for stacks, the top of the stack appears to the left. We have changed the notation from section 4 for convenience because the "top" of a category in CCGs is on the right also.)

$A[\ ] \rightarrow a$ $B[\ ] \rightarrow b$ $C[\ ] \rightarrow c$ $D[\ ] \rightarrow d$

$S_1[\ ] \rightarrow \epsilon$ $S_1[\backslash A/D/S_1 \backslash B/C] \rightarrow \epsilon$ $S_1[..] \rightarrow S_1[../C]C[\ ]$

$S[/S_1] \rightarrow \epsilon$ $S[..] \rightarrow S[../S_1]S_1[\ ]$ $S[..] \rightarrow S[../D]D[\ ]$

$S[..] \rightarrow A[\ ]S[..\backslash A]$ $S[..] \rightarrow B[\ ]S[..\backslash B]$

$S[..\backslash X_1 /X_2 /X_3 \backslash X_4] \rightarrow S[../S_1]S_1[\backslash X_1 /X_2 /X_3 \backslash X_4]$

for all $X_1, \ldots, X_4 \in V_N$.

5.2.2 TALs $\subseteq$ CCLs   We will just give the main idea of the construction of a CCG, G', from a TAG, G, such that G and G' are equivalent. It is important to appreciate that the order in which categories are combined is crucial in a CCG derivation, since the same categories combined in different orders give different strings.

Each of the auxiliary trees will result in certain assignments of categories by f to a terminal or the empty string. Each occurrence of adjunction will be mimicked by the use of a combinatory rule.

Adjunction into nodes to the right (left) of the foot node (which corresponds to concatenation) will be simulated by backward (forward) application. Adjunction into nodes dominating the foot node of a tree (which corresponds to wrapping) will be simulated in the CCG by composition. It is necessary to ensure that the subsidiary category in every occurrence of

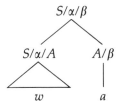 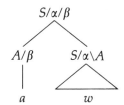

Figure 2.4
Context of composition

composition has just been introduced into the derivation by an assignment of f (see figure 2.4). This will correspond to the adjunction of an auxiliary tree that has not had any trees adjoined into it. It can be shown that composition is guaranteed only in this context.

Forward and backward application are restricted to cases where the secondary category is some X^a, and the left immediate component of the primary category is some Y^a.

Forward and backward composition are restricted to cases where the secondary category has the form $((X^c|_1 c_1)|_2 c_2)$, or $(X^c|_1 c_1)$, and the left immediate component of the primary category is some Y^a.

An effect of the restrictions on the use of combinatory rules is that the only categories that can fill the secondary role during composition are categories assigned to terminals by f. Notice that the combinatory rules of G' depend only on the terminal and nonterminal alphabet of the TAG and are independent of the elementary trees.

The construction depends on a particular normal form for TAGs. We will omit all the details here. The tree in figure 2.5 is encoded by the category

$$A \backslash A_1^a / A_2^c / A_3^a \backslash A_4^a.$$

EXAMPLE 10   Figure 2.6 shows an example of a TAG for the language $L_2 = \{a^n b^n | n \geq 0\}$ with crossing dependencies.

We give the CCG that would be produced according to this construction.

$$S^a \backslash S_1^a / S_2^c \in f(\epsilon) \quad S^c \backslash S_1^a / S_2^c \in f(\epsilon)$$

$$S_2^a / S^c / S_3^c \in f(\epsilon) \quad S_2^c / S^c / S_3^c \in f(\epsilon)$$

$$S_1^a \backslash A \in f(\epsilon) \quad S_1^c \backslash A \in f(\epsilon)$$

$$S_3^a / B \in f(\epsilon) \quad S_3^c / B \in f(\epsilon)$$

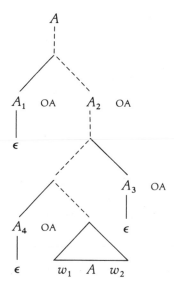

Figure 2.5
Tree encoding $A\backslash A_1^a / A_2^c / A_3^a \backslash A_4^a$

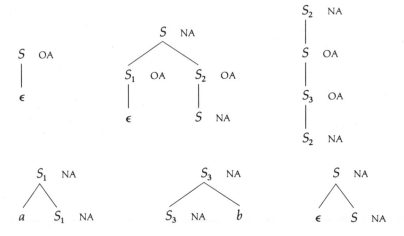

Figure 2.6
TAG for L_2

$A \in f(a)$ $B \in f(b)$

$S^a \backslash S_\epsilon \in f(\epsilon)$ $S^c \backslash S_\epsilon \in f(\epsilon)$

$S_\epsilon \in f(\epsilon)$

The CCGs produced according to the construction given here have the property that parentheses are redundant. It can be shown in general that the use of parentheses in CCGs does not increase the generative power of the formalism. Parenthesis-free CGs differ from CCGs (Friedman, Dai, and Wang 1986; Friedman and Venkatesan 1986). It can be shown that parenthesis-free CGs generate languages not generable by CCGs (Weir 1988).

For further details of this construction and a discussion of derivation trees, see Weir 1988.

6 Linear Context-Free Rewriting Systems

So far we have discussed a number of formalisms and shown equivalences among them. All these systems share certain properties that make them members of the so-called mildly context-sensitive grammar formalisms. All these systems involve some type of context-free rewriting. Vijay-Shanker, Weir, and Joshi (1987) and Weir (1988) have described a system, called *linear context-free rewriting system* (LCFRS), that attempts to capture the common properties shared by these formalisms.

6.1 Generalized Context-Free Grammars

We define *generalized context-free grammars* (GCFGs), first discussed, though with a somewhat different notation, by Pollard (1984).

DEFINITION 2   A GCFG, G, is written as $G = (V, S, F, P)$, where

    V is a finite set of variables,
    S is a distinguished member of V,
    F is a finite set of function symbols, and
    P is a finite set of productions of the form

$$A \rightarrow f(A_1, \ldots, A_n),$$

where $n \geq 0, f \in F$, and $A, A_1, \ldots, A_n \in V$.

The set of terms (trees), $T(G)$, derived from a GCFG, G, is the set of all t such that $S \overset{*}{\underset{G}{\Rightarrow}} t$, where the *derives* relation is defined as follows.

- $A \underset{G}{\Rightarrow} f(\ )$ if $A \rightarrow f(\ )$ is a production.
- $A \overset{*}{\underset{G}{\Rightarrow}} f(t_1, \ldots, t_n)$ if $A \rightarrow f(A_1, \ldots, A_n)$ is a production, and $A_i \overset{*}{\underset{G}{\Rightarrow}} t_i$ for $1 \leq i \leq n$.

Notice that in GCFGs, rewriting choices during the derivation are independent of context. GCFG will generate a set of trees that can be interpreted as derivation trees in various grammar formalisms. Based on GCFG, we can now define a formalism called *linear context-free rewriting systems* (*LCFRSs*), which captures the common properties shared by the formalisms discussed earlier. By giving an interpretation for each of the functions in F, each term (tree) in $T(G)$ can be seen as encoding the derivation of some derived structure. It can be shown that CFGs, HGs, TAGs, and MCTAGs are example of LCFRSs.[2]

In each of the LCFRSs that we have given, the functions (combining strings, trees, or sequences of strings and trees) share certain constrained properties. It is difficult to completely characterize the entire class of such functions that will be so constrained because we are considering formalisms with arbitrary structures. Instead, we will give two restrictions on the functions. We would like these restrictions to ensure that the functions do not "copy," "erase," or "restructure" unbounded components of their arguments. The result of composing any two structures should be a structure whose "size" is the sum of its constituents plus some constant. Every intermediate structure that a grammar derives contributes some terminals to the string that is yielded by the structure that is finally derived. However, the symbols in the yield of an intermediate structure do not necessarily form a continuous substring of the final string. In general, though, we can write the yield of an intermediate structure as a finite sequence of substrings of the final string. The composition operations are "size" preserving. Thus, with respect to the yield of the structures being manipulated, the composition operations do no more than reorder their arguments and insert a bounded number of additional terminals. It can be shown that LCFRSs are semilinear (and hence obey the constant growth property) and are parsable in polynomial time. (For further details, see Vijay-Shanker, Weir, and Joshi 1987 and Weir 1988.) Weir (1988) has also shown that languages generated by MCTAGs are equal to the languages generated by LCFRSs.

Kasami, Seki, and Fujii (1988) have studied a system called multiple context-free grammars, which is the same as LCFRSs. They have obtained some additional properties of the classes of languages generated by their system; in particular, they have shown that the "nonerasing" property does not change the power.

7 Feature-Structure-Based Tree-Adjoining Grammars and Restricted Feature-Structure-Based Tree-Adjoining Grammars

In this section we briefly present *feature-structure-based TAGs* (*FTAGs*), where adjunction becomes function application and unification, and *re-*

stricted FTAGs (*RFTAGs*), where the feature structures associated with each node in an elementary tree are bounded.

7.1 FTAGs

The linguistic theory underlying TAGs is centered around the factorization of recursion and localization of dependencies into the elementary trees. The "dependent" items usually belong to the same elementary tree.[3] Thus, for example, the predicate and its arguments will be in the same tree, as will the filler and the gap. Our main goal in embedding TAGs in a unificational framework is to capture this localization of dependencies. Therefore, we would like to associate feature structures with the elementary trees (rather than breaking these trees into a CFG-like rule-based system and then using some mechanism to ensure that only the trees produced by the TAG itself are generated).[4] In the feature structures associated with the elementary trees, we can state the constraints among the dependent nodes directly. Hence, in an initial tree corresponding to a simple sentence, we can state that the main verb and the subject NP (which are part of the same initial tree) share the agreement feature.

In unification grammars, a feature structure is associated with a node in a derivation tree in order to describe that node and its relation to features of other nodes in the derivation tree. In a TAG, any node in an elementary tree is related to the other nodes in that tree in two ways. Feature structures written in FTAG using the standard matrix notation, describing a node, η, can be made on the basis of

1. The relation of η to its supertree (that is, the view of the node from the top). Let us call this feature structure t_η.
2. The relation of η to its descendents (that is, the view from below). This feature structure is called b_η.

Note that both the t_η and b_η feature structures are associated with the node η. In a derivation tree of a CFG-based unification system we associate one feature structure with a node (the unification of these two structures) since both the statements, t and b, together hold for the node, and no further nodes are introduced between the node's supertree and subtree. This property is not true in a TAG. On adjunction, at a node there is no longer a single node; rather, an auxiliary tree replaces the node. We believe that this approach of associating two statements with a node in the auxiliary tree is consistent with the spirit of TAGs. A node with OA constraints *cannot* be viewed as a single node and must be considered as something that has to be replaced by an auxiliary tree. t_η and b_η place restrictions on the auxiliary tree that must be adjoined at η. Note that if the node does not have an OA constraint, then we should expect t_η and b_η to be compatible (that is,

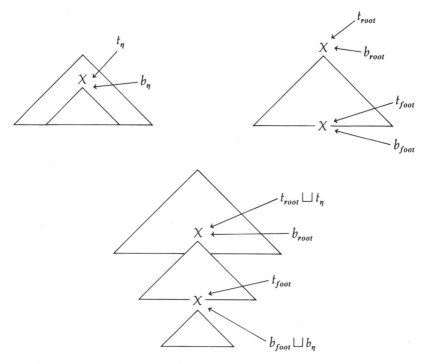

Figure 2.7
Feature structures and adjunction

unifiable). For example, in the final sentential tree, this node will be viewed as a single entity.

Thus, in general, with every internal node, η, at which adjunction can take place, we associate two structures, t_η and b_η. With each terminal node, we associate only one structure.[5]

Let us now consider the case when adjunction takes place as shown in figure 2.7. The notation we use is to write the t and b statements alongside each node, with the t statement written above the b statement. Let us say that t_{root}, b_{root} and t_{foot}, b_{foot} are the t and b statements of the root and foot nodes of the auxiliary tree used for adjunction at the node η. Based on what t and b stand for, it is obvious that on adjunction the statements t_η and t_{root} hold of the node corresponding to the root of the auxiliary tree. Similarly, the statements b_η and b_{foot} hold of the node corresponding to the foot of the auxiliary tree. Thus, on adjunction, we unify t_η with t_{root}, and b_η with b_{foot}. In fact, this adjunction is permissible only if t_{root} and t_η are compatible and b_{foot} and b_η are compatible as well. At the end of a derivation, the tree generated must not have any nodes with OA constraints. We check that by unifying the t and b feature structures of every node. More details of the definition of FTAG may be found in Vijay-Shanker 1987, Vijay-Shanker and Joshi 1988, and Joshi and Vijay-Shanker, to appear.

7.2 Restricted FTAGs

FTAGs as defined above are not constrained, just as CFG-based unification grammars are not constrained. However, if the feature structures associated with each node of an elementary tree are bounded, then RFTAGs can be shown to be equivalent to TAGs (Vijay-Shanker 1987). This restriction is the same as in GPSG; however, because of the larger domain of locality of TAGs and the operation of adjunction, RFTAGs are more powerful than GPSGs.

8 Lexicalized Tree-Adjoining Grammar

We call a grammar *lexicalized* if it consists of (1) a finite set of structures associated with each lexical item, which is intended to be the "head" of these structures, and (2) an operation or operations for composing these structures. The finite set of structures define the domain of locality over which constraints are specified, and these are local with respect to their "heads." It can be shown that, in general, a CFG cannot be lexicalized. Even if a CFG can be lexicalized, it is not always the case that we can guarantee that the lexical item associated with a structure is the linguistically appropriate "head." Both these results hold even if the domain of locality is extended to trees. This is so because the only operation available in CFG is substitution. If, however, we add adjunction as an operation, along with substitution, then we can appropriately lexicalize a CFG (see Schabes, Abeille, and Joshi 1988 for further details about lexicalized grammars, in particular, *lexicalized TAGs* (*LTAGs*)).

TAGs are "naturally" lexicalized because of their extended domain of locality and the operation of adjunction. In an LTAG we allow substitution in addition to adjunction. Adjunction can simulate substitution; however, in an LTAG we allow substitutions explicitly. The definitions of elementary trees are as before except that at the frontiers we can have nodes that are substitution nodes, in the sense that we have to substitute elementary or derived structures at the substitution nodes. Adjunction is defined as before. In the following example, the substitution nodes are marked by ↓.

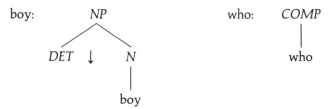

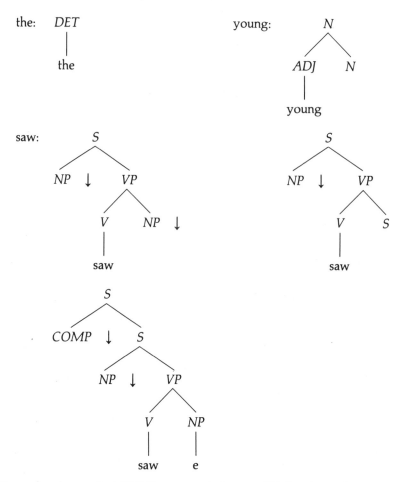

It can be shown that LTAGs are equivalent to TAGs. An Earley-type parser has been described in Schabes and Joshi 1988. For further details about LTAGs, see Schabes, Abeille, and Joshi 1988.

9 Tree-Adjoining Grammars—Local Dominance and Linear Precedence

9.1 TAG (LD/LP)

The extended domain of locality of TAGs has implications for how domination and precedence can be factored. We will now take the elementary trees of TAG as *elementary structures* (initial and auxiliary) specifying only domination structures over which linear precedences (LPs) can be defined. In fact, from now on we will define an *elementary structure (ES)* as consisting of the *domination structure plus a set of linear precedences*. Thus, α below is the domination structure of an ES.

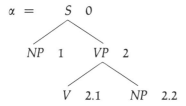

$\alpha =$ S 0

The addresses for nodes serve to identify the nodes. They are not to be taken as defining the tree ordering. They are just labels for the nodes.

Let LP_1^α be a set of linear precedence statements associated with α,

$$LP_1^\alpha = \begin{bmatrix} 1 < 2 \\ 2.1 < 2.2 \end{bmatrix},$$

where $x < y$ (x precedes y) if x and y are nondominating nodes (that is, x does not dominate y and y does not dominate x) and if x dominates z_1 and y dominates z_2, then $z_1 < z_2$.

Note that LP_1^α corresponds exactly to the standard tree ordering. Given LP_1^α, (8) is the only terminal string that is possible with the ES (α, LP_1^α), where α is the domination structure and LP_1^α is the linear precedence statement:

(8) $NP_1 \, V \, NP_2$.

Suppose that instead of LP_1^α, we have

$$LP_2^\alpha = \begin{bmatrix} 1 < 2.1 \\ 2.1 < 2.2 \end{bmatrix}.$$

First note that in $1 < 2.1$, 2.1 is not a sister of 1. We can define precedences between nonsisters because the precedences are defined over α, the domain of locality.

Once again, the only terminal string that is possible with the ES (α, LP_2^α) is

(9) $NP_1 \, V \, NP_2$,

but there is an important difference between (α, LP_1^α) and (α, LP_2^α) that will become clear when we examine what happens when an auxiliary tree is adjoined to α. Before we discuss this point, let us consider

$$LP_3^\alpha = \varnothing,$$

that is, the case where there are no precedence constraints. In this case we will get all six possible orderings:

$NP_1 \, V \, NP_2$, $NP_1 \, NP_2 \, V$, $V \, NP_2 \, NP_1$, $NP_2 \, V \, NP_1$, $V \, NP_1 \, NP_2$,

$NP_2 \, NP_1 \, V$.

Let us return to (α, LP_1^α) and (α, LP_2^α). As we have seen, both ESs give the same terminal string. Now let us consider an ES that is an auxiliary structure β (analogous to an auxiliary tree) with an associated LP, LP^β:

$$LP^\beta = [1 < 2].$$

We have

$$\beta = \qquad VP \quad 0 \qquad\qquad LP^\beta = [1 < 2].$$

$$V \quad 1 \qquad VP \quad 2$$

When β is adjoined to α at the VP node in α, we have

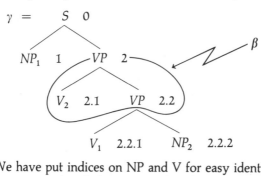

$$\gamma = \qquad S \quad 0$$

We have put indices on NP and V for easy identification. NP_1, V_1, NP_2 belong to α and V_2 belongs to β. If we have LP_1^α associated with α and LP^β with β, after adjunction the LPs are updated in the obvious manner:

$$LP_1^\alpha = \begin{bmatrix} 1 < 2 \\ 2.2.1 < 2.2.2 \end{bmatrix},$$

$$LP^\beta = [2.1 < 2.2].$$

The resulting LP for γ is

$$LP^\gamma = LP_1^\alpha \cup LP^\beta$$

$$= \begin{bmatrix} 1 < 2 \\ 2.1 < 2.2 \\ 2.2.1 < 2.2.2 \end{bmatrix}.$$

Thus, γ with LP^γ gives the terminal string

(10) $NP_1 \ V_2 \ V_1 \ NP_2.$

If we associate LP_2^α, rather than LP_1^α, with α, then after adjoining β to α as before, the updated LPs are

$$LP_2^\alpha = \begin{bmatrix} 1 < 2.1 \\ 2.2.1 < 2.2.2 \end{bmatrix},$$

$LP^\beta = [2.1 < 2.2]$.

The resulting LP for γ is

$$LP^\gamma = LP_2^\alpha \cup LP^\beta$$

$$= \begin{bmatrix} 1 < 2.2.1 \\ 2.1 < 2.2 \\ 2.2.1 < 2.2.2 \end{bmatrix}.$$

Thus, (γ, LP^γ) gives the terminal strings

(11) $NP_1\ V_2\ V_1\ NP_2$

and

(12) $V_2\ NP_1\ V_1\ NP_2$.

(11) is the same as (10), but in (12) NP_1 has "moved" past V_2. If we adjoin β once more to γ at the node VP at 2, then with LP_1^α associated with α, we will get

(13) $NP_1\ V_3\ V_2\ V_1\ NP_2$,

and with LP_2^α associated with α, we will get

(14) $NP_1\ V_3\ V_2\ V_1\ NP_2$,

(15) $V_2\ NP_1\ V_3\ V_1\ NP_2$,

and

(16) $V_3\ V_2\ NP_1\ V_1\ NP_2$.

Let us consider another LP for α, say LP_3^α:

$LP_3^\alpha = [1 < 2.1]$.

Then we have the following terminal strings for α (among others):

(17) $NP_1\ V_1\ NP_2$,

(18) $NP_1\ NP_2\ V$.

It can easily be seen that given LP_3^α associated with α and LP^β associated with β as before, after two adjunctions with β_1, we will get

(19) $NP_1\ V_3\ V_2\ V_1\ NP_2$,

(20) $NP_1\ V_3\ V_2\ NP_2\ V_1$,

(21) $NP_1\ V_3\ NP_2\ V_2\ V_1$,

(22) $NP_1\ NP_2\ V_3\ V_2\ V_1$,

and, of course, several others. In (20), (21), and (22), NP_2, the complement of V_1 in α, has "moved" past V_1, V_2, and V_3 respectively.

The ESs with their domination structure and the LP statements factor the constituency (domination) relationships from the linear order. The complex patterns arise due to the nature of the LP and the operation of adjunction. The main point here is that both the constituency relationships (including the filler-gap relationship) and the linear precedence relationship are defined on the ESs. *Adjunction preserves these relationships.* We have already seen in section 2 how the constituency relationships are preserved by adjunction. Now we have seen how the linear precedence relationships are preserved by adjunction. Thus, we have a uniform treatment of these two kinds of dependencies; however, the crucial difference between them clearly shows up in our framework. Joshi (1987b) has shown how this type of TAG can be used to account for several word order variations in Finnish, first described by Karttunen (1986).

The idea of factoring constituency (domination) relationships and linear order is basically similar to the immediate domination/linear precedence (ID/LP) format of GPSG. However, there are important differences: the domain of locality is the ES (and not the rewrite rules or local trees), and we have defined the LP for each ES. Of course, a compact description of LP over a set of ESs can easily be defined; but when it is compiled out, it will be in the form we have given here. We will call a TAG in which the (local) domination (LD) relationships and linear precedence (LP) relationships are factored out, a TAG in the LD/LP representation, or a *TAG(LD/LP)*.

In order to give further insight into the degree of word order variation possible in TAG(LD/LP), we will give an example.

Let $G = (I, A)$ be a TAG (LD/LP) where

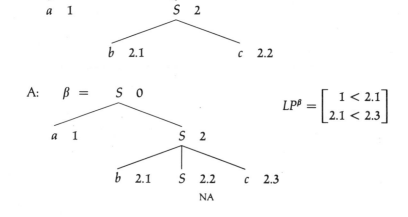

If G were a regular TAG (that is, if α and β were trees), then clearly the language generated by G, $L(G)$, is (as we have shown in section 2)

$$L(G) = \{a^n b^n c^n \mid n \geq 1\}.$$

However, G is a TAG(LD/LP). It is clear that the only string that corresponds to α is

abc.

If we adjoin β to α at the node 2 in α, we get

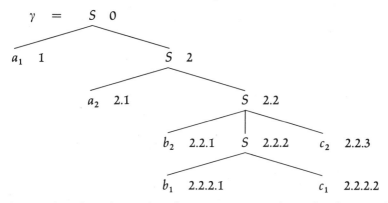

(We have indexed a's, b's, and c's for convenience.) The updated LP^α and LP^β are

$$LP^\alpha = \begin{bmatrix} 1 < 2.2.2.1 \\ 2.2.2.1 < 2.2.2.2 \end{bmatrix},$$

$$LP^\beta = \begin{bmatrix} 2.1 < 2.2.1 \\ 2.1 < 2.2.3 \end{bmatrix}.$$

Hence,

$$LP^\gamma = LP^\alpha \cup LP^\beta$$

$$= \begin{bmatrix} 1 < 2.2.2.1 \\ 2.2.2.1 < 2.2.2.2 \\ 2.1 < 2.2.1 \\ 2.2.1 < 2.2.3 \end{bmatrix}.$$

Thus, some of the possible strings corresponding to γ are

(23) $a_1 a_2 b_2 b_1 c_1 c_2$,

(24) $a_1 a_2 b_2 b_1 c_2 c_1$,

(25) $a_1 a_2 b_1 b_2 c_1 c_2$,

(26) $a_1 a_2 b_2 b_1 c_2 c_1$,

(27) $a_1 b_1 c_1 a_1 b_1 c_1$,

(28) $a_2 b_2 c_2 a_1 b_1 c_1$,

(29) $a_1 a_2 b_1 c_1 b_1 c_2$.

There are 20 strings in all. Each string contains 2 a's, 2 b's, and 2 c's. The corresponding a's, b's, and c's appear in the order a, b, c. This example shows that the elements of an auxiliary structure can "scatter" in a fairly complex manner over the elements of the ES to which it is adjoined, the complexity arising out of the specifications for LP and the adjunction operation itself.

If in the TAG(LD/LP) above both LP^α and LP^β are empty (that is, there are no LP statements), then the language generated by G is the so-called MIX language (or Bach language), which consists of strings of equal numbers of a's, b's, and c's in any order. MIX can be regarded as the extreme case of free word order. It is not known yet whether TAG, HG, CCG, and LIG can generate MIX. This has turned out to be a very difficult problem. In fact, it is not even known whether an IG can generate MIX.

9.2 Languages of TAG(LD/LP)

It is clear that the languages of standard TAG (that is, when the elementary structures are trees with the standard tree ordering) are contained in the class of languages of TAG(LD/LP). Whether the containment is proper or not is not known at present. Languages of TAG(LD/LP) continue to satisfy the constant growth property, hence cannot generate languages of the form $L = \{a^{n^2} | n \geq 1\}$, $L = \{a^{2^n} | n \geq 1\}$, and so on.

Notes

1. Note that f can assign categories to the empty string, ϵ, though, to our knowledge, this feature has not been employed in the linguistic applications of CCG.
2. Weir (1988) has examined derivation trees associated with CCGs. Although the derivation trees traditionally associated with CCGs differ from those of LCFRSs, this does not preclude the possibility that there may be an alternative way of representing derivations. Weir (1988) gives a normal form for CCGs that allows them to be classified as LCFRSs.
3. It is sometimes possible for "dependent" items to belong to an elementary tree and the auxiliary tree that is immediately adjoined in it.
4. Such a scheme would be an alternative way of embedding TAGs in a unificational framework. However, it does not capture the linguistic intuitions underlying TAGs, and it loses the attractive feature of localizing dependencies.
5. It is possible to allow adjunctions at nodes corresponding to prelexical items. For example, we may wish to obtain verb clusters by adjunctions at nodes that are labeled as verbs. In such a case we will have to associate two feature structures with prelexical nodes as well.

References

Ades, A. E., and M. J. Steedman. 1982. On the order of words. *Linguistics and Philosophy*, 3:517–558.

Aho, A. V. 1968. Indexed grammars: An extension of the context-free grammars. *Journal of the ACM* 15:641–671.

Ajdukiewicz, K. 1935. Die syntaktische Konnexität. *Studia Philosophica* 1:1–27. English translation in S. McCall, editor, *Polish Logic 1920–1939*. Oxford University Press, Oxford.

Bar-Hillel, Y., C. Gaifman, and E. Shamir. 1964. On categorial and phrase structure grammars. In Y. Bar-Hillel, editor, *Language and information*. Addison-Wesley, Reading, MA.

Berwick, R., and A. Weinberg. 1984. *The grammatical basis of linguistic performance*. MIT Press, Cambridge, MA.

Bresnan, J. W., R. M. Kaplan, P. S. Peters, and A. Zaenen. 1982. Cross-serial dependencies in Dutch. *Linguistic Inquiry* 13:613–635.

Culy, C. 1985. The complexity of the vocabulary of Bambara. *Linguistics and Philosophy* 8:345–351.

Friedman, J., D. Dai, and W. Wang. 1986. The weak generative capacity of parenthesis-free categorial grammars. In *11th Intern. Conf. on Comput. Ling.*

Friedman, J., and R. Venkatesan. 1986. Categorial and non-categorial languages. In *24th Meeting Assoc. Comput. Ling.*

Gazdar, G. 1982. Phrase structure grammars. In P. Jacobson and G. Pullum, editors, *The nature of syntactic recognition*. D. Reidel, Dordrecht, Holland.

Gazdar, G. 1985. Applicability of indexed grammars to natural languages. Technical report CSLI-85-34, Center for the Study of Language and Information, Stanford University.

Gazdar, G., E. Klein, G. K. Pullum, and I. A. Sag. 1985. *Generalized Phrase Structure Grammar*. Basil Blackwell, Oxford. Also published by Harvard University Press, Cambridge, MA.

Higginbotham, J. 1984. English is not a context-free language. *Linguistic Inquiry* 15:225–234.

Hopcroft, J. E., and J. D. Ullman. 1979. *Introduction to automata theory, languages, and computation*. Addison-Wesley, Reading, MA.

Joshi, A. K. 1985. How much context-sensitivity is necessary for characterizing structural descriptions: Tree adjoining grammars. In D. Dowty, L. Karttunen, and A. Zwicky, editors, *Natural language parsing: Psychological, computational and theoretical perspectives*. Cambridge University Press, New York. Originally presented in May 1983 at the Workshop on Natural Language Parsing at the Ohio State University.

Joshi, A. K. 1987a. An introduction to tree adjoining grammars. In A. Manaster-Ramer, editor, *Mathematics of language*. John Benjamins, Amsterdam.

Joshi, A. K. 1987b. Word-order variation in natural language generation. In *Proceedings of the Annual Conference of the American Association for Artificial Intelligence (AAAI-87)*, Seattle, July 1987.

Joshi, A. K., and L. S. Levy. 1977. Constraints on structural descriptions: Local transformations. *SIAM Journal of Computing* 6:272–284.

Joshi, A. K., L. S. Levy, and M. Takahashi. 1975. Tree adjunct grammars. *Journal of Computer and System Sciences* 10:136–163.

Joshi, A. K., and K. Vijay-Shanker. To appear. Unification-based tree adjoining grammars. In J. Wedekind, editor, *Unification-based grammars*. MIT Press, Cambridge, MA.

Kasami, T., H. Seki, and M. Fujii. 1988. *Generalized context-free grammars, multiple context-free grammars and head grammars*. Technical report, Department of Information and Computer Science, Osaka University, Osaka, Japan.

Kroch, A. S. 1986. Asymmetries in long distance extraction in a tag grammar. In M. Baltin and A. S. Kroch, editors, *New conceptions of phrase structure*. University of Chicago Press, Chicago, IL.

Kroch, A. S. 1987. Subjacency in a tree adjoining grammar. In A. Manaster-Ramer, editor, *Mathematics of language*. John Benjamins, Amsterdam.

Kroch, A. S., and A. K. Joshi. 1985. Linguistic relevance of tree adjoining grammars. Technical report MS-CIS-85-18, Department of Computer and Information Science, University of Pennsylvania, Philadelphia.

Kroch, A. S., and A. K. Joshi. 1986. Analyzing extraposition in a tree adjoining grammar. In G. Huck and A. Ojeda, editors, *Syntax and semantics: Discontinuous constituents*. Academic Press, New York.

Kroch, A. S., and B. Santorini. To appear. The derived constituent structure of the West Germanic verb-raising construction. In R. Freidin, editor, *Principles and parameters in comparative grammar*. MIT Press, Cambridge, MA.

Pareschi, R., and M. J. Steedman. 1987. A lazy way to chart-parse with categorial grammars. In *25th Meeting Assoc. Comput. Ling.*

Peters, S., and R. W. Ritchie. 1972. Context-sensitive immediate constituent analysis: Context-free languages revisited. *Mathematical Systems Theory* 6:324–333.

Pollard, C. 1984. Generalized phrase structure grammars, head grammars and natural language. Doctoral dissertation, Stanford University.

Pollard, C. 1985. Lecture notes on head-driven phrase-structure grammar. Center for the Study of Language and Information, Stanford University.

Pullum, G. K. 1982. Free word order and phrase structure rules. In J. Pustejovsky and P. Sells, editors, *Proceedings of NELS 12*. GLSA, University of Massachusetts, Amherst.

Roach, K. 1987. Formal properties of head grammars. In A. Manaster-Ramer, editor, *Mathematics of language*. John Benjamins, Amsterdam.

Rounds, W. C. 1988. LFP: A logic for linguistic descriptions and an analysis of its complexity. *Computational Linguistics* 14.4:1–9.

Schabes, Y., A. Abeille, and A. K. Joshi. 1988. Parsing strategies with "lexicalized" grammars: Applications to tree adjoining grammars. In *12th Intern. Conf. on Comput. Ling.*

Schabes, Y., and A. K. Joshi. 1988. An Earley-type parsing algorithm for tree adjoining grammars. In *26th Meeting Assoc. Comput. Ling.*

Shieber, S. M. 1985. Evidence against the context-freeness of natural language. *Linguistics and Philosophy* 8:333–343.

Steedman, M. 1985. Dependency and coordination in the grammar of Dutch and English. *Language* 61:523–568.

Steedman, M. 1986. Combinators and grammars. In R. Oehrle, E. Bach, and D. Wheeler, editors, *Categorial grammars and natural language structures*. Foris, Dordrecht, Holland.

Steedman, M. 1987. Combinatory grammars and parasitic gaps. *Natural Language and Linguistic Theory* 5:403–439.

Steedman, M. 1990. Gapping as constituent coordination. *Linguistics and Philosophy* 13:207–263.

Vijay-Shanker, K. 1987. A study of tree adjoining grammars. Doctoral dissertation, University of Pennsylvania.

Vijay-Shanker, K. and A. K. Joshi. 1985. Some computational properties of tree adjoining grammars. In *23rd Meeting Assoc. Comput. Ling.*

Vijay-Shanker, K., and A. K. Joshi. 1988. Feature structure based tree adjoining grammars. In *Proceedings of the 12th International Conference on Computational Linguistics*. Budapest, Hungary.

Vijay-Shanker, K., D. J. Weir, and A. K. Joshi. 1986. Tree adjoining and head wrapping. In *11th Intern. Conf. on Comput. Ling.*

Vijay-Shanker, K., D. J. Weir, and A. K. Joshi. 1987. Characterizing structural descriptions produced by various grammatical formalisms. In 25th *Meeting Assoc. Comput. Ling.*

Weir, D. 1988. Characterizing mildly context-sensitive grammar formalisms. Doctoral dissertation, University of Pennsylvania. Also published as Technical Report MS-CIS-88-74, Department of Computer and Information Science, University of Pennsylvania.

Weir, D. J., and A. K. Joshi. 1988. Combinatory categorial grammars: Generative power and relationship to linear context-free rewriting systems. In 26th *Meeting Assoc. Comput. Ling.*

Weir, D. J., K. Vijay-Shanker, and A. K. Joshi. 1986. The relationship between tree adjoining grammars and head grammars. In 24th *Meeting Assoc. Comput. Ling.*

Wittenburg, K. B. 1986. Natural language parsing with combinatory categorial grammar in a graph-unification based formalism. Doctoral dissertation, University of Texas at Austin.

Chapter 3

Sentence Processing and the Mental Grammar
Janet Dean Fodor

---

1 Introduction

Charting the mental operations involved in the production and perception of sentences is an interesting project in itself, and one that obviously stands to gain much from the results of formal and descriptive linguistics. In this chapter I consider whether psycholinguistics can give anything in return. Can the study of sentence processing reveal properties of the mental "competence" grammar?

We know that psycholinguistics can tidy up the data for linguistics. The classic example is Miller and Chomsky's (1963) argument that multiply center-embedded sentences are merely unprocessable, not ungrammatical. Psycholinguistics may also provide explanations for constraints that do render certain sentences ungrammatical. For example, such constraints may serve to eliminate complexities or ambiguities that would otherwise impede sentence processing. Since some of these constraints are rather odd-looking from a linguistic point of view, a linguist might be glad to know that they are highly motivated on practical grounds and so are not necessarily indicative of deep properties of Universal Grammar. (See, for example, Hankamer 1973; Bever 1970; Fodor 1978.) On a somewhat grander scale, there have even been arguments to the effect that one or another theory of grammars offers the best account of how efficient sentence processing is possible. (See, for example, Berwick and Weinberg 1984, 1985; Fodor 1985.) I will not discuss this functional explanation research in any detail here, but will concentrate on what can be learned about the grammar from experimental investigations of sentence parsing.

Some history to start with. In the early years of generative linguistics, psycholinguists investigated the "psychological reality" of the grammatical

This chapter was written in late 1986 for the CSLI conference at Santa Cruz in January 1987. In the nearly four years since then, psycholinguistics has continued its lively progress. Rather than trying to update the discussion of all the topics covered here, I have just added a note or two to flag the existence of later results, and I would refer interested readers to the papers and bibliographies in recent collections such as Altmann 1989, Carlson and Tanenhaus 1989, and Swinney and Fodor 1989.

rules and representations proposed by linguists. The results were upsetting; grammatical derivations were not confirmed by the experiments. Fodor, Bever, and Garrett (1974) came to the conclusion that the human sentence-processing mechanism does not make direct use of the rules of the mental grammar studied by linguists. Instead, it employs heuristics for piecing together certain important aspects of the derivation of a sentence, heuristics that reflect some of the information contained in the grammar, but not in the format in which the grammar represents it. If this is true, then it follows that we can learn nothing about the format of the mental grammar by studying sentence processing. Competence and performance are not nicely interlocked in a way that would let us reason from discoveries about one to conclusions about the other. Psycholinguistics will not illuminate linguistics.

In the last few years there has been a resurgence of research in experimental psycholinguistics based on the working assumption that one can uncover facts about the mental grammar by reference to the way in which sentences are processed. I will try to explain the reasons for this renewed optimism, and I will review some of the recent experimental studies. In the course of doing so, I will draw attention to a variety of methodological problems, ranging from specific issues about the proper interpretation of experimental data, to broad limitations on the kinds of questions that can be addressed by experimental methods. But though many of my specific comments will be critical, and my estimate of what we have learned so far will be largely negative, I do not by any means intend to imply that the general project is ill conceived, that psycholinguists should narrow their sights and settle for mapping out low-level implementation details.

On the contrary, my hope is that this (partial) survey will illustrate that psycholinguistics can be simultaneously responsible and interesting—that it can pose questions of general theoretical relevance, and that it can set about establishing the answers to them. All I ask is that it not be judged by harsher standards than we apply to "pure" linguistics. None of us conclude that linguistics is hopeless just because linguists (smart, serious linguists) are capable of disagreeing about the proper formulation of Subjacency or the level at which the Case Filter applies, or even when we recognize that nobody has a clue what to do about certain apparent violations of c-command, and so forth. So I will take the risk here of exposing some of the disagreements and uncertainties we face in sentence-processing research, in the interest of giving linguists and computationalists an inside view of what psycholinguists are working on these days and what it is like to do so.

Several things have changed since the earlier period of grammar-testing experiments. I will identify four important changes and discuss them in turn.

1.1 Advances in Experimental Methods

In the early days, when an experiment did not confirm the motivating hypothesis, it was tempting to put more faith in the hypothesis than in the experimental findings. Nowadays we may still debate the validity of experimental data, but there is less uncertainty, there are more fixed points to hold onto.

This is not just because we have gone high-tech, and use computers to present stimuli and to time responses. It is in part because a richer variety of experimental paradigms have been devised over the years. But also, importantly, it is because we have gained wisdom in using them; we have a better idea of which tasks are good for which purposes, how the results of different tasks should relate to each other, what extraneous factors need to be controlled out, and so on. (For examples, see Morton and Long 1976; Mehler, Segui, and Carey 1978; Swinney 1979, 1983; Tanenhaus, Carlson, and Seidenberg 1985; and references therein.)

1.2 Alternative Theories of Grammar

When Fodor, Bever, and Garrett concluded that the mental grammar was not the source of information consulted on-line by the parser, there was only one theory of grammar in the field, the Standard Theory of Chomsky's *Aspects of the Theory of Syntax*. Chomsky had moved from the *Syntactic Structures* model to the Standard Theory, and to most (generative) linguists it was clear that now we'd got things right—in general outline, though of course there were plenty of details still to be filled in. So when the experimental results persisted in disconfirming the Derivational Theory of Complexity—where derivational complexity was defined by "the" theory of the mental grammar—it was natural to conclude that the grammar does not direct linguistic performance.

Joan Bresnan (1978) broke out of this line of reasoning that dooms psycholinguistics to linguistic irrelevance, by developing an alternative theory of grammars that fit the experimental data better and could also be argued to have merit as linguistics. This theory was the precursor of Lexical-Functional Grammar (LFG; see Bresnan 1982). We now have a variety of other linguistic theories that must be taken seriously: Government-Binding (GB) Theory, which retains some of the ideas of earlier transformational theories (see Chomsky 1981, 1986), Generalized Phrase Structure Grammar (GPSG; see Gazdar et al. 1985), Relational Grammar (see Perlmutter 1983), and others. So now psycholinguists need not ask merely whether "the" grammar is or is not the data base for sentence processing; they can ask which theory of grammars comes closest to providing an explanation for the experimental results obtained.[1]

1.3 Implementability

If the early psycholinguistic experiments had confirmed direct use of a Standard Theory transformational grammar in sentence parsing, it would have been something of an embarrassment. Experimental results aside, it was absurd to suppose that perceivers reconstructed Standard Theory derivations for sentences. Reconstructing "forward" derivations by analysis by synthesis was hopelessly unwieldy; reconstructing "backward" derivations was hampered by the irreversibility of many transformational rules and the lack of rules for computing well-formed surface structures prior to computing their deep structures. (See Fodor 1979 for a summary of problems.)[2] The Standard Theory was an implementation disaster.

By contrast, current theories of grammar, both transformational and nontransformational, appear to be much more "user-friendly." It is easier to see how they could be put to work in parsing algorithms. (See Berwick and Weinberg 1984; Kaplan and Bresnan 1982; Crain and Fodor 1985b; Abney and Cole 1986.)[3] So it becomes plausible to reinstate the methodological assumption that the mental grammar directly guides the parser's behavior. This is only a working hypothesis. The data may yet force us to abandon it. But meanwhile it reduces the degrees of freedom we must contend with, focuses debate, provides some falsifiability, and allows us to at least try to give psycholinguistic research some grip on theoretical linguistic issues.

Admittedly, there is no precisely defined notion of a "direct" processing implementation of a given grammar. Typically, there are choices to be made about just how a grammar is to be used by a parser. And exact predictions from a grammar concerning millisecond-by-millisecond parsing operations are out of the question in the absence of assumptions about accessing mechanisms, buffer memory, and all sorts of nonlinguistic matters. Nevertheless, there is a measure of informal agreement about what would be a more direct, or a less direct, way of putting a given grammar to work; or, looking at it the other way around, about which of several alternative models of the grammar could more directly account for some psycholinguistic observation (that is, with least reliance on ancillary assumptions about heuristics, timing of operations, and other matters that do not reflect aspects of the grammar itself). There is still plenty of room for disagreement, and for adjustments to theory in the face of otherwise disconfirming data, but there is enough content to the notion of directness of implementation to make it possible to get on with the project of choosing between competence theories by reference to how well they fit performance.

1.4 Focus on Fundamental Aspects of Grammar

This is not really a departure from the earlier approach, but it should be mentioned. One way to get around (even if not solve) the variability in experimental predictions due to uncertainties about implementation algorithms is to concentrate on properties of grammars so basic that they should be relatively immune to different implementation decisions. The studies described below have addressed such fundamental issues as whether there are levels of syntactic representation other than a surface level, and whether and how grammatical information is divided among different components ("modules").

It is worth noting that these basic questions about the design of the mental grammar are the most difficult ones to resolve by linguistic methods. Just because they are most central, they are the farthest removed from confirmation or disconfirmation by empirical linguistic observations. That is why responsible linguists who agree about the facts that must be characterized can hold such divergent opinions about the form of the grammars that characterize them. It would be highly satisfactory, then, if these were the questions that psycholinguistics was best suited to answer. If the issue is how relative clauses are formed in Swahili, or how c-command should be defined for purposes of the binding theory, linguistic methods are likely to be a much quicker route to a solution than psycholinguistic experiments. But in linguistics we frequently confront cases where two theories can both accommodate the linguistic facts but do so in different ways, with different levels of representation, different ways of grouping phenomena under general principles, different formal mechanisms. At least for linguists who are prepared to present their theories as theories of the mental representation of linguistic knowledge, these formal differences are differences of substance. And psycholinguistics ought to be helpful here, since psychology is in the business (among other things) of trying to identify how human knowledge is mentally encoded.

What I would like to suggest, then, is that it is not merely self-indulgent of psycholinguistics to try to attack the "glamorous" problems, the ones whose answers we would most like to know. Linguistic questions may very well respond to psycholinguistic methods, at least if they are broadly enough stated, and if we are prepared to adopt some fairly obvious working strategies: assume as direct an implementation of a grammar as possible; and compare alternative grammars, accepting at each step the one that accounts for the processing data most directly.

2 An Experimental Study of Levels of Syntactic Representation

One property of grammars that meets the criteria of being fundamental and of distinguishing between different linguistic theories is whether grammatical derivations include a single level of syntactic representation or multiple levels. Despite some dissent (for example, Aoun 1983), GB Theory retains from earlier transformational theories the concept of a sequential syntactic derivation from a "deep" level (now D-structure) to a "surface" level (S-structure), and then on to the new syntactic level of Logical Form (LF). Other current theories, such as LFG and GPSG, characterize only a surface level of syntactic structure.

Freedman (1982) has argued that there is experimental evidence for the level of D-structure. (This argument has since been modified, as I will explain below, to support the GB level of S-structure, but it is interesting to consider the earlier version.) Prior to this work, the best evidence for D-structure was due to Wanner (1974), who found that a prompt word facilitated recall of a sentence more effectively the more often it appeared in the (Standard Theory) deep structure of the sentence. But occurrence of a word in a deep structure could not be dissociated from presence of the corresponding word-concept as a constituent of the sentence meaning. In these experiments, then, the influence of D-structure was inevitably, frustratingly, confounded with the influence of sentence meaning.

Freedman's approach does not face this problem. The idea is to show the existence of D-structure by showing that sentences that have a well-formed D-structure are easier to respond to (in a sentence-matching task, described below) than sentences that lack a well-formed D-structure. Since the sentences without D-structures will necessarily be ungrammatical, a fair comparison requires that the sentences that have D-structures should be ungrammatical too—in other words, that although their syntactic derivations start out well enough, they break down later as a result of violating some syntactic constraint. Thus the comparison is between nonsentences that do not satisfy the principles of the base (which have been called in the psycholinguistic literature, rightly or wrongly, *rule violations*) and non-sentences that satisfy the principles of the base but not all of the constraints on transformational operations or outputs (dubbed *constraint violations*). Freedman took agreement violations and quantifier placement violations, as in (1) and (2), as examples of the first kind, and Subjacency violations and Specified Subject Condition violations, as in (3) and (4), as examples of the second kind.

(1)   *Mary were writing a letter to her husband.

(2)   *Lesley's parents are chemical engineers both.

(3)   *Who do the police believe the claim that John shot?

(4)   *Who did the duchess sell Turner's portrait of?

Note that although they are ungrammatical, all of these sentences are quite easily interpretable.

In the sentence-matching task, one sentence appears on a screen, and 2 seconds later a second sentence appears beneath it. The subjects' task is to indicate, as quickly as possible, whether the two sentences are identical or not. For all the sentences of interest, the correct answer is "yes"; mismatched sentence pairs are interspersed among the matched pairs so that subjects can respond correctly only by reading both sentences carefully. The measure of interest is how long it takes subjects to respond correctly, for the different types of sentences.

What Freedman had originally expected was that response times would be higher for ungrammatical sentences than for closely comparable grammatical control sentences. What she observed, and repeatedly confirmed, was that this was true only for the rule-violating sentences. For the constraint-violating sentences there was no effect of the ungrammaticality at all. Freedman attributed this to the fact that the constraint violations have well-formed D-structures. If we suppose that subjects decide whether sentences match by mentally comparing their D-structure representations, then matching should be easy for sentences with well-formed D-structures (that is, grammatical sentences and constraint violations), but difficult for sentences lacking a D-structure representation (that is, rule violations). (I note in passing that this is not at all what Freedman was looking for in her original experiments. This is an elegant example of the extraction of theoretical significance from an accidentally discovered phenomenon.)

This D-structure explanation of the experimental findings had to be relinquished in the face of various linguistic problems—for example, that number agreement violations cannot be determined at the D-structure level, and that the quantifier placement violations could be analyzed as violations of constraints on a Quantifier Float transformation.[4] But the original explanation can be translated into an explanation referring to S-structure representations, which is also of theoretical interest. This S-structure approach is developed in Freedman and Forster 1985.

Suppose all of the traditional constraints on movement (including Subjacency) are reformulated as constraints on trace binding that operate between S-structure and LF. Then it could be argued that sentences like (1) and (2) (which I will continue, for convenience, to refer to as "rule violations") lack well-formed S-structures, whereas sentences like (3) and (4) ("constraint violations") have well-formed S-structures and fail only at LF. And suppose also that we change our earlier assumption about sentence matching, taking it now to involve comparison of S-structure representations. Then it is predicted as before that constraint violations will be as easy to match as grammatical sentences, but matching of rule violations will be hindered. If this is the right explanation, it still favors GB Theory over alternative theories (such as GPSG) that do not define any syntactic level that has the relevant properties of S-structure—in other words, a level such that phrasal structure has been assigned but the legitimacy of antecedent-trace relations has not yet been checked. Strong implications for linguistic theory thus follow if this S-structure explanation can plausibly be argued to be correct.

The only way to argue for it is to argue that no other hypothesis explains the findings so well. But Crain and Fodor (1985a, 1987) proposed an alternative hypothesis and obtained further experimental results suggesting that this alternative is superior. Specifically, Crain and Fodor suspected that the rule/constraint contrast was confounded, in Freedman and Forster's sentence materials, with a contrast between ungrammaticalities that are easily (even irresistibly) mentally corrected, as in the rule-violating sentences, and ungrammaticalities that cannot be corrected except by an elaborate paraphrase, as in the constraint-violating sentences. If subjects in the sentence-matching task automatically correct the rule violations as they process the sentences on the screen, they may then be confused about what to compare with what—the original ungrammatical input, or the mentally corrected version of it. And this confusion could slow down their responses, relative to responses on sentences that they are not tempted (or are unable) to correct.

To test this correctability explanation of the sentence-matching data, one needs to unconfound the two factors, by including two additional sentence types in the experiment: highly correctable constraint violations, and uncorrectable rule violations. Crain and Fodor's attempts to construct such sentences are illustrated in (5) and (6) respectively.

(5) *How many dancers did they say that would be in the show?
     *What kind of sauce did Sam serve the pork chops and?

(6) *Part of when the screen went blank.
     *The plumber took what the time was to finish the job.

The suspected differences in correctability between the sentence types were confirmed by having subjects correct the sentences in a pencil-and-paper editing task and rate how difficult they found it to do so. Then sentence-matching times were obtained for all four sentence types. They showed a highly significant effect of correctability but no significant effect of the rule/constraint (or $\pm$S-structure) contrast.

There are many wrinkles in the analysis of the data that I will not go into here, and comparable results for another task used by Freedman (the so-called Rapid Serial Visual Processing or RSVP task) must also be accounted for. But the conclusion of Crain and Fodor's discussion was that Freedman and Forster's experiments do not, after all, provide support for a level of syntactic structure prior to the application of constraints on the binding of *wh*-traces. There is (as yet) no evidence that parsing a sentence involves computing its GB S-structure representation. The debate is not over yet; see Forster and Stevenson 1987 for the next installment.[5] But I will leave it at this point, to comment on one of the limitations of experimental research anticipated in section 1.

Let us imagine, for the moment, that there did exist some experimental results showing that perceivers compute GB S-structure representations. Then it would be a more or less secure conclusion that the mental grammar generates these S-structure representations and that any linguistic theory that denies this is incorrect. By contrast, if the data do *not* indicate that S-structure representations are computed, then we can draw no conclusion at all about the mental grammar. The first state of affairs would support GB Theory as against GPSG, but the second state of affairs would fail to discriminate between them. This is the notorious problem of null results that looms over every psycholinguistic experiment. If the sentence-matching studies fail to reveal mental representations of S-structure, that might be because there are none, or it might be because the sentence-matching task is not sensitive to them. Perhaps matching takes place at the level of D-structure or LF, or at the orthographic equivalent of Phonetic Form (PF) (essentially, the sequence of words as it appears on the screen); then the matching times would not reflect S-structure differences between sentence types even if S-structures are mentally computed. Or possibly matching does involve S-structure, but its effects are so small that they are swamped by theoretically uninteresting factors such as correctability. Yet another possibility, of course, is that the mental grammar characterizes S-structures but perceivers do not compute them; in other words, it is possible that our working assumption of direct implementation of the grammar is invalid.

When a theory makes a prediction, failure to confirm that prediction can be construed as disconfirmation of the theory only if it is reasonable to suppose that confirming evidence would have been obtained if the prediction were true. This is not a novel observation. But it is one that cuts deeper in psycholinguistics than in linguistics, just because there are so many ways in psycholinguistics of failing to find the evidence that would be confirmatory. The problem does arise in linguistics. Suppose, for example, that some linguistic theory entails that the class of possible human languages includes languages with some "exotic" property P. Since a possible human language need not actually have been used by humans, and since even some that have are inaccessible or have not yet been adequately analyzed, the absence of any known language with property P cannot falsify the theory that entails that P is possible. Nevertheless, the data for linguistics are certainly *more* accessible than they are for the experimental sciences (a point on which we often congratulate ourselves). To use Tony Kroch's clever simile, data gathering in linguistics is like scanning the pebbles on a beach, whereas data gathering in experimental psycholinguistics is like having to turn over rocks to see what is beneath them.

In testing the psychological reality of S-structure, we may not yet have looked underneath the right rock. But the fact that one can't tell in advance whether an experiment will be informative doesn't mean it isn't worth doing. If the sentence-matching findings had turned out otherwise (or if Freedman and Forster's interpretation of them can yet be defended against the correctability interpretation), the theoretical payoff would have been considerable.

3 Experimental Studies of Modularity within the Syntactic Component

The treatment of empty categories is another important point on which current linguistic theories differ. I will restrict the discussion again to GB Theory and GPSG. GB Theory treats long-distance *wh*-dependencies as the result of movement, with trace binding subject to constraints at LF. (This glosses over many variations that won't concern us here, such as the possibility that the Strict Cycle and Subjacency are constraints on rule application rather than on representations, or that some constraints hold at S-structure, and so on.) GPSG treats long-distance dependencies as trace binding mediated by "slash features" in (surface) phrase structure trees. GB Theory treats local NP rearrangements as in Passive and Raising as syntactic movement leaving traces; GPSG treats them as lexical operations not creating empty categories. GB Theory treats control as the binding of PRO at S-structure or LF; GPSG treats it as an aspect of semantic interpretation, with a bare VP complement and no empty category as its subject in the syntactic tree (but a Control Agreement Principle in the syntax to establish agreement relations between the controlling NP and the VP complement).

The meanings assigned to sentences will be the same on both theories. But if psycholinguistic experiments can tap intermediate stages of processing, they may be able to choose between the formal mechanisms by which these interpretations are assigned. There are two obvious points of attack. We can try to develop tests that will tell us which syntactic constructions do and do not contain empty categories.[6] And we can try to establish where the boundaries fall between components ("modules") of the grammar by looking for similarities and differences among the operations by which perceivers assign interpretations to these empty (or nonexistent) categories.[7]

In these investigations, too, there will be evidential asymmetries. For example, success in establishing a module boundary in the parser would constitute prima facie evidence for a corresponding module boundary in the grammar, but failure to find a module boundary in the parser would provide no decisive information about the modular structure of the grammar. (It is hard to see how the parser could segregate kinds of linguistic information if the grammar integrates them, but easy to see how the parser could combine them even if the grammar does not.) So once again, we can't tell how informative an experiment will be until we have run it and found out which way the facts fall. Nevertheless, there are some possible results that would be well worth looking for. For example: a separation in the parsing routines between phrase structure assignment and *wh*-trace binding would favor GB Theory;[8] an association of phrase structure assignment and *wh*-trace binding, but delayed analysis of raising and control constructions, would tend to favor GPSG.

3.1 Control

Frazier, Clifton, and Randall (1983) (henceforth FCR) established an important program of research (continued in Clifton and Frazier 1986) with their investigation of the processing of PRO. FCR observed difficulties in the comprehension of certain sentences containing PRO, which they took to show that the parser applies information about legitimate control relations quite late relative to its assignment of phrase structure, perhaps only during a second pass through the input. FCR reasoned, as above, that if information relevant to phrase structure assignment and information relevant to control were intertwined in the grammar, they could not be disentangled by the parser and applied at different times. Thus, FCR's experimental data would appear to support a linguistic theory in which phrasal structure and control are handled by different modules. There are various problems with this interpretation of the data, which I will outline. They are worth considering because they point the way to more decisive studies of this topic in the future.

The first problem is that this finding does not discriminate, as FCR suggest it does, between GB Theory and GPSG, because both theories assign control and phrase structure principles to different modules. (Whether the modules in question are syntactic or semantic is not addressed in these experiments.) Thus the processing phenomenon discovered by FCR, if it does concern control, could at best confirm a module boundary that is not in dispute. However, it is not clear that the processing phenomenon does concern control. It might, as I will show, concern subcategorization or *wh*-trace binding, in which case it might indeed distinguish different theories of grammar.

The sentence types tested by FCR are illustrated in (7)–(10). (Here and throughout, *t* indicates a trace.)

(7)   This is the woman$_i$ [who$_i$ the child$_j$ begged [PRO$_j$ to sing the songs for t$_i$]].

(8)   This is the woman$_i$ [who$_i$ the child begged t$_i$ [PRO$_i$ to sing the songs]].

(9)   This is the woman$_i$ [who$_i$ the child$_j$ tried [PRO$_j$ to sing the songs for t$_i$]].

(10)   This is the woman$_i$ [who$_i$ the child forced t$_i$ [PRO$_i$ to sing the songs]].

(I have simplified the examples here; the actual sentences tested included *Everyone liked the woman who the little child begged to sing those stupid French songs for last Christmas*.) Subjects were required to read the sentences and to indicate as quickly as possible after each one either "got it" or "missed it" (that is, whether they understood the sentence right away or felt the need to reread it in order to understand it). The greater the number of "missed it" responses, and the slower the "got it" responses, the harder we can assume the sentence is to process.

In (7) the PRO in the lowest clause is controlled by the subject of its matrix clause (the relative clause). In (8) the PRO is controlled by the matrix object (the *wh*-trace in the relative clause). But these sentences are temporarily ambiguous. The correct analysis of the sentence at the PRO position is not determined until the end of the sentence, where there either is, or is not, a "gap" that can be analyzed as the *wh*-trace that must be present in the relative clause. If there is, analysis (7) is correct; if there is not, analysis (8) is correct. FCR discovered that when such sentences end as in (8) they are more difficult to comprehend than when they end as in (7). They concluded that the parser adopts the analysis (7) in cases of temporary ambiguity (that is, where the grammar does not uniquely determine the correct analysis by the time the PRO is encountered) and therefore "garden paths" on (8) (not necessarily consciously). The garden path is illustrated in (11); when no gap has been found by the end of the relative clause to associate with the *wh*-filler, this analysis will be recognized as incorrect and must be revised.

(11)   This is the woman$_i$ [who$_i$ the child$_j$ begged [PRO$_j$ to sing the songs]].   ????!!

This kind of asymmetry in processing difficulty for temporarily ambiguous sentences, depending on which way the sentence ends, is familiar in psycholinguistics; it is the standard sign of serial processing of alternative structural hypotheses.[9] A more striking result in FCR's experiment was that sentences like (10) were more difficult than those like (9), despite the fact that these sentences involve no temporary ambiguity. FCR took the similarity between the results for (9)/(10) and those for (7)/(8) to suggest that there must be a garden path in the processing of (10) also. But this could be so only if the parser is not making immediate use of the information in the grammar that renders (10) unambiguous.

So now we must ask, What information about (10) renders it unambiguous? It is this information that the parser temporarily ignores, and which therefore must be represented separately from the information that it applies immediately. There are several possibilities to consider. If the garden path analysis computed by the parser is (12), comparable to (11), it is subcategorization information (the transitivity of *force*) that is being ignored.

(12)   This is the woman$_i$ [who$_i$ the child$_j$ forced [PRO$_j$ to sing the songs]].

If the parser misanalyzes (10) as (13), then it is ignoring the principles (case and theta theory principles in GB Theory) that prevent the binding of the *wh*-trace object by the subject NP of the same clause.

(13)   This is the woman$_i$ [who$_i$ the child$_j$ forced t$_j$ [PRO to sing the songs]].

(Note that (13) actually represents two different misanalyses, depending on whether the index on PRO is *i* or *j*.) If the misanalysis is (14), then the parser is indeed making a mistake about control.

(14)   This is the woman$_i$ [who$_i$ the child$_j$ forced t$_i$ [PRO$_j$ to sing the songs]].

(I will ignore here some possible variants of these three hypotheses about the nature of the parser's error; for further discussion, see Fodor 1988.)

A subcategorization error such as (12) would suggest that general principles of phrase structure are encoded in the grammar separately from lexical specifications and would thus tell against a theory such as GB that assumes that phrase structure is largely projected from lexical entries. A *wh*-trace binding error such as (13) would suggest separation of phrase structure principles and binding principles and would thus tell against a theory like GPSG in which the two are closely associated. As noted earlier, a control error such as (14) would be compatible with both theories (perhaps all current theories). So it matters a great deal just what the parser is doing wrong. But the data from an end-of-sentence task like the "got it" task can reveal only the existence of a parsing problem, not its nature.

A valuable next step in this research project would therefore be to test the same materials with an on-line task that permits the parser's operations to be tracked throughout the sentence. Some relevant results are presented in Crain and Fodor 1985b. But best of all would be a task that can indicate not only whether an error has occurred in the assignment of antecedents, but also *which* antecedents have been assigned. A priming paradigm has these virtues. Priming tasks have been used in the study of "filler-gap" dependencies, though they have not yet been applied to the sentence constructions used by FCR.[10] I will describe some priming experiments in detail below, but the general idea is this. If an NP is assigned as antecedent to an empty category, we can hope to find signs of the mental activation of that NP at the position of the empty category. A priming experiment looks for this activation by seeing whether responses to an item associated in some way with the NP are primed (facilitated) at the gap position.

In FCR's sentences, one would investigate, at various positions through the sentence, the degree of priming by the main clause subject and by the relative pronoun (or head of the relative clause). In general, this would be expected to vary inversely with the distance of the NP in question from the point of testing. But at the clause boundary in (10), where the trace and PRO occur, we should observe a sharp increase in priming by whichever NP(s) the parser assigns as antecedent. If there is priming at the clause boundary by the matrix subject NP only, that would indicate disregard of subcategorization or the constraints on *wh*-trace binding (= error (12) or (13)). If there is priming by both the subject and the relative pronoun, that would suggest a control error (= error (14). If there is priming by the relative pronoun only, that would indicate that no binding or control error has occurred at all.

This last possibility deserves consideration, since the claim that an error occurs is a crucial ingredient in the reasoning from the observed processing difficulty to the existence of modular organization in the grammar. The linking assumption is that an error occurs because of a delay in applying one of the grammar modules. If this argument is to go through, it is essential to defend the claim that the difficulty in sentences like (10) does consist in the making of an error (a garden path) and its subsequent correction, rather than reflecting a heavy processing load involved in correctly parsing the sentence—for example, in correctly identifying and interrelating the two empty categories when they are adjacent as in (8) and (10).

One thing psycholinguistics is confident of is how to tell a garden path from a processing load effect. A difficulty due to a garden path will afflict only a temporarily ambiguous sentence; it will not be present in a comparable unambiguous sentence. But the materials used by FCR defy this classic line of argument, because they are claimed to have the special property of creating garden paths even when *un*ambiguous. Therefore in this case the unambiguous sentences cannot be used to establish a neutral baseline. There are some other, more subtle criteria by which a garden path effect could be identified (for discussion, see Crain and Fodor 1985b and Fodor 1988), but the clearest way to settle the issue would be to find out which antecedents the parser assigns on its first pass through the sentence. So priming experiments, and other techniques that can provide qualitative data, can be expected as the next step in this line of research.[11]

3.2 *The Speed of* WH-*Trace Binding*

We have seen that FCR's and Clifton and Frazier's studies could conceivably turn out to bear on *wh*-trace binding rather than control. A number of other experiments have addressed the binding of *wh*-traces, and they give some estimate of how rapidly this occurs. The relevance of this, as above, is that a temporal delay in processing would indicate separation of information sources in the mental grammar.

Tanenhaus, Carlson, and Seidenberg (1985) (henceforth TCS) used a rhyme-priming task with sentences like (15), presented visually word by word.

(15)   The man was surprised at which $\begin{Bmatrix} \text{beer}_i \\ \text{wine}_i \end{Bmatrix}$ the judges awarded the first prize to t_i.

Four hundred milliseconds after presentation of the last word, a string of letters appeared on the screen and the subject had to make a lexical decision (that is, indicate as quickly as possible whether the string was a word). For (15) the lexical decision target was *fear*. Responses were faster when the word *beer*, which rhymes with *fear*, had appeared earlier in the sentence than when the word *wine* had appeared. This facilitation of *fear* by *beer* was comparable in strength to the facilitation obtained when the priming item was the last word of the sentence, presented right before the target word. These results are explicable if we assume that the word *beer* is mentally activated at the end of the sentence, even though it appeared seven words earlier. And this activation can be attributed to the fact that *which beer* is the antecedent for the trace at the end of (15). An earlier experiment had shown *no* facilitation due to a rhyming item seven words earlier in the sentence if it was *not* the antecedent for a later empty category.[12]

This study indicates that an antecedent is assigned to a *wh*-trace within a second after the parser encounters the information that signals the existence of the trace (in this case, the end of the sentence). The lexical decision target appeared 400 milliseconds after the end of the sentence, and response times in this experiment averaged approximately 600 milliseconds. The reading of the target item and the physical response probably occupy 300 or 400 milliseconds of the total response time. So if there is any systematic delay in the binding of traces attributable to the modular structure of the grammar, it is quite short. Unfortunately, the fact that the gaps were sentence final in TCR's materials leaves open the possibility that binding is systematically postponed not by some fixed amount of time, but until the end of a clause or of the sentence, so that the rapidity of binding here is atypical.

Swinney, Ford, Bresnan, and Frauenfelder (1988) (henceforth SFBF) tested *wh*-traces in nonfinal positions, in a slightly different paradigm that permits a tighter bracketing of the time interval. Their sentences were spoken, at a normal rate, and the lexical decision target appeared on a screen during the presentation of the sentence. SFBF used semantic priming; that is, the target item was a semantic associate, rather than a rhyme, of the item of interest in the sentence. Their materials are illustrated in (16).

(16)   The policeman saw the boy$_i$ that$_i$ the crowd at the
party accused t$_i$ of the crime.

1   2   3

The lexical decision target was presented at one of three positions: between *party* and *accused*, between *accused* and *of*, and simultaneous with the *the* preceding *crime*. Note that the second position is the position of the trace associated with the relative pronoun. At the first position, responses to the target item *group* (a semantic associate of *crowd*) were significantly faster than responses to a control target item (that is, a word not related to a word in the sentence but matched for length and frequency with *group*). But responses to *girl* (a semantic associate of *boy*) were not faster than responses to an unrelated target. Thus, there was priming by *crowd* but not by *boy* at the first position, before the *wh*-gap had occurred. This finding is consistent with the expected effect of distance on degree of priming. At the second and third positions, however, responses to *girl* showed priming, but responses to *group* did not. These results suggest that the relative pronoun, or the head noun *boy*, was assigned as antecedent to the trace that follows *accused*.[13] Similar results were obtained in a second experiment in which the task was to read the target word aloud (the "naming" task). In this experiment it was even clearer that only the correct antecedent had a priming effect at the gap position; responses showed no priming either by *crowd* or by *policeman*, which was also tested. Responses in these experiments occurred, on average, 600 milliseconds after presentation of the target word, indicating a rapid decision about the interpretation of the trace.

Thus, this study also shows no clear sign of a systematic delay of trace binding in relation to phrase structure assignment. The parser binds traces as fast as we can measure—so far. Can we draw the measurements even closer? It may be possible to eliminate the physical button-pushing responses required in these experiments, by monitoring brain activity directly. The measurement of evoked potentials is a technique that has been hovering in the wings for some years; it may now be sufficiently refined to be put to work in sentence-processing studies, and it could bring response times down to around 400 milliseconds. (For discussion, see Garnsey, Tanenhaus, and Chapman 1987; Kutas and Hillyard 1983.)

However fast we may show trace binding to be, we don't really know how fast is fast enough. That is, we don't know how much time is required simply for the recognition of an empty category in the phrase structure and its interpretation by reference to the antecedent. Only if the actual processing time exceeds this unknown minimum could we conclude that the binding principles are accessed and applied by the parser later than the phrase structure principles. Because of this uncertainty, only the demonstration of a huge delay in trace binding could be convincing, and the currently available results suggest that that is unlikely to occur. If so, the conclusion would not be that structure assignment and binding are simultaneous in processing, much less that they are inseparable in the mental grammar, but only that this kind of timing argument cannot serve to show that they are separate.

3.3 Constraints on WH-Trace Binding

Fortunately there is another way in which delayed application of the binding principles could reveal itself. Incontrovertible evidence would be the occurrence of temporary errors of binding prior to correct binding. Once again the argument is one-sided. The modular hypothesis does not entail that errors will occur before the binding module is engaged, since the parser might hold back from making any decisions about empty categories and their antecedents until it was in a position to make the right decisions. But *if* temporary errors occur, that would strongly favor the modular hypothesis.

FCR's delay hypothesis is an example of a temporary error hypothesis. Their proposal was that the parser, while waiting for the relevant grammatical information to become accessible, selects an antecedent for a gap by a "dumb" strategy; in particular, they proposed that for PRO the parser picks the most recent potential filler (or perhaps the most recent *nonempty* potential filler). Can a comparable claim be established for trace binding? TCS's and SFBF's results do not encourage such a claim, since they indicate that the parser is sensitive to at least some of the constraints on trace binding. There would have been no priming by the correct antecedent if an incorrect one were always assigned. And there should have been some priming by *crowd* and *policeman* in SFBF's example (16) if the parser were selecting at random and did not respect the case and theta theory principles requiring the antecedent of a *wh*-trace to be in a preclausal nonargument position.[14]

Other experiments have investigated whether the parser also respects the bounding constraints that establish extraction "islands." That is, assuming now that the parser does correctly select an antecedent in nonargument position for a *wh*-trace, does it restrict its choice to those within the same extraction island as the trace? Of course, it might do so for the wrong reasons, such as a preference for recent fillers. So we must include tests in which a more distant but correct filler is pitted against a closer but incorrect one. Priming experiments would clearly be useful here too. But other tests are possible if the question is turned the other way around. That is, given a *wh*-filler, does the parser restrict its choice of gap to those that are not separated from the filler by an island boundary?

The first experiment on this topic was by Stowe (1983, 1984). She showed that the parser anticipates the appearance of a gap in legitimate positions following a *wh*-antecedent, but she found no gap anticipation within a subject island. This suggests that the parser has immediate access to the bounding constraints that block extraction from islands.

Stowe used a self-paced reading task, in which a sentence is presented visually word by word, and subjects press a button after each word to indicate that they have read it and are ready for the next one. The reading time for each word is taken as a measure of the difficulty of integrating that word into the structure for the sentence. Anticipation of a gap in nonisland contexts was revealed by what I will call the *filled gap effect*. If a lexical NP appears in a position that might have contained the gap, reading time for the initial word of the NP is often high (relative to reading time for the same word in the same local context but with no *wh*-antecedent in the sentence). A high reading time at the beginning of the lexical NP suggests that the parser is surprised not to find the trace in that position. Consider the sentences in (17), from Stowe's experiment.

(17)   a. The teacher asked what$_i$ the team laughed about Greg's older brother fumbling t$_i$.
       b. The teacher asked if the team laughed about Greg's older brother fumbling the ball.

The word *Greg's* is the potential locus for a filled gap effect. In (17a) the NP that begins with *Greg's* is in a legitimate gap position, since *The teacher asked what$_i$ the team laughed about t$_i$* is well formed.[15] (17b) establishes a baseline for identifying a filled gap effect in (17a), since (17b) has no *wh*-antecedent and the parser should not expect a gap at the position of *Greg's*.

The following examples illustrate the island-containing sentences that Stowe tested.

(18)   a. The teacher asked what$_i$ [the silly story about Greg's older brother] was supposed to mean t$_i$.
       b. The teacher asked if [the silly story about Greg's older brother] was supposed to mean anything.

In (18a) the *Greg's* NP is inside a subject phrase *(the silly story about Greg's older brother)* where a trace associated with *what* cannot legitimately appear; a sentence like *The teacher asked what$_i$ the silly story about t$_i$ was supposed to mean something* is not grammatical. A filled gap effect at *Greg's* in (18a) would thus indicate that the parser expects gaps in islands. (18b), which contains no *wh*-phrase, serves as comparison for (18a).

Stowe found a significant filled gap effect in (17a) relative to (17b), but no significant effect in (18a) relative to (18b). This is just what would be expected if the parser does respect island boundaries when it associates antecedents and traces. However, the technique used here may not be ideal for establishing this conclusion. The reason is that a filled gap effect would be expected to occur only when the parser positively *expects* a gap in that sentence position. But there might be reasons why the parser would not actively predict a gap with a subject phrase even if it were (temporarily) unaware that such a gap is prohibited. Thus the absence of a filled gap effect within an island is not the strongest test of the parser's use of the constraints in the grammar.[16] It cannot rule out the possibility that the parser would *accept* a gap within the island if the sentence offered one. Yet passive acceptance of a gap would equally indicate lack of concern for grammatical principles.

A more subtle test is provided by the *decoy gap effect* exploited by Clifton and Frazier (reported in Frazier 1985). A decoy gap is a possible but false gap that precedes the true gap in a sentence. In (19a), for example, the true gap follows *at*, but there is a decoy gap between *win* and *at*. Since *win* may be transitive or intransitive, the sentence is temporarily ambiguous at this point; only when the parser discovers that there is no lexical NP following *at* can it conclude that this is where the trace belongs, rather than after *win*.

(19) a. What$_i$ did the girl win at t$_i$?
      b. What$_i$ did the girl excel at t$_i$?

In (19b), by contrast, there is no decoy gap since *excel* is unambiguously intransitive and could not be followed by the trace. Sensitivity to a decoy gap, resulting in a garden path analysis, would be a sign that the parser is prepared to accept a gap in that position.

Clifton and Frazier's subjects gave grammaticality judgments to visually presented sentences; long judgment times were taken to indicate greater processing difficulty. Sentences like (19a) were found to be more difficult than matched sentences like (19b) containing no decoy gap, indicating that the parser can indeed be temporarily deceived by a decoy gap. Clifton and Frazier also tested sentences like those in (20), where the decoy gap after *won* in (20a) appears inside a relative clause island.

(20)   a. What$_i$ did the girl [who$_j$ t$_j$ won] receive t$_i$?
        b. What$_i$ did the girl [who$_j$ t$_j$ excelled] receive t$_i$?

In this case, as well, comparison of the results for the two sentences suggested that the parser might temporarily have taken the decoy gap after *won* in (20a) to be the real gap. But this, it was argued, would constitute a violation of Subjacency (or whatever principle, in theories other than GB, makes a relative clause an island); only if the parser ignored Subjacency, at least temporarily, could it have been taken in by the decoy gap in (20a).

However, the decoy gap effect in (20a) was smaller than in (19a) and was statistically marginal. Moreover, it admits of possible explanations other than delay in the parser's application of Subjacency. For one thing, the relative clause in (20a) contains its own *wh*-filler, the relative pronoun *who*, which needs a gap. Its gap, being in subject position, would be found before the decoy gap position was encountered. But the parser might nevertheless not have discontinued its search for a gap to associate with the relative pronoun; and for that, of course, the island constraint is irrelevant. It is worth noting in this regard that Stowe (1983, 1985/86) found a small (nonsignificant) filled gap effect at positions following an unambiguous subject gap, such as the position of *us* in (21).

(21)   My brother wanted to know who$_i$ t$_i$ will bring us home to Mom at Christmas.

This is compatible with the idea that the parser may not always terminate its gap search when it has found the true gap. So the marginal decoy effect in Clifton and Frazier's experiment might be attributable to the *wh*-phrase inside the relative clause, rather than to the illegitimate *wh*-antecedent outside it. Testing other kinds of islands, such as the subject islands of Stowe's experiment, would avoid this possible problem with *wh*-islands.

More importantly, though the trace of an external *wh*-phrase cannot appear within a relative clause or subject island, a secondary or "parasitic" gap associated with it can appear there. In fact, (20a) is actually a well-formed parasitic gap construction, though it needs some circumstantial padding, as in (22), to make it a natural one. (Here and throughout, *p* indicates a parasitic gap.)

(22)   Which prize$_i$ did the girl [who won p$_i$ at the fair] not receive t$_i$ in the mail until six months later?

(Note that since the gap position after *won* is ambiguous, (20a) and (22) also have an interpretation without the parasitic gap.) The gap pattern for the relevant reading of (20a) and (22) is comparable (ignoring the question/relative clause difference and other details) to that of the example (23), cited as acceptable by Chomsky (1986).

(23) He's a man that$_i$ anyone [who talks to p$_i$] usually likes t$_i$.

So even if there had been a strongly significant decoy gap effect at the object position in the relative clause of (20a), this would not necessarily signify a disregard of Subjacency. The parser might simply be alert to the possibility of a parasitic gap if a likely one is offered. (I concede that the typical undergraduate subject in a psycholinguistics experiment may be less sensitive to parasitic gaps than linguists now are.) For more decisive evidence we would want to apply the decoy gap paradigm to locally ambiguous gap positions where the grammar prohibits both "primary" *and* parasitic gaps. An example of this is the position after *paying* in (24).

(24) Which boy$_i$ did [Mary's attempt to see the show [without
      paying for a ticket]] annoy t$_i$ most?

The position after *paying* is inside an adjunct island that is itself inside a subject island, and even a parasitic gap is excluded there. Thus there is no legitimate interpretation of this sentence in which *paying* is transitive and has *boy* as its understood object. A fully constraint-sensitive parser should show no decoy gap effect in (24). It is probably worth testing such constructions, but it would be no surprise to discover that these materials are just too complicated for subjects to cope with.

Grodzinsky and Johnson (1985) have suggested a different approach that avoids all possibility of contamination by parasitic gaps. Their idea is that we could find out whether the parser applies island constraints by investigating gap positions that are outside of islands. A parser sensitive to island constraints will know not only that the true gap *cannot* appear *inside* an island, but also that the true gap *must* appear *outside* an island. Suppose we concentrate on islands that are not likely to be followed by the gap. This is the case for postverbal adverbial clauses, as suggested by the dubious acceptability of examples like (25).

(25) What$_i$ did you phone Mary [while feeling depressed] for t$_i$?

If the parser knew that the (primary) gap could not legitimately be inside the island, and if it could guess that the gap was unlikely to follow the island, then it could reasonably infer that the gap would precede the island. In other words, the gap must be found by the time the island begins. All we have to do, therefore, is to provide a locally ambiguous gap prior to an island boundary, and see whether the parser is especially eager to accept this as the true gap—more eager than if there were no following island boundary. If it is, then it apparently can recognize islands and knows their significance for its gap hunt. Note that this reasoning is unaffected by the possibility that the island contains a second (parasitic) gap.[17]

Grodzinsky and Johnson illustrated this point with the example sentence (26).

(26)   Who$_i$ did you walk t$_i$ [after talking to p$_i$]?

The verb *walk* tolerates (though it does not prefer) a direct object (as in *walk the dog*), so there is a possible gap between *walk* and the adjunct island introduced by *after*. This particular example (which also contains, irrelevantly, a parasitic gap within the adjunct) is awkward and doesn't inspire confidence that the parser will be influenced by the island boundary to recognize the gap after *walk* as the true gap. But more natural examples can easily be constructed. Fodor and Quinn (in progress) propose to test sentences like those shown in (27).

(27)   a.   !To which concerto did John complain because you forced
             him to listen against his will?
        b.   To which concerto did John complain that you forced him
             to listen against his will?
        c.   To which friend did John complain because you forced
             him to listen against his will?
        d.   To which friend did John complain that you forced him to
             listen against his will?

Subjects will be instructed to respond as quickly as possible if they detect a semantic anomaly in the sentence presented. They should indicate an anomaly in (27a) soon after the occurrence of *because*, if they are aware that the *because*-clause cannot contain the trace associated with *to which concerto*, for then *to which concerto* will have to modify *complain*, which is silly. (27b) is not anomalous, since the trace of *to which concerto* can modify *listen* in the *that*-clause; the *that*-clause is a complement, not an adjunct, and therefore is not an island. (27c) and (27d) make sense with the trace in the *complain*-clause. (27b), (27c), and (27d), together with a variety of anomalous sentences not involving islands, will serve to establish baselines for accuracy and speed of anomaly detection.

The sentences in (27) are still not perfectly natural; fronting a prepositional phrase (pied piping) is stilted in modern English and thus these examples are less than ideal for psychological testing. A fronted NP would be more natural, but then instead of a verb like *complain* the main clause would need a verb that takes an optional postverbal NP and an optional complement clause (that is, [_____ (NP)(S̄)]) such that the NP when present is extractable. But with the dubious exception of *promise* (for example, *Which friend did John promise that/because he was loyal (to)?*), English seems not to have any such verbs. This illustrates another common problem in psycholinguistic experimentation: having painstakingly constructed a recipe for exactly the right sentences to test, one discovers that nothing in the language satisfies the recipe.

In the present case it is possible to adapt Grodzinsky and Johnson's proposal slightly so that it can, after all, use sentences with fronted NPs rather than PPs. Instead of providing a syntactic gap that results in a semantic anomaly, we can fail to provide any gap at all before the island begins. The crucial sentence is then ungrammatical rather than merely anomalous, so we must switch the task from anomaly detection to ungrammaticality detection. Then we can use verbs like *complain* again, as in (28).

> (28) a. *Who did John complain because you forced him to listen to?
>
>   b. Who did John complain that you forced him to listen to?

There is no NP-shaped gap in the main clause in either (28a) or (28b). (28b) is grammatical because the filler can be associated with a gap in the *that*-clause, but (28a) is ungrammatical because the filler cannot be associated with a gap in the *because*-clause island, and hence it has no legitimate gap at all. If the parser is sensitive to adjunct islands, an on-line ungrammaticality detection task should produce "ungrammatical" responses to (28a) soon after the occurrence of *because*. (28b) will serve as control, to check that the parser doesn't panic when it encounters *any* subordinate clause before it has found a gap. Other controls, such as in (29) and (30), could be used to show that a difference in responses between (28a) and (28b) is not due just to a lexical difference between *that* and *because*.

> (29) a. Did John complain because you forced him to listen to Albert?
>
>   b. Did John complain that you forced him to listen to Albert?
>
> (30) a. *Did John convince because you forced him to listen to Albert?
>
>   b. *Did John convince that you forced him to listen to Albert?

These proposed studies have the disadvantage noted earlier, that there is no precise prediction about how rapidly subjects should respond. As soon as bounding constraint information becomes available to the parser, it should be able to reject (28a) without waiting to examine the *because*-clause for possible gap positions. But just how fast would the response have to be, to prove that bounding information is *immediately* accessible? The best one can do here is to see whether the response to *because* is as speedy as the response to other types of ungrammaticality. But despite this remaining source of imprecision, this approach should usefully complement the studies by Stowe and by Clifton and Frazier, since it seeks a positive effect of respect for islands, whereas the others looked for a positive effect of disrespect for islands. This double-pronged attack is optimal. I should stress that no data are available yet from Fodor and Quinn's studies. Intuitive judgments on sentences like (27)–(30) suggest that the anomalies/ungrammaticalities *are* readily detectable and hence that the linguistic constraints *are* rapidly applied; but as usual with psycholinguistic experiments it would be wise to wait and see.

4 An Experimental Comparison of Types of Empty Category

A characteristic shared by all the experiments I have described so far is that the hypothesis that is tested derives from the GB model.[18] GPSG makes negative predictions—that no evidence will be found for nonsurface levels of syntactic representation, or for a module boundary between phrase structure and *wh*-trace binding principles. So the plausibility of GPSG could be enhanced only by consistent failure of the search for such phenomena. It would be interesting to turn things around, by finding a positive prediction of GPSG to test. One possibility concerns the range of empty categories. For GPSG, only *wh*-trace is a genuine empty category in syntactic trees, and only *wh*-trace is linked to its antecedent by syntactic principles. So, under a reasonably direct implementation, GPSG predicts differences between the processing of *wh*-trace and the processing of constructions that GB Theory regards as containing NP-trace and PRO. Whether these differences could be expected to have detectable effects in available experimental paradigms is another question, but at least we have here something that we can go out and look for.

Bever and McElree (1988) have used a priming paradigm to investigate the interpretation of different kinds of empty categories. They employed a self-paced reading paradigm like Stowe's, but with successive presentation of whole phrases rather than single words. The subjects' task was to indicate as rapidly as possible whether an adjective presented after the sentence had occurred in the sentence or not. In all cases of interest, the adjective did appear in the sentence. In fact, it appeared in an NP that was the correct antecedent for an empty category later in the sentence. Also tested, for comparison purposes, were sentences in which the adjective-containing NP appeared but there was no associated empty category. If the response to the adjective was faster for the experimental sentence (containing an empty category) than for its matched control sentence (with no empty category), this was taken as evidence that the adjective-containing NP had been associated with the empty category by the parser, thus boosting the accessibility of the adjective for the end-of-sentence task.

I will discuss just one of Bever and McElree's experiments, in which PRO, NP-trace in raising constructions, and *wh*-trace in *tough* constructions were compared with overt lexical pronouns.[19] Sample materials are shown in (31); the priming target in all cases was *astute*.

(31) a. The astute lawyer who faced the female judge strongly
          hoped PRO to argue during the trial. [PRO construction]
      b. The astute lawyer who faced the female judge was certain
          NP-trace to argue during the trial. [raising construction]
      c. The astute lawyer was hard for the judge to control
          wh-trace during the very long trial. [*tough*-movement
          construction]
      d. The astute lawyer who faced the female judge hoped he
          would speak during the trial. [lexical pronoun construction]
      e. The astute lawyer who faced the female judge hated the
          long speech during the trial. [control sentence; no anaphor]

Significant priming effects were observed in all of (31a–d), compared with the control sentence (31e). Bever and McElree took this as an indication that binding of an empty category was occurring in (31a–c), comparable to the binding of an overt pronoun in (31d). It was also found that both kinds of trace gave rise to stronger priming effects than PRO, and this was taken as evidence for a GB taxonomy of these constructions, rather than a GPSG or LFG taxonomy according to which neither the NP-trace nor PRO constructions actually contain empty categories.

These are initial studies in a valuable new line of research, and further work may refine the information they provide. The end-of-sentence task is rather far from the crucial gap position, and response times were high (on the order of 1 second). Since the theoretically critical finding that NP-trace patterned with *wh*-trace rather than with PRO was evident only in the error data, not in the response time data, it would be good to replicate this study with a more tightly timed task. Also, though the existence of priming in all of (31a–c) appears to be statistically solid, the slowness of the responses raises the possibility, which Bever and McElree note, that this task may tap semantic interpretation rather than syntactic processing. If so, the existence of priming in all three cases would be consistent with almost any linguistic theory—that is, with any theory that claims that raised NP constructions are interpreted like related unraised NP constructions, and that clauses with no subjects may be interpreted in the same way as clauses with overt subjects.

Here we confront yet another wrinkle in the interpretability of experimental results. In the timing studies described earlier, it is of no great importance whether the tasks tap semantic or syntactic processing, since evidence of rapid semantic processing of empty categories would be sufficient to show rapid syntactic processing of empty categories. (Though if we were interested in how *slow* syntactic processing of empty categories is, evidence from semantic processing would not be helpful, since slow semantic processing does not necessarily imply slow syntactic processing —assuming that syntax feeds semantics but not vice versa.) However, when the issue is the uniformity or nonuniformity of syntactic processing of different kinds of empty categories, only syntactic processing evidence will do. Similarities and differences in syntactic processing could be obscured by similarities and differences in semantic processing. For example, Bever and McElree point out that only in the case of PRO do the antecedent and the empty category have independent theta roles. So if the PRO construction behaves differently than the others, this might be a fact about its semantics and might not reflect at all on the syntactic status of PRO.

Wright and Garrett (1984) have shown how syntactic and semantic priming effects can be dissociated, by looking for syntactic priming where all the relevant items are semantically anomalous and hence equally unexpected on purely semantic grounds. They compared sentence fragments such as those in (32), followed by the lexical decision target *formulate*.

(32)   a. If your bicycle is stolen, you must
        b. For now, the happy family lives with

They found that priming occurred in (32a), where the verb target was syntactically compatible with the preceding sentential context, but no priming occurred in (32b), where the verb target was not a syntactically legitimate continuation of the sentence fragment. So far, this semantics-free task has not been adapted to gap filling, to establish syntactic priming profiles for different types of empty category, but this would be a good approach to try in the attempt to isolate the stage of processing at which the effects found by Bever and McElree occur.

5 Conclusion

Rather than attempt to summarize all that has gone before, I will end with a projection for the future. If I were to make a guess, it would be that further experimentation will continue to show that the human sentence-parsing mechanism does most of the things it has to do both quickly and accurately. The places where parsing breaks down are striking and interesting; but most of them involve temporarily ambiguous constructions where the grammar does not provide the relevant information at the point at which the parser is faced with a choice. No parser could be blamed for sometimes making a wrong decision in such circumstances. In *un*ambiguous constructions, errors seem to be quite rare and may be attributable to simple processing overload (as in the case of multiply center-embedded constructions). I see very little indication that the parser makes mistakes because it ignores the grammar, or applies it late, or applies it improperly.

Now suppose that this is indeed what future research shows. In one way it would be disappointing. To the extent that the parser exhibits no idiosyncratic or "stupid" behavior, it presents us with the familiar problem of not being able to tell how a mechanism works when it's working well. Its surface will be too smooth to reveal its underlying character. On the other hand, if the human parser is indeed a highly efficient, well-oiled system, that is in itself an important empirical finding, one that couldn't have been anticipated, and one that should constrain future theory building. The most plausible variety of grammar (other things, such as descriptive coverage, being equal) would be the one that is optimal as the data base for an efficient parser.

This makes the project highly interdisciplinary. The need for psychological sophistication is clear; we have seen how carefully experimental methods must be chosen, and how potentially confounding factors must be identified and controlled out. The need for linguistic sophistication is also clear, from its role in both the design of experimental materials and the precise statement of hypotheses to test. The finding that the human parser makes highly efficient use of the grammar would call for understanding of efficiency arguments of the kind that computational linguistics can provide, tempered perhaps by neuropsychological findings about what is efficient for the human brain.

Notes

1. I will assume throughout this discussion that the mental grammar cannot be expected to provide an algorithm for sentence processing, but only the information about the language that the processor needs to draw on. The rules-as-process approach has not proved fruitful.

2. The "superstrategy" approach developed in Fodor 1979, borrowing from ideas in augmented transition network (ATN) theory, offered solutions to these problems. But as noted there, that approach was really consonant with a different theory of grammars—the Extended Standard Theory, or one putting even heavier emphasis on surface syntactic representations.

3. The discussion of GB-based parsing in what follows will not reflect the recent ideas of Abney and Cole (1986) and Abney (1987), partly because I have not thought through their relation to the experimental data, and also because this model has not yet been extended in detail to long-distance movement, which will be my main focus here.

4. Also, this D-structure explanation conflicted with the most influential GB-based parsing model (Berwick and Weinberg 1984), which does not assume that D-structure representations are computed during sentence comprehension. (Incidentally, this means that Berwick and Weinberg's model does not constitute a very direct implementation of the competence grammar they assume.)

5. Anyone interested in contributing to this debate might want to consider the possibility of inserting a wedge into Forster and Stevenson's argument at the point at which they equate the correctability scales across different experiments.

6. For convenience, in what follows I will refer to movement operations, and to empty categories such as NP-trace and PRO, but without intending to prejudge the differences between linguistic theories.

7. See Caplan and Hildebrandt 1988 for an investigation of the processing of different kinds of empty categories by aphasics, in relation to differences between GB Theory and LFG.

8. GPSG does employ a distinct formal device (the slash category) for handling trace binding; but since slash features are subject to the same percolation principles as other syntactic features, I think that a delay in adding slash features to trees would constitute a devious implementation. The most natural implementation, I assume, would be one in which all features in a local tree are established (as far as is possible) before moving on to the next one.

9. However, see Gorrell 1987 for an account of such findings in terms of a parallel processing model that does not posit garden paths.

10. This is no longer true. See note 11.

11. Experiments by Nicol (1988) show priming by the relative pronoun only, at the gap position in sentences like (10). This is compatible with there being no garden path, which would undermine FCR's argument for grammar modules. But this result needs to be interpreted against the background of other recent experiments that have looked for priming by the controller of PRO. See Nicol 1988, Nicol and Swinney 1989, McElree and Bever 1989, and Fodor 1989.

12. TCS recommend caution in interpreting these results until the seven-word delay is tested both with and without the empty category in the same experiment.

13. The existence of an empty category after *accused* is not clear until after *of* is processed (since the sentence might have continued as in *The policeman saw the boy that the crowd at the party accused Sam of insulting*). We must assume that the parser anticipates possible gaps (see the later discussion of Stowe's experiments), or else that its response to the visual target was sensitive to the spoken words that occurred right after presentation of the target.

14. If priming by *party* had also been tested, it would have been possible to see whether there was any tendency for the parser to select the linearly most recent NP in violation of the c-command requirement; *crowd* was the most recent c-commanding candidate.

15. Many speakers consider that the actual gap position after *fumbling* in (17a) is not fully acceptable. This does not bear *directly* on the hypothesis being tested, since the actual gap does not occur until after the "filled gap" position that is of interest; but it is an unfortunate aspect of the stimulus materials, since one would not want subjects in this experiment to start expecting ungrammatical sentences.

16. A possible sign of this is that Stowe's experiment revealed no sensitivity to potential parasitic gaps; see the discussion below.

17. Does this approach completely rule out the possibility that the parser would tolerate a primary gap in the island? All we can really show is a shift in the parser's betting strategies about the status of the possible pre-island gap, in response to the island boundary. However, in the proposed experiments the response of interest is a rejection of certain sentences, and for the parser to be making this rejection it would have to be anticipating no possible amelioration by a gap in the island. Even so, it might be worthwhile to try to explore the confidence levels of these judgments.

18. I have worded this point carefully, because it is actually GPSG that is put to the test in these experiments. GB Theory makes positive claims about the existence of nonsurface

levels and of a binding module; but as noted earlier, null results might be explained away, leaving GB Theory unharmed. GPSG makes negative claims about the non-existence of these constructs and is therefore open to falsification by positive experimental results.

19. I should emphasize again that this is GB terminology, used for convenience here even though it conflicts with the claims of other linguistic theories; see below.

References

Abney, S. 1987. Licensing and parsing. In *Proceedings of North Eastern Linguistic Society* 17. GLSA, University of Massachusetts, Amherst.

Abney, S., and J. Cole. 1986. A government-binding parser. In *Proceedings of North Eastern Linguistic Society* 16. GLSA, University of Massachusetts, Amherst.

Altmann, G., ed. 1989. Special issue on parsing and interpretation. *Language and Cognitive Processes* 4.3/4.

Aoun, J. 1983. The status of movement rules. In T. Borowsky and D. Finer, eds., *Occasional papers in linguistics* 8. University of Massachusetts, Amherst.

Berwick, R. C., and A. S. Weinberg. 1984. *The grammatical basis of linguistic performance: Language use and acquisition.* Cambridge, Mass.: MIT Press.

Berwick, R. C., and A. S. Weinberg. 1985. Deterministic parsing and linguistic explanation. *Language and Cognitive Processes* 1.2, 109−134.

Bever, T. G. 1970. The influence of speech performance on linguistic structure. In G. B. Flores d'Arcais and J. M. Levelt, eds., *Advances in psycholinguistics.* Amsterdam: North Holland.

Bever, T. G., and B. McElree. 1988. Empty categories access their antecedents during comprehension. *Linguistic Inquiry* 19, 35−43.

Bresnan, J. 1978. A realistic transformational grammar. In M. Halle, J. Bresnan, and G. A. Miller, eds., *Linguistic theory and psychological reality.* Cambridge, Mass.: MIT Press.

Bresnan, J., ed. 1982. *The mental representation of grammatical relations.* Cambridge, Mass.: MIT Press.

Caplan, D., and N. Hildebrandt. 1988. *Disorders of syntactic comprehension.* Cambridge, Mass.: MIT Press.

Carlson, G. N., and M. K. Tanenhaus. 1989. *Linguistic structure in language processing.* Dordrecht, Holland: Kluwer Academic Publishers.

Chomsky, N. 1981. *Lectures on government and binding.* Dordrecht, Holland: Foris.

Chomsky, N. 1986. *Barriers.* Cambridge, Mass.: MIT Press.

Clifton, C., and L. Frazier. 1986. The use of syntactic information in filling gaps. *Journal of Psycholinguistic Research* 15.3, 209−224.

Crain, S., and J. D. Fodor. 1985a. Rules and constraints in sentence processing. In *Proceedings of North Eastern Linguistic Society* 15. GLSA, University of Massachusetts, Amherst.

Crain, S., and J. D. Fodor. 1985b. How can grammars help parsers? In D. R. Dowty, L. Karttunen, and A. M. Zwicky, eds., *Natural language parsing: Psychological, computational and theoretical perspectives.* Cambridge: Cambridge University Press.

Crain, S., and J. D. Fodor. 1987. Sentence matching and overgeneration. *Cognition* 26, 123−169.

Fodor, J. A., T. Bever, and M. Garrett. 1974. *The psychology of language.* New York: McGraw-Hill.

Fodor, J. D. 1978. Parsing strategies and constraints on transformations. *Linguistic Inquiry* 9, 427−473.

Fodor, J. D. 1979. Superstrategy. In W. E. Cooper and E. C. T. Walker, eds., *Sentence processing: Psycholinguistic studies presented to Merrill Garrett*. Hillsdale, N.J.: Lawrence Erlbaum Associates.

Fodor, J. D. 1985. Deterministic parsing and subjacency. *Language and Cognitive Processes* 1.1, 3–42.

Fodor, J. D. 1988. On modularity in syntactic processing. *Journal of Psycholinguistic Research* 17, 125–168.

Fodor, J. D. 1989. Empty categories in sentence processing. In Altmann 1989.

Fodor, J. D., and D. Quinn. In progress. Parsing adjunct islands. Ms., Graduate Center, CUNY, 1987.

Forster, K. I., and B. J. Stevenson. 1987. Sentence matching and well-formedness. *Cognition* 26, 171–186.

Frazier, L. 1985. Modularity and the representational hypothesis. In *Proceedings of North Eastern Linguistic Society* 15. GLSA, University of Massachusetts, Amherst.

Frazier, L. 1986. Natural classes in language processing. Paper presented at the MIT Cognitive Science Seminar, November 1986.

Frazier, L., C. Clifton, and J. Randall. 1983. Filling gaps: Decision principles and structure in sentence comprehension. *Cognition* 13, 187–222.

Freedman, S. A. 1982. Behaviorial reflexes of constraints on transformations. Doctoral dissertation, Monash University.

Freedman, S. A., and K. I. Forster. 1985. The psychological status of overgenerated sentences. *Cognition* 19, 101–131.

Garnsey, S. M., M. K. Tanenhaus, and R. M. Chapman. 1987. Evoked potential measures of parsing for sentences with local structural ambiguity. Paper presented at BABBLE conference, Niagara Falls.

Gazdar, G., E. Klein, G. K. Pullum, and I. A. Sag. 1985. *Generalized Phrase Structure Grammar*. Cambridge, Mass.: Harvard University Press.

Gorrell, P. 1987. Studies of human syntactic processing: Ranked-parallel versus serial models. Doctoral dissertation, University of Connecticut.

Grodzinsky, Y., and K. Johnson. 1985. Principles of grammar and their role in parsing. Ms., MIT.

Hankamer, J. 1973. Unacceptable ambiguity. *Linguistic Inquiry* 4, 17–68.

Kaplan, R. M., and J. Bresnan. 1982. Lexical-Functional Grammar: A formal system for grammatical representation. In Bresnan 1982.

Kutas, M., and S. A. Hillyard. 1983. Event-related potentials to grammatical errors and sentence anomalies. *Memory and Cognition* 11, 539–550.

McElree, B., and T. G. Bever. 1989. The psychological reality of linguistically defined gaps. *Journal of Psycholinguistic Research* 18, 21–35.

Mehler, J., J. Segui, and P. Carey. 1978. Tails of words: Monitoring ambiguity. *Journal of Verbal Learning and Verbal Behavior* 17, 29–35.

Miller, G. A., and N. Chomsky. 1963. Finitary models of language users. In R. D. Luce, R. R. Bush, and E. Galanter, eds., *Handbook of mathematical psychology*, Vol. II. New York: Wiley.

Morton, J., and J. Long. 1976. Effect of word transitional probability on phoneme identification. *Journal of Verbal Learning and Verbal Behavior* 15.1, 43–51.

Nicol, J. 1988. Coreference processing during sentence comprehension. Doctoral dissertation, MIT.

Nicol, J., and D. Swinney. 1989. The role of structure in coreference assignment during sentence comprehension. *Journal of Psycholinguistic Research* 18, 5–19.

Perlmutter, D., ed. 1983. *Studies in Relational Grammar*, 1. Chicago: University of Chicago Press.

Stowe, L. A. 1983. Models of gap location in the human parser. Doctoral dissertation, University of Wisconsin. Distributed by Indiana University Linguistics Club, Bloomington.

Stowe, L. A. 1984. A subject/object asymmetry in parsing. In *Proceedings of North Eastern Linguistic Society* 14. GLSA, University of Massachusetts, Amherst.

Stowe, L. A. 1985/86. Parsing WH-constructions: Evidence for on-line gap location. *Language and Cognitive Processes* 1.3, 227–245.

Swinney, D. 1979. Lexical access during sentence comprehension: (Re)consideration of context effects. *Journal of Verbal Learning and Verbal Behavior* 18, 645–659.

Swinney, D. 1983. Theoretical and methodological issues in cognitive science: A psycholinguistic perspective. In W. Kintsch, J. Miller, and P. Polsow, eds., *Methods and tactics in cognitive science.* Hillsdale, N.J.: Lawrence Erlbaum Associates.

Swinney, D. A., and J. D. Fodor, eds. 1989. Special issue on sentence processing. *Journal of Psycholinguistic Research* 18.1.

Swinney, D., M. Ford, J. Bresnan, and U. Frauenfelder. 1988. Coreference assignment during sentence processing. In M. Macken, ed., *Language structure and processing.* Stanford, Calif.: CSLI.

Tanenhaus, M. K., G. N. Carlson, and M. S. Seidenberg. 1985. Do listeners compute linguistic representations? In D. R. Dowty, L. Karttunen, and A. M. Zwicky, eds., *Natural language parsing: Psychological, computational and theoretical perspectives.* Cambridge: Cambridge University Press.

Wanner, E. 1974. *On remembering, forgetting, and understanding sentences.* The Hague: Mouton.

Wright, B., and M. F. Garrett. 1984. Lexical decision in sentences: Effects of syntactic structure. *Memory and Cognition* 12.1, 31–45.

Chapter 4
Principle-Based Parsing
Robert C. Berwick

1 Introduction: Principle-Based Parsing and Rule-Based Parsing

This chapter describes a new approach to processing natural language, *principle-based parsing*, that has been developed at the MIT Artificial Intelligence Laboratory over the past five years. Principle-based parsing replaces the traditionally large set of rules used to parse sentences on a language-by-language basis with a much smaller, fixed set of parameterized, universal principles. The principles interact deductively to replace many rules.

In the past few years there has been much talk of a dramatic shift away from rules in linguistic theories to systems of interacting principles. Principles-and-parameters models (in one instantiation, known as Government-Binding or GB Theory) have been regarded as leading this charge: for example, there are no particular transformational "rules" in this kind of theory. On this view, there is no single "rule" of passive; rather, passive constructions result from the interactions of deeper morphological and syntactic operations (case absorption, thematic role assignment, and free movement).[1] These interacting principles happen to have, as surface realizations, sentence forms that may be described as "active" and "passive," and were so described in earlier theories, for example, by transformations, or even by pairs of context-free rules related by metarules.

But this shift is certainly not unique to principles-and-parameters theory. Many other current linguistic theories, among them Generalized Phrase Structure Grammar (GPSG) and Head-Driven Phrase Structure Grammar, have gradually shifted to declarative constraints that are not construction specific. For instance, modern GPSG theory is full of principles that fix the well-formedness of surface strings without spelling out explicitly their detailed phrase structure: the Foot Feature Principle, the Head Feature

Research on principle-based parsing at the Artificial Intelligence Laboratory at MIT has been supported by NSF grant DCR-85552543 under a Presidential Young Investigator's Award to Professor Robert C. Berwick, by a grant from the Lotus Development Corporation, by the Kapor Family Foundation, and by the IBN Graduate Research Fellowship Program. This chapter was originally written in the fall of 1986 and substantially revised in 1987; it was further revised in 1989.

Convention, and the Control Agreement Principle replace explicit phrase structure rules with constraint sets. These theories too no longer contain large numbers of particular rules, but declarative schemas constrained according to syntactic and morphological principles.

We may contrast a principle-based approach with a *construction-based* approach to language. A construction-based approach attempts to describe sentences typologically by spelling out surface order and morphological patterns—passive, dative, and the like. A principle-based approach aims to reconstitute the vocabulary of grammatical theory in such a way that surface and language-particular constructions like passive follow from the interactions of a different set of primitive elements than before. Roughly and intuitively, the analogy is that doing construction-based linguistics is like doing chemistry without molecular and atomic theory: though one can describe the various chemical compounds that appear, one cannot say why certain chemicals and not others are found—this requires a new scientific vocabulary that consists of basic elements and their principles of combination, exactly what the principle-based approach seeks.

But what exactly does this shift to principles imply for *parsing*? A host of important issues arise, most of which are only just now being explored. Though the rest of the chapter will address these in more detail, I would like to set the stage with some general remarks.

What is principle-based parsing? Perhaps it is easiest to say what it is *not*. It is not like more traditional parsing that relies on many thousands of individual, language-particular rules, exemplified by augmented transition network systems (ATNs) or most systems based on context-free grammars. These rule-based parsing systems attempt to describe sentences typologically by spelling out shallow word surface order and spelling patterns—passive, dative, and the like.

For instance, consider a "passive" sentence: *The ice cream was eaten.* To understand this sentence, at the very least a parser must be able to analyze *ice cream* as the object of *eat*—the thing eaten. This is triggered (in English) by the form of the verb *be* (here, *was*) plus the *en* ending on the verb *eat*. A typical rule-based parser might capture this left-to-right pattern in an if-then rule:

> If: subject filled, *be*–Verb + ed, no object
> Then: make the subject the object

Note that this if-then rule directly encodes the left-to-right order of the English passive pattern, along with all its particular features. It is appropriate only for English, and only for this particular kind of passive form.

The basic idea of principle-based parsing is to replace this rule with a much deeper, smaller, explanatory set of basic principles. In some ways, this is much like the shift in medical expert systems from a shallow, descriptivist approach to an explanatory theory based on, for example, a knowledge of kidney physiology.

The motivation for the shift from rules to principles is the same in both domains. Rule systems have many problems. They are too inflexible, too specific, too fragile, too hard to maintain, and too large. As we will see, principle-based parsing repairs each of these defects:

• What happens when a sentence is only partially well formed? Sentences like *What do you wonder who likes* or *John is proud Bill*, though hard to understand, don't cause people to collapse like a rule-based system would. Rather, people understand such sentences uniformly. Rule-based language systems have traditionally handled such possibilities by adding weights or more rules that can describe the wrong sentences. But this makes the rule set larger still.

• What happens if the rule system is missing a rule that is almost, but not quite, like the one that handles passives? Consider the sentence *The ice cream got eaten*. This is a simple dialect variant, but unless it has been preprogrammed into the rule base—often one programmer's dialect—the full system will fail on such an example. Of course, once the problem is known, a system can be patched by adding a new rule, but there is no end to the patches, the maintenance problems, and the size of the rule system.

• What happens in other languages? The French sentence fragment *faire manger la pomme par Jean* 'to have the apple be eaten by John' is like the English passive, but there is no *be* form, and the object can follow *eat* (*manger*). Thus, the entire system must be retooled for new dialects and languages, and this in fact has been the traditional approach. In a principle-based approach, we can view such cases as variations on a basic theme. Instead of writing a completely new, specialized if-then rule, we can regard the French (and English) examples as parameterized variants of a set of more primitive, underlying components. Section 6 describes principle-based translation in more detail.

• What happens when the rule set becomes too large? Because rules are fine grained and language particular, existing rule-based natural language systems use thousands of rules. Since parsing algorithms run as a function of grammar size, an inflated rule size forces poor system performance. Too much effort is expended trying to build special-purpose algorithms or hardware when the real source of the problem is an overly large rule system that attempts to capture all the different possible placements of adjunct phrases (prepositional phrases and the like). For example, one recent language system developed at Boeing contained many thousands of individual rules for a portion of English. As is so often the case, even a single sentence could be analyzed in a thousand different ways or more (Harrison 1988).

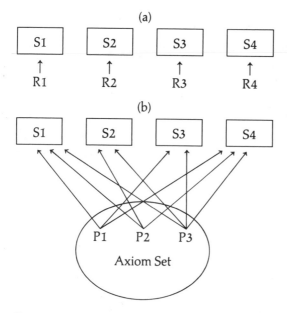

Figure 4.1
These two figures illustrate the difference between rule-based and principle-based systems. (a) A rule-based system. Each sentence construction type, like passive, is described by a distinct rule. (b) A principle-based system. Sentence types are derived from a smaller basis set of more fundamental principles that deductively interact to yield the effect of constructions like passive. See section 2 for more details on just how this works.

1.1 A Few Principles Can Replace Many Rules

In contrast, a principle-based approach aims to reconstruct the vocabulary of grammatical theory in such a way that surface and language-particular constructions like passive *follow* from the interactions of a small set of primitive elements. Figure 4.1 illustrates the difference. The top half of the figure shows a conventional rule-based approach. Each sentence type (a *construction* like passive) is described by a different rule. The bottom half of the figure shows a principle-based approach.

Principles and word meaning building blocks are like atoms in chemistry, or axioms in a logic system. By combining just a few dozen atoms, we can build up a huge number of chemical compounds (sentence rules and word meanings) instead of listing each compound separately. In the language domain, we can replace the surface effect of many rules with longer deductive chains of just a few axioms. Note that one can get the multiplicative effect of $n_1 \times n_2 \times \cdots$ rules by the interaction of $n_1 + n_2 + \cdots$ autonomous modules. Thus, by supplying a dozen or so principles, each with two or three degrees of freedom, we can encode many thousands of rules. By varying the parameters, we can describe different dialects and even different languages. Naturally, no single principle accounts for all the variation we see in a language, just as no single molecule accounts for all chemical compounds and reactions. It is the interaction that matters.

Of course, the principle-based approach raises many questions for parsing. The next sections of this chapter will attempt to answer these key questions:

• Are parsers based on principles really any different from those based on rules? If so, how?
• Are principle-based parsers more efficient than rule-based parsers? Or must they somehow be "multiplied out" into a more efficient, individual rule-like form? After all, at first blush it would seem that working directly with principles rather than surface constructions could lead to a slower parser, since one might have to laboriously recalculate, each time, the permitted surface arrangements of phrases: since principles lead to a more circuitous connection between what sequence of words actually appears on the surface and the principles beneath, principle-based parsing would seem to demand a *larger* number of computational steps to map between surface sentence and underlying form. What then if anything is gained by grounding parsers on principles instead of rules? We will see that the trade-off between multiplying out principles off-line versus using them on-line is quite subtle.
• Contrary to what is often assumed, a "direct" or "principle-based" implementation of a linguistic theory need not assume a close correspondence between the formal operations of a generative grammar and the computational operations of linguistic processing. The usual assumption is that the grammatical theory ought to reproduce the clustering of properties observed in psycholinguistic experiments (Frazier 1986). But there is a subtle fallacy here: this position fails to distinguish between the *temporal* sequence of operations in parsing and the *logical* sequence of operations in a derivation. If these do not correspond, it is often said that a parser is an "indirect" implementation of a grammatical theory (and as a corollary it is claimed that the grammatical theory is correspondingly lacking). On just these grounds, Frazier (1986) argues from certain experimental evidence that a principles-and-parameters theory is flawed. However, we will see (section 2.3) that one can build a language-processing system that intuitively *does* directly incorporate principles-and-parameters theory, even though it need not directly reflect the clusters of psycholinguistic properties we see "on the outside." In other words, psycho-

linguistic results may not clearly tell us whether or not people use a principle-based parser.

• What does it mean to say that grammatical principles are used *directly* or *indirectly* in parsing? Is it just the difference between using an axiom system and using its theorems to deduce whether a sentence is well formed, as suggested above?

• What is the range of algorithms possible for principle-based parsers? What representations—or, more broadly, *information structures*—must they, can they, or should they use?

• What can principle-based parsers do well that rule-based parsers cannot?

Though I will defer detailed answers to these questions to later sections, I can offer a glimpse at them now.

Consider first a simple example of how general principles can replace specific rules. One general principle says that action-expressing phrases in a sentence must either *begin* with a verb in some languages or *end* with a verb in others. This basic description of the tree shapes in a language, dubbed $\bar{X}$ *theory*, gives us part of the variation between languages like English and Spanish, on the one hand, and languages like German and Japanese, on the other. In English the verb must come first, with the object after. A second principle, called the *Case Filter*, says that all pronounced nouns like *ice cream* must receive case, either from an active verb like *ate* or from an auxiliary verb like *was*; the adjective-like verb *eaten* does not do the job. Taken together, these two principles plus a few others conspire to push *ice cream* into its position at the front of a sentence if the sentence contains a verb sequence like *was eaten*. There is no explicit Passive rule. (Figure 4.3 shows the interactions between these various constraints in a more complete version of the same model.)

Section 3 on principle-based parsing for Warlpiri shows how these principles can be used to build a parser that does not use individual rules. Drawing on research carried out by Michael Kashket (1986), it also shows how the same principles can be made to work with a language that is very different from Romance languages or German—in this case, the Australian aboriginal language Warlpiri. Warlpiri is a good test case for the principle-based model because its structure seems at first so different from that of English, German, or Romance languages.

Many principles operate like constraint filters. This lets them handle the problem of partially well formed sentences. A principle-based parser can accommodate language "mistakes" by constraint relaxation. If a sentence is ill formed, it is simply because one or another principle fails to hold. In fact, in the principle-based approach, there really is no such thing as an ungrammatical sentence—this notion doesn't even really apply. Every string of sounds is assigned some interpretation. Some of these happen to "pass" all the principles, whereas some fall short in one area or another.

For example, consider the sentence *This is the ice cream that I don't know whether it was eaten by John.* Technically this sentence is ill formed, and it would break existing language interfaces because they would have no special rule that could apply in such cases. In contrast, a principle-based system would degrade gracefully. In this example, a locality principle that limits the distance between words like *it* and *ice cream* is at fault, but importantly all other principles hold. In particular, the principle that every sentence has a subject (*it*) and a verb (*eaten*) still holds. Sentence analysis would proceed as before, simply taking note of this violation, which does not impede inference or understanding. No special "weights" or extra rules are required.

The principle that a sentence needs a subject and object is also parameterized, illustrating how principles can ease the task of language translation. In languages like Spanish and Italian, and under degraded situations in English, the subject need not be expressed. These and other similar, but simple, parameters are what makes English different from Spanish or Italian. Thus, our parser does not need special rules to analyze Spanish or another English dialect; it simply sets its parameters to those values required for Spanish, such as "The subject may be missing." Only the dictionary changes from language to language. Section 6 describes an implemented system, UNITRAN (Dorr 1987, 1990), that adopts this approach.

1.2 Rules and Principles: The Key Differences

Before we proceed, it is important to clear away some possible misunderstandings about the differences between rules and principles. It should be evident that most rules could just as well be expressed as declarative principles. For instance, one could just use a definitional language like Rounds's (1988) first-order formalism (LFL), or definite clause grammars (DCGs), to transform concatenative context-free rules into declarative constraints. For instance, in Rounds's formalism we might write

$$S \rightarrow NP\ VP \Rightarrow S(x) \Leftrightarrow \exists yz.NP(y) \land VP(z) \land x = yz.$$

On this view, a set of context-free rules expressed via definite clause grammars could just as well be called a set of principles, since indeed they fit our definition as a "set of statements, well-grounded on general empirical evidence, such that a range of phenomena follow from their interaction."

Similarly, any principle A can be converted into a procedural rule that simply says, "Apply principle A." Evidently, then, there is nothing to be gained at this level of discussion. Indeed, the rule-principle distinction here nearly smacks of the declarative-procedural controversy in artificial intelligence research: are facts about some domain best stated in a program (procedurally) or declaratively? I think that pursuing a formal rule-principle distinction will be about as fruitful as this older dispute—which is to say, not very fruitful at all. But even though in this superficial formal sense there seems to be little point in pursuing a distinction between rules and constraints, from a *practical* point of view—how the notions of "rule" and "principle" have been distinguished in linguistic practice—the difference looms large.

In practice, though, "rules" have nearly always been used to describe language-particular constructions like passive or raising-to-object, whereas principles (such as the A-over-A Condition) have been taken to be language universal. For example, the first-order formalization of the rule expanding S given above is presumably language particular, hence, colloquially, a "rule."

Thus, we seem to have at least two notions at work here: one is *language particular* versus *non—language particular*, and the other is *construction specific* versus *non—construction specific*. This yields four possible distinctions. The usual notion of a rule such as Passive is language particular and construction specific. A principle is language universal and non—construction specific (though this is of course relative to how abstract we take the notion of a construction to be); a paradigm example is the principle Move α. What of the other two possibilities? In modern theories, the language-specific and non-construction-specific option is filled by *parameterizing* universal principles: thus, a language may contain Move α or not; or it may select the option that phrasal heads are first (as in English) or final (as in Japanese). The remaining language-universal and construction-specific category would apply to a theory such as that proposed by Bach (1965), positing language-universal but construction-specific rules such as *wh*-movement; for example, a language could either have *wh*-movement rules or not.

In the remainder of this chapter, then, we will take *principles* to be language-universal statements, parameterized to handle the case of particular languages, and *principle-based parsers* to be those that in some sense use language-universal statements to analyze sentences, that is, to associate linguistic descriptions with sentences.

A further distinction has to do with whether principles themselves can or ought to be stated declaratively or not. At least superficially, it appears that most modern syntactic theories can be stated purely declaratively, though it is not obvious that all linguistic levels of representation can be so stated.[2] If this is correct, then a declarative grammatical formulation of at least the D- and S-structure components of GB Theory should be possible, though the difficulties in doing so are perhaps not fully appreciated. (Section 2 sketches some of the problems in broad outline.) For example, consider the important constraint of GB Theory, as outlined by Van Riemsdijk and Williams (1986: 292, after Chomsky 1981), that an empty category must be "properly governed." (This is called the *Empty Category Principle*, or *ECP*.) Proper government is a declarative constraint that rules out sentence configurations like (1) while admitting sentences like (2):

(1)   *John was tried [*trace* to be promoted].

(2)   Who do you [think (that) Bill saw *trace*]?

Van Riemsdijk and Williams define the relevant principle(s) this way:

> *Empty Category Principle*: [*e*] (an empty element like a *trace* or a non-lexical pronominal) must be properly governed.
>
> *Proper government*: X properly governs Y if and only if X governs Y and X is either X^0 (that is, V, N, A, P), or NP_i where $Y = NP_i$.
>
> *Government*: X governs Y if and only if Y is contained in the maximal $\overline{X}$ projection of X, Xmax, and Xmax is the smallest maximal projection containing Y, and X c-commands Y.
>
> *C-command*: X c-commands Y if and only if the first branching node dominating X also dominates Y, and X does not itself dominate Y.

To illustrate how this very simple but basic constraint might be formulated in declarative terms, we could try defining proper government, at least for pairs of nodes:

$properly\_governs(X, Y) \leftarrow governs(X, Y)$
        $\wedge\ lexical\_category(X).$

It's easy to see that this follows the English account. Putting aside the straightforward problem of defining the predicate *lexical_category*, we note that we must now define a new predicate, *governs*, again following Van Riemsdijk and Williams. This predicate in turn requires four new predicates:

$governs(X, Y) \leftarrow maximal\_projection(X, Xmax)$
        $\wedge\ dominates(Xmax, Y)$
        $\wedge\ least\_maximal\_projection(Y, Xmax)$
        $\wedge\ c\_commands(X, Y).$

Again, I defer the definitions of the tree predicates *maximal_projection*, *dominates*, and *least_maximal_projection*, defining only *c_command* in terms of *dominates* and *first_branching_node*:

$c\_commands(X, Y) \leftarrow first\_branching\_node\_from(X, BrNode)$
        $\wedge\ dominates(BrNode, Y)$
        $\wedge\ \neg dominates(X, Y)$
        $\wedge\ \neg dominates(Y, X).$

124   Robert C. Berwick

A complete set of declarative constraints for principles-and-parameters theory would involve similar conditions for each of its many modules, applied to all potentially well formed tree structures. If this program could be carried out in full detail, then one would be able to apply the theorem-proving techniques of logic programming, developing a *provably* faithful principle-based parsing system (see Stabler, forthcoming, for a worked-out example of such an approach). Section 2 briefly describes some of the parsing techniques that would be applicable.

Many obstacles remain. For example, the proper government predicate only defines when one node properly governs another, but proper government of a particular empty category holds only if *there exists* some X that properly governs the empty category. Though in general it's easy to write simple declarative statements for constraints that operate essentially under tree sisterhood, and therefore it's easy to write a declarative formulation of principles-and-parameters theory that "works" for bounded sentences of one sentence domain or two, it's a bit trickier to properly formulate declarative *chain constraints*—constraints that apply globally to an entire parse tree, like the ECP. More recently, Fong (Berwick and Fong 1989, 1990), Stabler (forthcoming), and Johnson (1988) have all worked out systems that declaratively express entire sections of GB Theory.

A further, practical difference between rules and principles—the way they have been actually used in linguistic theories—lies with the differing conceptions of language that each entails. Since this difference is important to parsing, I will review it here.

At heart, the rule-based view of language connects to traditional grammars with their emphasis on language-specific constructions as well as to formal language theory with its idea that we have some set of rules—a grammar—that generates a distinguished set of strings—the grammatical sentences—and no others. The rule-based generative grammar/formal language theory tradition *starts* with a distinguished corpus of grammatical strings to be described—"the language." This (extensional) set of strings thus becomes of central importance, since it serves as the touchstone for the rule system's success. A key issue, then, is where this special set comes from. It demands some justification; one cannot just pick out a set of strings at random.[3]

A principle-based theory starts from quite a different vantage point. On the constraint-based view, *all* sounds are assigned *some* description, depending upon which admissibility constraints they pass or which principles they abide by; there is no (artificial) division into "grammatical" and "ungrammatical" strings. Rather, some sounds pass all admissibility constraints (and so are dubbed fully grammatical), whereas others violate a range of constraints (and so vary in their apparent acceptability).[4] In a sense, then, the principle-based view rejects the traditional formal language theory account whereby the aim of the grammar is to generate a special set of strings and structural descriptions.

From this deep division in conceptual foundations a great many of the rule-based/principle-based distinctions flow, many with computational implications.

Rules and principles view language differently:

- Rule-based systems are construction oriented; they tend to focus on string sets rather than grammars. This follows from their historical roots in traditional grammars and formal language theory. In contrast, principle-based systems aim from the start to describe grammars, not languages; although they too must of course account for the variety of constructions observed in natural languages, their emphasis is different. For instance, the context-free rule VP → V NP says only that a noun phrase lies immediately to the right of a verb in a verb phrase; this describes the construction. In contrast, a principle-based account strives to say *why* the noun phrase lies to the right (because in English verbs case-mark NPs under adjacency, and $\overline{X}$ theory says that complements lie to the right).
- Rule-based systems must be greatly altered to handle so-called ungrammatical input. Usually new rules or scoring functions are added. Since parsing time varies directly with grammar size, this has computational impact. In contrast, a principle-based system naturally accommodates ill-formed input; it is designed from the start to be able to parse any string.
- Grammar rules generally have been taken to mean rules like S → NP VP, or Passive, Raising, and the like. Further, the notion of derivation and rewrite rules makes phrase structure a central focus of rule-based systems. In contrast, for principle-based systems *admissibility conditions* or *licensing relations* are central. Phrase structure is derivative. For instance, in a GB-based parser we might only have to recover what governs what, plus thematic assignments, rather than an explicit phrase structure tree; phrase structure is simply derivative from these more basic relations. Abney (1986) gives an example, assuming thematic relations plus three other basic licensing relations: *Subjecthood, Functional selection,* and *Modification,* illustrated in figure 4.2. Note that the phrase structure tree is not needed at all in order to fix the grammatical relationships for a sentence such as *John would like pictures of Mary,* but it may be easily recovered from these relationships if so desired (as shown by the dashed lines). Thus, principle-based parsing turns ordinary context-free parsing on its head: its primary job is to recover whatever information structures are necessary to build up grammatical relations, and these are not necessarily the same as tree structures.

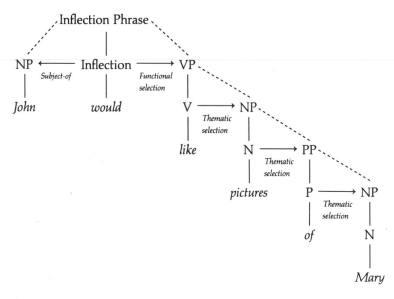

Figure 4.2
For a principle-based parser, phrase structure may be derivative. The dashed lines in this figure indicate phrase structure that is read off of other licensing relations such as thematic selection. (After Abney 1986.)

As we will see, this difference has enormous implications for the range of parsing algorithms one can think of for principle-based systems; it opens up a world of parsing possibilities that would not be thought of with phrase-structure-based systems.

- (Context-free) rule-based parsers have difficulty handling so-called free-word-order languages in a linguistically grounded way, whereas principle-based parsers can tackle them successfully. Since rules have often meant context-free rules, and since context-free rules encode both linear precedence and hierarchical information in a *single* format, such systems cannot easily tease apart the spectrum of free-word-order variation found across natural languages. In Warlpiri, for instance, morpheme order is fixed, and hence precedence information needs to be recorded here; but phrasal ordering is by and large free, and so only hierarchical information needs to be used at the phrasal level. By parceling out distinct informational constraints among distinct principles and representations, a principle-based theory can separate morpheme precedence from phrasal hierarchy and describe a language that has fixed morpheme order and free phrasal order. (We will go through this example in more detail in section 3.)

• A rule-based parser does not easily yield an account of cross-linguistic variation. A rule-based theory will typically contain very different rules for each language, with no obvious connection between the two. Consider any context-free rule-based translation system, for instance, Slocum's Spanish-English translation program (1984). Slocum's system requires an entirely different set of context-free rules for English-Italian translation, simply because there need be no constraint relating, say, Spanish and English, beyond saying simply that the rules for both are context free. The rules have nothing else in common at all. In the best case, a principle-based system will confront cross-linguistic variation head-on, describing parametric variation *within* one set of principles that accounts for the full space of natural language possibilities. Translation systems based on principles consist of a large central core, common to all languages, plus variations sanctioned by the principles—not context-free rules that have nothing in common. We will look at a specific example in section 6.

• Rules breed uniformity; principles do not. The reason is simple: with rules, the great temptation is to add one or more new rules to cover each new sentence example. Since it is usually possible to shoehorn any single natural language sentence into a context-free rule format, or, for that matter, any single rule format, rule systems tend to exhibit a certain uniformity. (Of course, this is being a bit too glib; we are talking here only of syntactic coverage.) Again we obtain large, hard-to-manage grammars. In contrast, principle-based systems try to assign distinct information-bearing tasks to each principle—for example, each kind of licensing has a special job of its own to do, whereas binding operates in a different domain, with its distinct principles and representations. This *information factoring* is central to the enterprise of principle-based grammatical description, and its resulting modularity lends itself naturally to the solution of cross-linguistic variation and, as pointed out by Barton, Berwick, and Ristad (1987), even to efficient parallel processing. This of course does not *bar* a rule-based system from having many different kinds of rules—a case in point being the immediate dominance/linear precedence formalism (ID/LP), in which immediate dominance rules are separated from linear precedence rules. It's just that things seem to run in the direction of uniformity precisely because so much attention is paid to string set coverage. It also does not rule out the possibility of compiling principles into complex rule systems, a point to which we will return in section 2.

It should be noted here that the advantage of such knowledge factoring is recognized even in rule-based systems. Context-free systems often use one kind of principle-based device: it is often remarked that we can describe natural languages "as if" they consist of context-free skeletons plus feature augmentations imposed on top of these; hence the current interest in such context-free augmented systems in one variety or another.

Taking that point to its logical conclusion, we ought to view possible surface sentences built up in a kind of layer-cake fashion, as the *linear superpositioning* of several autonomous modules, each with its own constraints. This has an obvious direct interpretation in so-called logic-based formalisms.[5] Figure 4.3 illustrates one way that the modules in a principles-and-parameters theory might be divided.

1.3 An Outline of the Chapter
Section 2 sets out a general framework in which to describe principle-based parsers and probes what it means to say that a parser *directly* implements a grammar or whether a grammar is transformed into another, perhaps more efficient format. The term *compilation* has sometimes been used for this process, but this is somewhat misleading. A more accurate but more cumbersome term would be *source-to-source translation*: most often grammatical statements are replaced with combinations of other statements. Whatever the terminology, the notion of compilation demands careful treatment. Most accounts are too weak or too strong. Section 2 explores a specific formal language theory example that brings this question into sharp relief and proposes a particular way of looking at how grammars can be implemented as parsers. Section 2 goes on to propose a particular way of looking at how grammars might be "used" by language processors. In particular, we would like to reconcile various psycholinguistic facts about the automaticity or fluency of language processing with a principle-based approach, as noted by Frazier (1986).

My chief aim will be to exhibit a variety of ways of building principles into a parser, drawn from implemented systems, and to examine just how this affects parsing. It appears that there are roughly three basic kinds of translation that have been used in implemented principle-based systems, two *internal* to representational levels and one applying *across* representational levels: (1) parameter fixing within a representational level (for instance, the language is head first or head final); (2) substitution of values within a particular linguistic level (for instance, expanding an $\overline{X}$ skeleton by substituting lexical values for the X as preposition, noun, verb, adjective); (3) substitution across representational levels, by folding together declarative constraints (multiplying out the various "landing sites" for empty categories would be an instance of substitution across the D-structure and S-structure levels).

Evidently each of these translations is no more than the sort of partial evaluation one often finds in Prolog programs, and one might take the

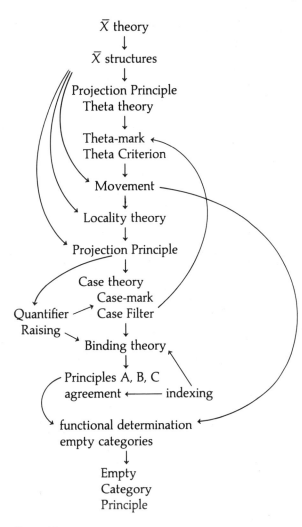

Figure 4.3
A design for a principle-based parsing system. Each module component varies over a limited parametric range. The joint interaction of all modules replaces the effects of many language-particular rules.

notion of partial substitution as one way to systematically examine the space of possible "compiled" parsers. Efforts along these lines are derived from the work of Tamaki and Sato (1984) on *fold/unfold* transformations in logic programs. More recently this approach has been explored by Johnson (1988) and Fong (Berwick and Fong 1989, 1990). This is a useful technique since Tamaki and Sato's transformations preserve correctness. In section 2 we will briefly examine three distinct logic-as-grammar approaches to principle-based parsing.

There have been two basic results from *practical* studies of principle transformations. First, in some compiled parsers, notably Dorr's (see section 6), psycholinguistic effects do not (need not) cluster along the fault lines of the principle module. If this is true, then psycholinguistic results indicating a different clustering than that dictated by a principle theory need not undermine that theory. Second, in several principle-based parsers where partial evaluation has been explored, limited partial evaluation generally speeds up parsing, but it can also slow things down. We will consider these results in detail, developed by Fong (1990), below. It all depends on whether the combined statements cut down the space of possibilities as quickly as possible, or whether they expand the space of possibilities. For example, combining $\overline{X}$ and Move α components will generally expand possibilities. If Move α is combined with an $\overline{X}$ component, this will increase the number of possible structures, since the number of valid surface structures includes those licensed by $\overline{X}$ theory plus those contributed by movement. In contrast, factoring in a "filtering" component that can only rule out possibilities, like case theory, can only cut down on the possibilities, since the number of well-formed structures that meet both $\overline{X}$ and case theory is far fewer than the number that meet either constraint alone.

The remainder of this chapter will explore working principle-based parsers. Section 3 describes free-word-order parsing for Warlpiri, comparing rule-based and principle-based approaches in the context of a parser implemented by Kashket (1986). Section 4 shows how rule-based and principle-based parsers deal differently with so-called ungrammatical sentences.

Section 5 covers two principle-based parser designs, showing how to avoid explicit (context-free) phrase structure rules and indicating the range of algorithm possibilities that a principle-based approach allows: Abney's licensing model and the direct use of $\overline{X}$ rules in a deterministic parser. These examples will serve as a springboard for a discussion of how principles might be carved up in a parsing system. I will argue that there are three basic principle-based component clusters: (1) topological relations (like adjacency and hierarchy, often taken in context-free systems to mean simply general phrase structure rules, but in principle-based systems to mean $\overline{X}$ topology); (2) lexical relations (like subcategorization and case marking), simply overlaid on or projected through the basic configurational relations (along the layer-cake or "autosegmental" model); and (3) binding relations (like *wh*-movement and anaphor-antecedent relations generally), again overlaid on basic licensed structures.[6]

Section 6 turns to language translation, comparing a Spanish-English principle-based design implemented by Dorr (1987) with a standard context-free rule-based approach. Dorr's parser uses a bipartite division by grouping principle cluster (1) separately from (2) and (3): she exploits the topological information in an underspecified $\bar{X}$ theory to drive an Earley-type parser that is coroutined (operates in tandem) with principles-and-parameters government constraints, idiosyncratic subcategorization, and the like. Whenever the skeletal $\bar{X}$ parse can no longer be extended, the principles-and-parameters constraint system is called to weed out under-constrained parses or propose parsing extensions. Dorr's parser shows that principles may be clustered in a variety of ways.

Finally, section 7 concludes with exploration of the computational power of modular, principle-based systems, along with possibilities for speed-up using parallel computation.

2 Principles and Parameters in Parsing Design: A Framework for Principle-Based Parsing

2.1 Introduction

To begin, let us answer the first question about principle-based parsing raised earlier: Can a small number of principles describe natural language? This is a question about linguistic description, so we rely on linguistic theory to answer it. Currently, we have adopted a variant of the *principles-and-parameters* theory developed at MIT and elsewhere (sometimes called *Government-Binding* or *GB Theory* (Chomsky 1981; Lasnik and Uriagereka 1988)). Figure 4.3 shows the topology of the system currently used. It pictures about a dozen modules or *theories*, most of which are described more fully in the next paragraph. Lines between the modules mark logical dependencies—certain constraints are defined in terms of others.

Let's see just what these principles mean and how they work together to account for passive sentences.

- $\bar{X}$ *theory* describes the basic tree shapes allowed in a language. Roughly, natural languages allow two basic tree forms: function-argument form, as in English where the verb begins a verb phrase, a preposition begins a prepositional phrase, and so forth (*eat the ice cream, with a spoon*); and argument-function form, as in Japanese and much of German.
- The *Theta Criterion* says that every verb must discharge its thematic arguments—its placeholders that flesh out who did what to whom.

Thus, a main sentence with *eat* must mention the eater and optionally the thing eaten, whereas a main sentence with *put* must mention the thing that is put somewhere and the place where it is put (one can't have *John put the book*).

• The *Case Filter* says that pronounced (*overt*) noun phrases like *ice cream* must receive case. What is meant by case? In simplest terms, it is much like what is found in a traditional Latin grammar: the subject noun phrase receives nominative case; the direct object of the verb receives accusative case; the object of a preposition receives oblique case. The pale residue of this *case-marking* system shows up in English in the use of *her* as an object versus *she* as a subject: *Mary likes her; She likes Mary*. This is what accounts for the difference between (well-formed) sentences like *It is likely that John will win* and (ill-formed) sentences like *It is likely John to win*. In the first sentence *John* receives nominative case from *will*; in the second there is no tensed verb or verb-like element to give *John* case, and so the sentence violates the Case Filter.

• *Binding theory* spells out how pronouns may be related to their antecedents in certain configurations. For example, compare the following sentences:

John thinks that he likes ice cream.
He thinks that John likes ice cream.

In the first sentence *John* and *he* may refer to the same person; in the second they cannot.

• *Locality theory* and the *Empty Category Principle* restrict where "silent" noun phrases (*empty categories*) can appear. A silent noun phrase is not pronounced but is still needed to understand a sentence. For example, in the sentence

John wants to like ice cream

there is a silent noun phrase, which we can denote *e*, that acts as the subject of *to like ice cream*; just like a pronoun, it refers to *John*:

John wants to *e* like ice cream.

Empty categories cannot appear too far away from their antecedents (locality) and can appear only in certain configurations (the ECP). The first example below shows a violation of locality—the empty category *e* is too far away from *John*—and the second a violation of the ECP. (We will not be concerned in this chapter with exactly how constraints like the ECP are formulated.)

John seems it is certain *e* to like ice cream.
John was wanted to *e* like ice cream.

- The *Movement Principle* says basically that any phrase can be moved anywhere. For example, we can change *John likes ice cream* to *Ice cream, John likes*. (Of course, this freedom may violate other principles.)

Having covered these basic principles, we can now see in detail how they interact to yield *The ice cream was eaten*. If we think of the principles as axioms, the passive construction emerges as a theorem. But the deductive chain is much longer than in a simple if-then rule system, where there is a direct, one-step connection between passive sentences and rules. The following sequence outlines the steps shown in figure 4.3.

$\overline{X}$ theory sets the basic function-argument order of English
↓
was eaten the ice cream
↓
Eaten is an adjective, and so does not assign case
↓
Ice cream must receive case
↓
So *ice cream* moves to subject position
where it receives nominative case
↓
This leaves behind an empty category, linked to *ice cream*
(so that *eat* can meet the Theta Criterion and
make *ice cream* the thing eaten)
↓
the ice cream was eaten e

This may seem like a lot of deductive work for one sentence, but the important point is that the *same* principles combined in different ways yield different sentences, just as the same molecules can combine in different ways to make many different chemical compounds. For example, in the sentence *It was believed that the ice cream was eaten* no movement is required because *ice cream* already receives nominative case from *that*. (This would show up more clearly if *ice cream* were replaced with a pronoun. Then the pronoun would have its nominative form: *It was believed that he was eaten*.)

2.2 Principles and Parsing
So far, all that we have done with principles is describe sentences. How can we use principles to parse sentences—that is, to assign structure to sentences that shows what the subject and object are, what the thematic roles are (who did what to whom), and so forth? In some way we must reproduce the deductions that connect axioms to sentences. Of course, all we have to start with is the input sentence, a dictionary, and the principles themselves.

Although there are several possible approaches, it is useful to divide the principles into two classes: *generators* and *filters*.

Generators produce or hypothesize possible structures. For example, consider $\overline{X}$ theory. Given a string of words, say, *eat the ice cream,* $\overline{X}$ theory would say that *eat* is possibly the beginning of a verb phrase, with *the ice cream* as its argument. Similarly, movement theory creates possible structures. Given a valid $\overline{X}$ structure, movement theory can displace various noun phrases like *ice cream* to create new ones. Binding theory also generates new output possibilities from old ones. For example, given the sentence *John thinks that he likes ice cream, he* can refer either to *John* or to someone else not mentioned in the sentence, thus generating two candidate outputs.

Filters weed out possible structures. Most of the remaining boxes in the module picture are filters—the Case Filter, the Theta Criterion, the ECP, and locality theory. For example, if the structure *John is proud ice cream* is input to the Case Filter, it will be filtered out as a violation (it should be *proud of ice cream,* where *of* assigns case to *ice cream*).

Given this generator-filter model, the simplest way to build a parser is as a cascaded sequence of principle modules, as shown in figure 4.4a. (For reasons of space the figure does not show all the possible principle modules.) The input sentence, *The ice cream was eaten,* passes into the first module, in the figure $\overline{X}$ theory, which produces several output possibilities indicated by multiple arrows (depending on word and structural ambiguities). The basic point is that these hypotheses are driven from the input in a bottom-up way. Given a verb, the system posits that a verb phrase must start; given a preposition, it posits that a prepositional phrase must start; and so on. Note that this requires access to a dictionary. As usual, these hypotheses are subject to numerous ambiguities (words may be either nouns or verbs, for example), but we will defer these standard problems here. All the usual techniques for efficient bottom-up processing, such as lookahead, can be useful here.

Alternatively, such a system could enumerate all possible function-argument structures *before* even looking at the input until it hits upon one that matches the input. Such a straightforwardly hallucinatory approach is known to be fraught with hazards unless special precautions are taken (it may not terminate, for example). For this reason, almost all existing principle-based systems attempt to access the information in the input sentence as quickly as possible, and this will be the case in all the principle-based parsing systems described in the rest of this chapter.

Continuing with our rough conceptual picture, the hypotheses output from the $\overline{X}$ component are fed into the next module down the line, the movement component, which also expands the number of hypothesized structures. Binding also generates multiple hypotheses. Finally, the ECP

(a)

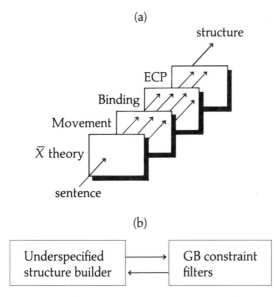

(b)

| Underspecified structure builder | GB constraint filters |

Figure 4.4
Principles may be classified as *generators* and *filters* and then organized into parsers in a variety of ways. (a) A sequential parser design. The input sentence is successively expanded and collapsed into a series of structural hypotheses. Generators expand the hypothesis space, whereas filters narrow it down. (b) A coroutine parser design, as used by Dorr in her translation system. Structure-building generators operate in tandem with constraint modules.

whittles these multiple hypotheses down to just one: the output structure *the ice cream$_i$ was eaten e$_i$* (the subscript *i* indicates that the empty category following *eaten* is linked to *ice cream*). In each step, important information from a dictionary or lexicon may be accessed. For instance, it is the lexicon that says just what thematic roles a verb requires—that *eat* needs an eater and an optional thing eaten. This information must figure in the hypotheses that are generated and filtered.

Since many of the constraints depend on particular structural configurations as inputs, the principle modules can be ordered only in certain ways. For instance, case is often assigned only under a particular local structural arrangement—the element receiving case is an immediately adjacent sister to a verb or a preposition. These logical dependencies must be respected in any principle-based parser design.

As an alternative to the straightforward sequential design it is possible to *coroutine* the operation of filters and generators, alternating between structure-building $\overline{X}$ and movement components, and filters (see figure 4.4b). This approach has been adopted by Dorr for her translation system. Dorr exploits the structure information in $\overline{X}$ theory to drive an Earley-type parser that is coroutined (operates in tandem) with filtering constraints. Whenever the $\overline{X}$ parse can no longer be extended, filters and some generators are called to weed out underconstrained parsers or propose parsing extensions. See section 6 for more details on this coroutine design.

2.3 What Is a Principle-Based Parser?
The fundamental question we turn to next is this: What does it mean to have a principle-based parser at all? Intuitively, the answer is clear: It means that grammatical principles are *accessed* and *used* in parsing. Unfortunately, what it means to use a principle is unclear; further, it's even less clear what it means to *directly* use a (grammatical) principle. This point is important because principle-based parsers are usually assumed to be direct, and therefore evidence that parsing is somehow indirect may be cited as a count against principle-based parsing.

This section examines what it means to implement a principle-based parser, either directly or indirectly.

- First, we will see that the notion of "direct" use of grammatical principles demands clarification, and we will look at a formal language theory example that helps to bring this issue into sharp relief. We will also examine how logic-based grammars give us the three distinct notions of how principles might be used in parsing: directly, via metagrammatical interpretation, and via source-to-source translation.[7]
- Second, we will define principle-based parsers in terms of the information clusters they use—for example, whether they group $\overline{X}$ theory together with case theory or not. We will use this taxonomy to group various principle-based parsing proposals. We will also look in more detail at one possible account of source-to-source translation, based on the logical notions of substitution or partial evaluation.
- Third, we will examine the psycholinguistic arguments put forth by Frazier (1986) claiming that principle-based parsers do not look like good models for human sentence processing, whereas parsers that directly access and use ordinary phrase structure rules (that do not contain detailed lexical information) do fit the psycholinguistic facts.

What it means to use a principle or rule is complex in the case of grammars because several different senses of "use" are relevant. For example, one classic notion is that of inferential use: the rules or principles are axioms, and to use the rules for parsing means to employ them deductively to analyze sentences. The complication is that grammars themselves play many functional roles. Grammars can be used for language acquisition, or for sentence analysis or sentence production. Logically speaking, then, representations of grammars could be used in one of those domains but not in another. For example, one could propose that grammatical universals are used for language acquisition but not for parsing. This was the essence of Fodor, Bever, and Garrett's (1974) idea that grammars are used for learning, but then only their surface effects (surface word order cues such as the appearance of *that* before embedded complements) are consulted for parsing. To take an extreme version of this proposal, suppose the acquired grammar generated only a finite number of sentences. Then one could, in principle, first learn this grammar and then generate all possible sentences. One could then throw away the grammar and parse by consulting just the table of sentences. Still, one would properly say that the grammar was "used," since grammatical representations were used to carry out the construction of the sentence table. More realistically, an LR (*L*eft-to-right scan, *R*ightmost derivation in reverse) parser uses (finite-state) tables that are systematically constructed from an underlying unambiguous context-free grammar. As is well known from the compiler literature, such a parser can even handle ambiguous context-free grammars if one adds external oracles that resolve ambiguities that arise during the parse and show up as multiple entries in the table construction. In this case, the augmented parser is even more indirectly related to its grammar, though it is still systematically related.

This example shows that the relationship of "use" could be an indirect one, with "use in parsing" decoupled, in an explanatory sense, from "use in acquisition." Grammars can be represented in many different ways, and any of these could be used to generate the required sentence table. From the standpoint of the sentence analyzer, any of these grammars would be the same.

Such a possibility suggests that the attribution of principles or rules really does just follow from "best explanation": we say that people follow rules or access representations because in so doing we gain the best account we have of language acquisition and use. This is a completely unremarkable position but for some reason seems to have stirred wide controversy in the cognitive sciences. To see how unremarkable it is, consider a similar problem in Ullman's theory of the recovery of structure from visual motion. A key element in the theory is what Ullman (1979) calls the "rigidity assumption": any set of elements undergoing a two-dimensional transformation that has a unique interpretation as a rigid body moving in space is so interpreted. Suppose we take this principle as the "best explanation" we have of how people compute the structure of an object from viewing successive snapshots of it in motion. Then we can ask whether the Rigidity Principle (RP) is "used." Evidently, the answer is yes, even though we have no idea what its realization might be. Note that no one supposes that the RP is literally inscribed in the brain. Presumably, there is some physical basis for the RP itself, where the RP is not literally expressed. But this does not detract from the RP idealization, which successfully explains the operation of the visual system. The visual system apparently acts as if it used the RP.

It seems, then, that there is at least a strong and a weak sense of how a system might "use" a set of principles. In a strong sense, the principles might be literally represented as such, individually, and used directly on-line as data structures for parsing. For example, this is roughly how the rules of a context-free grammar might be used in, say, Earley's algorithm (though the analogy is imperfect because as a matter of course the literal rules are never encoded as such but are usually broken down into a more efficient tabular form). In a weaker sense, principles might be *interpreted*. This could admit varying degrees of partial evaluation: for example, as suggested in section 1, one could fold together constraints on $\overline{X}$ structures to get a set of partially instantiated trees with defined heads, rather than just underdetermined $\overline{X}$ skeletons. Though it's clear what this comes to in the case of simple substitution of values for variables and partial evaluation, it's not so clear what this means when we admit *any* kind of transformation of the original principles.

To see whether we can distinguish between these two cases, we will look at a particular artificial language where the direct use of a system is especially clear, as a litmus test to dispose of some proposed definitions. We will then turn to three ways of looking at the same problem using logic grammars.

2.4 The Notion of "Direct" Use of Principles or Rules

What does it mean to use a grammatical rule or principle? Many definitions have been offered, but the notion of implementation remains unclear, because we do not know what counts as an implementation, or what we are allowed to do to build our parser. For example, suppose that the sentences of a language contain only an even number of words. Is this a fact that the parser is allowed to consult in order to figure out how to process a sentence? Should parsers be allowed to count? If so, would this still be a direct implementation of a grammar? Consider, for example, word fre-quency effects, or Fodor-Bever-Garrett type heuristics ("Take N–V bound-aries to mark a sentence"). Suppose we can derive reliable surface cues from our principle theory; can these be used in a principle-based parser? Should we demand that surface cues be universal or language particular? Many questions arise; unfortunately, we don't have answers to most of them.

In order to maintain our intuitions about the connections between gram-mars and language processors, it seems clear that not just *any* fact of language counts as a direct implementation of a principle-based (or rule-based) parser. Below I use a particularly clear cut case from formal language theory to drive home this point. Our moral will be that principles are used *directly* as long as they obey the representational encapsulations provided

by the grammatical theory; as soon as we carry out substitutions or transformations that destroy the original representational levels described by
the grammar, then the principles are being used *indirectly*.[8]

2.4.1 A Formal Language Theory Example   Let's turn first to the formal
language example. Our case study centers on two example parsers modeled after an idea of Aho and Ullman (1972:272). Both parsers output the
same structural descriptions—they are strongly equivalent. But the first
parser follows grammar rules directly, the second indirectly. The first
accesses—"uses"—the rules of its corresponding context-free grammar,
while respecting the representational integrity of those rules. The second
uses the grammar derivatively by computing some (global) property of the
grammar and then accessing that derived conclusion.

The language is a^+b. The grammar generating this language is given as
follows (with rules numbered for later reference):

(1) $S \rightarrow AC$

(2) $A \rightarrow AB$

(3) $A \rightarrow a$

(4) $B \rightarrow a$

(5) $C \rightarrow b$

For example, the sequence of steps used to generate the string *aaab* by a
rightmost derivation in the grammar would be these:

1. S
2. AC (via rule (1))
3. Ab (via rule (5))
4. ABb (via rule (2))
5. Aab (via rule (4))
6. $ABab$ (via rule (2))
7. $Aaab$ (via rule (4))
8. $aaab$ (via rule (3))

For our purposes here, a suitable output description of the parse of *aaab*
would simply be the string of symbols 1524243, corresponding to the
application of the rules of the grammar in their proper order, or the reverse
order 3424251. An abstract description of the parsing problem for this
sentence, then, is that the machine is given the string *aaab* and must output
either string of numbers.

How should this be done? The first parser we will look at will, in a clear
sense, access and use the rules (1)–(5) directly. At all times its memory will
hold exactly those tokens and strings of tokens admitted by the grammar

in its derivation of the sentence in question. No other computation, no other "reasoning" will be permitted.[9]

The second parser will work differently, although it will recover exactly the same representation as the first.[10] The second machine does not consult a representation of the grammar at all, but rather relies on a fortuitous connection between the tokens of the language generated by the grammar and the underlying grammar.[11] In fact, for other context-free languages and grammar—for example, $aa^+b + aa^+c$—Aho and Ullman show that a "natural" deterministic parser may not even exist.

The first parser operates by carrying out the rightmost derivation described earlier, but in reverse, using the "standard" simulation of a grammatical derivation via a pushdown automaton. This gives a so-called "canonical" LR parse. The device is a simple bottom-up parser that uses a single pushdown stack and two simple parsing actions: (1) *push* a nonterminal symbol of the grammar on the stack and (2) *replace* a sequence of symbols on the stack (corresponding to the right-hand side of some rule expansion) with the left-hand side of that grammar rule.

Crucially, each action manipulates just left-hand and right-hand sides of grammatical rules. We add an output action that is associated with each *replace* action that simply prints the corresponding rule number. In addition, at each step in the parse (that is, after each parser action) strings of tokens on the stack must be *isomorphic* to the corresponding line in the rightmost derivation, up to the point where terminal elements are encountered. A parsing action is defined by a stack string, input token pair, where the stack string may consist of several tokens (with an upper bound fixed in advance).

The operating rules of the parser are as follows. The machine starts with its pushdown stack empty and scanning the leftmost token of the input sentence. Besides the rules listed below, all other combinations of stack and input symbols lead to rejection of the input sentence.

1. If the leftmost input token is an *a*, and the top of the stack holds the end-of-stack symbol, then push *A* on the stack, output the number 3, and read the next input token.

2. If the leftmost input token is an *a*, and there is an *A* on the top of the stack, then push *B* on the stack, output the number 4, and read the next input token.

3. If a *B* is on the top of the stack, and an *A* is the second token on the stack, then replace these with the token *A* and output the number 2.

4. If the leftmost input token is a *b*, and *A* is on the top of the stack, then push *C* on the stack, output the number 5, and read the next input token.

5. If a *C* is on the top of the stack, and *A* is the second token on the stack, then replace these with the token *S* and output the number 1.

6. If *S* is on the top of the stack, and the second token on the stack is the end-of-stack symbol, and there are no more input tokens, then accept the sentence and halt.

The sequence of parsing operations for analyzing *aaab* would run as in figures 4.5 and 4.6. The important point to stress is that the successive "snapshots" of the stack configuration plus the remaining input duplicate (in reverse) the rightmost derivation. This correspondence is exact. For each line in a derivation, there is a corresponding parser configuration, and vice versa. More precisely, there is a one-to-one correspondence between strings of machine configuration tokens and derivation line string tokens.

Now let us look at the second parser that does the same job (figure 4.6). This machine will *not* consult the token strings of rightmost derivations at all. Instead, it will use a fortuitous property of this grammar that relates derivations to its surface language: we can use the *a*'s to "count" how many occurrences of the $A \rightarrow AB$, $B \rightarrow a$ productions there have been. Here are the second parser's rules:

1. If the leftmost token of the input is an *a*, then push *a* onto the stack and read the next input token.

2. If the leftmost token of the input is a *b*, then push *b* onto the stack and read the next input token.

3. If the top of the stack is a *b*, and there are no more tokens in the input, then replace *b* with the empty string (this "pops" *b* off the stack) and output the numbers 1, 5.

4. If the top of the stack is an *a*, the next stack symbol is not the end-of-stack symbol, and there are no more tokens in the input, then replace *a* with the empty string and output the numbers 2, 4.

5. If the top of the stack is an *a* and the next stack symbol is the end-of-stack symbol, then output the number 3 and halt, accepting the sentence.

Note that this second machine does not mention the right-hand or left-hand sides of grammar rules at all. Still, it is easy to see that this parser will output precisely the same structural descriptions as the first. And it uses exactly the same number of elementary steps.

Let's make this contrast explicit. The first parser actually refers to the grammar's literal constituent parts in order to decide what move to make. For example, if the first parser sees the unit *AB* on the stack, corresponding to the right-hand side of its rule (2), then it replaces that part with the left-hand side of rule (2). The form of the rules is directly implicated in the operation of the first machine.

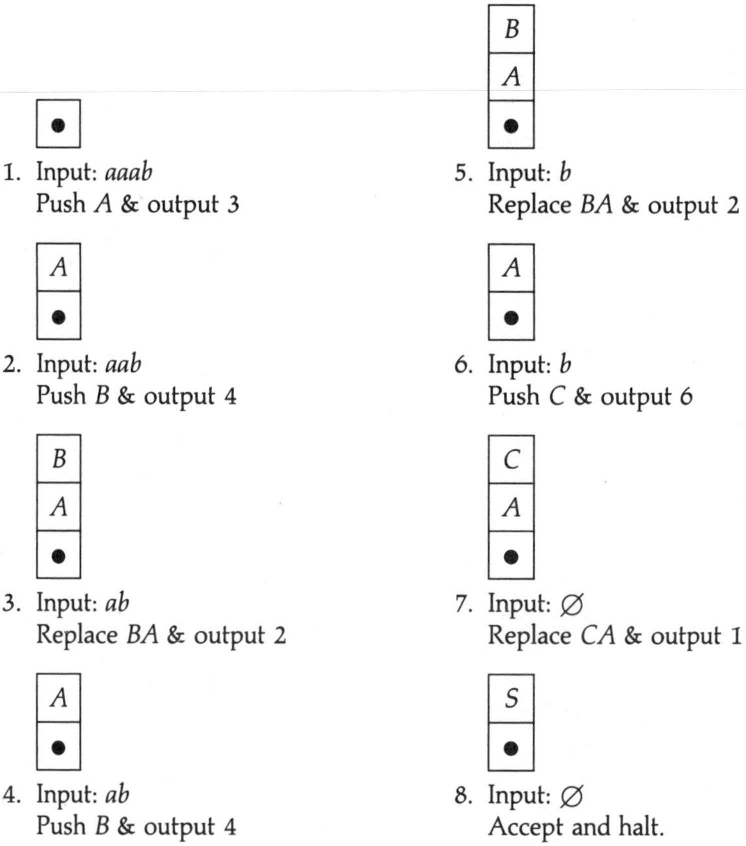

B
A
•

1. Input: *aaab*
   Push *A* & output 3

A
•

2. Input: *aab*
   Push *B* & output 4

B
A
•

3. Input: *ab*
   Replace *BA* & output 2

A
•

4. Input: *ab*
   Push *B* & output 4

5. Input: *b*
   Replace *BA* & output 2

A
•

6. Input: *b*
   Push *C* & output 6

C
A
•

7. Input: ∅
   Replace *CA* & output 1

S
•

8. Input: ∅
   Accept and halt.

Figure 4.5
This figure shows the machine operations of a "direct" implementation for the grammar described in the text.

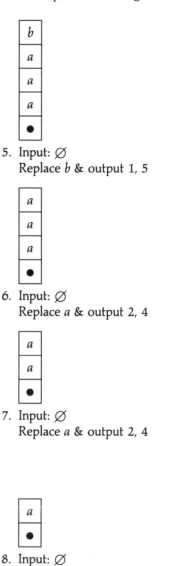

1. Input: *aaab*
   Push *a*

2. Input: *aab*
   Push *a*

3. Input: *ab*
   Push *a*

4. Input: *b*
   Push *b*

5. Input: ∅
   Replace *b* & output 1, 5

6. Input: ∅
   Replace *a* & output 2, 4

7. Input: ∅
   Replace *a* & output 2, 4

8. Input: ∅
   Output 3, accept, and halt.

Figure 4.6
This figure shows the machine configurations for a parser that implements a "nontranspar-ent" version of the same grammar. Note that it produces the same structural descriptions as the first machine, even though it has a different internal structure.

In contrast, the second parser "uses" the grammar—indirectly, to determine just what derivation number to output. Unlike the "direct" parser, it does not refer to any of the units of the grammar—the left- or right-hand side components of rules. But it still uses facts about the language—indirect facts, but facts nonetheless. One would be hard pressed to say that the parser actually follows the grammar in parsing the language.

To see what the alternatives might be, let us first note that for the first sort of parser we can carry out the conversion to a parser mechanically. No matter what the rules of the grammar, there is a straightforward relationship between the right- and left-hand sides of grammar rules and the *push* and *replace* operations. Putting aside questions of the ambiguity of derivations, for every rule of the form $A \rightarrow w$, w a string of terminal tokens, the machine pushes an A onto its stack whenever w appears in an input sentence. Similarly, if there is a rule of the form $A \rightarrow \phi$, ϕ a string of nonterminals, then whenever ϕ appears on the stack, the machine can replace it with the symbol A. This means that the transparent relationship of the parser to the grammar will be invariant under counterfactual changes in the form of the grammar. Adding or subtracting a rule will not significantly alter the connection between grammar and parsing operations.

The property of conversion under counterfactual changes to the original grammar does not hold for the second parser: here, adding just a single new rule to the original grammar will destroy the relatively fragile counting property that the parser exploited.

For example, consider the language consisting of just triples of a's, using the rules (1) $S \rightarrow aaSa$ and (2) $S \rightarrow \lambda$. A "derived" analyzer for this language could just count the number of a's and divide by 3, then output that number of 1's followed by a 2. If we now replace rule (2) with $S \rightarrow a$, then this parsing strategy no longer holds. In fact, the "Divide by 3" algorithm has all the properties of a parsing heuristic suggested by Fodor, Bever, and Garrett (1974):

> A parsing heuristic is ad hoc, in the sense that it may not work for all grammars.
> In other words, a parsing heuristic is language particular, perhaps based on language-particular surface word cues.

This is suggestive; but it is not clear that this is a sufficient property to distinguish the two cases, since it is possible to take a context-free grammar—an LR(k) grammar—that has a systematically associated parser, and then destroy the LR(k)-ness by adding or subtracting one rule. But this means that an indirect system will generally lack explanatory power, because it cannot, in general, hold up under counterfactual conditions. This is the potentially great weakness of a "derived" machine (when in fact the surface behavior is derivable from other principles).[12]

In any case, the example deflates some other proposed criteria for "direct" parser embeddings. Consider Pylyshyn's complexity measure (1984): Pylyshyn suggests that one process is computationally equivalent to another if one process executes in time n whereas the second operates in time kn, k a constant fixed in advance. But this is plainly not a sufficient condition, since both parsers 1 and 2 take the same number of steps; both run in linear time in the length of input sentences. We can refine Pylyshyn's criterion from a *linear* time constraint to a *real-time* constraint. A machine is *real-time* if it takes at most a bounded number of computational steps between consecutive times an input token is read, with the bound fixed in advance. Parser 1 is real-time, but parser 2 is not, since it takes a linear number of steps after all tokens of the input are read.

In its strongest form, then, we could say that a *direct* implementation is allowed to use only the bare axioms of the grammar—the individual grammatical principles themselves. Weakening this somewhat, an indirect—though still principle-based—parser could be obtained by allowing any variable substitution or axiom system partial evaluation while still respecting the representational levels in the original grammar. For example, in a context-free grammar, if we had the preterminal chain rules NP → Noun, Noun → Name, then we ought to be able to substitute *Name* for *Noun*.[13]

To take another simple example of "compilation," consider the three-part definition of *properly_governs* from section 1. We can "fold" this definition together into one clause by simple substitution to eliminate the intermediate predicate *c-command* and save some other steps:

$$properly\_governs(X, Y) \leftarrow maximal\_projection(X, Y) \land$$
$$dominates(Xmax, X) \land$$
$$least\_maximal\_projection(Y, Xmax) \land$$
$$first\_branching\_node\_from(X, BrNode) \land$$
$$dominates(BrNode, Y) \land$$
$$\neg dominates(X, Y) \land$$
$$\neg dominates(Y, X).$$

Note that this sort of partial evaluation still abides by the informational encapsulation of the original grammar even though it is a derived fact about the grammar. Or consider the usual LR table construction. Here a particular table entry represents an equivalence class of all left-hand sentence contexts that "lead to the same state." LR table entries reflect globally derived properties of their grammars, but still respect their grammars' original derivational structures. Put another way, the table entries and the parser's individual computation steps are transparently interpretable as grammatical derivation steps. But that is not true of our unnatural parser 2: here, the association between derivation steps and parser operations is only interpretable as such because we have externally supplied the interpretation relation; it is not mechanically connected to the grammar as with the LR tables.[14]

More generally, given a set of declarative constraints (an axiom system), a direct, principle-based parser could still allow variable substitution (as in the chain rule example above), or partial evaluation of those axioms. The parser would be an indirect, principle-based system if it used derived theorems that did not reflect the information encapsulation of the original system—for instance, if it used for parsing the fact that all sentences of a language began with *the*.

2.4.2 An Application of the Definition

Let's apply this test for direct-indirect principle/rule use to a real example, and then turn in the next subsection to a logical analysis of direct-indirect parsers.

Consider Marcus's parser, in particular how Marcus's parser analyzes passive sentences. The parser has a rule that inserts a trace into the position just after a verb, if that verb is marked passive; in turn, this marker is present just in those cases where the verb in question is passivizable and where passive morphology has been detected earlier. But this parsing rule does not *directly* use the grammatical principles of modern transformational theory (the GB Theory). The rule says only to "Insert a trace if the verb is passive." But there is no such "rule" in principles-and-parameters type theories. Rather, the possibility of this action is licensed (and forced, in English) by a constellation of other principles: the Projection Principle forces an NP to appear as a complement to a passivizable verb; the head-complement order of English puts this position just after the verb; passive morphology eliminates the possibility of case assignment by the verb to this NP, so it must move to subject position; hence, there must be an empty element that can survive the Case Filter in the position just after the verb. Marcus's rule is implied by these more basic principles, as a theorem is implied by an axiom system. Plainly this is a derived rule.

Matthews (1984) argues that Marcus's parser—crucially, as originally programmed—does not *directly* embed a transformational grammar. The rules that Marcus's parser accesses to guide its operation do not "look" like transformational rules. As we saw in the case of passive, there need be no one-to-one correspondence between Marcus parser rules and transformational rules. Pushed to its extreme, in fact, Marcus's parser could operate using just Fodor, Bever, and Garrett "heuristic strategies," in the manner of parser 2 described earlier. (One can write Marcus parser rules that "implement" the rules of parser 2, for example.)

On the other hand, it is also possible to write other Marcus parser rule sets in the manner of parser 1, so that the rules *do* directly reflect the representations of transformational rules, at least according to certain formalizations of transformational rules. Let us take as an example Lasnik and

Kupin's (1977) formalization. One can show that Marcus-type rules can be written that mirror Lasnik and Kupin's definition of transformations. A full account would take us far afield, so here we will simply look at just one example. In Lasnik and Kupin's framework, the structural changes described by a transformation must be written in one of the following forms:

$(A_1 A_2 A_3, i/j)$,

$(A_1 A_2 A_3, (i + j_r))$,

$(A_1 A_2 A_3, (i + j_l))$,

where

$1 \leq i \leq n, \quad i \neq j.$

These changes correspond to movement and right or left adjunctions. In addition, deletion and insertion transformations are defined as follows:

$(A_1 A_2, \varnothing/j)$,

$(A_1 A_2, b/j), \quad 1 \leq j \leq n,$

where b is a member of "some language-specific set of 'insertable elements'" (Lasnik and Kupin 1977 : 180). The elements A_i are associated with particular phrase structure analysis fragments called *subreduced phrase markers*. Very roughly, these fragments correspond to tree fragments as specified by a Marcus parser's rule-triggering pattern. Of course, since the Marcus parser is mapping from a surface sentence to an annotated surface structure instead of mapping from a D-structure representation to an annotated surface string, the parsing rules must "undo" the structural changes themselves.

In Lasnik and Kupin's formalization a structural change can have at most three terms. Lasnik and Kupin also note that there are *implied* variables between terms: that is, there may be some arbitrary tree material between each two A_i's. Thus, five elements are possible in a structural change: three explicit items, and two implicit "don't care" positions. This property is easily replicated in the Marcus parser design by using the five possible elements of a rule pattern, the three buffer cell elements and the two active node stack items.

For example, consider (the inverse of) *wh*-movement. In Lasnik and Kupin's framework, this may be stated as

(COMP WH, (2/1));

that is, the *wh*-element replaces the COMP. The inverse operation must move a *wh*-item from a COMP position to a "landing site." The corresponding Marcus-type rule would simply be stated as follows:

Cyclic node: COMP + wh;
Action: Insert trace into the buffer.

This structural change is, of course, restricted to operate according to a
whole battery of conditions: Strict Cyclicity, Subjacency and Tensed-S
Conditions, and so forth. These conditions are not part of transformational
rules themselves—they do not appear in the *form* of the rules. Rather, they
are universal conditions that apply, as it were, to the operation of transformational derivations generally. Again, the operation of our modified
Marcus machine is similar: the parser is built so that it obeys the conditions
of Strict Cyclicity, Subjacency, and so forth; these conditions are not present
in rule statements. Most of the constraints that prevent overgeneration are
actually encoded in these general principles. In addition, unlike the problem
of mapping from D- to S-structure, Marcus's parser needs some way to
guarantee that it is building an analysis that conforms to D-structure principles. This is assumed by Lasnik and Kupin; the transformational analysis
starts with a well-formed D-structure representation. To capture these constraints, Marcus's parser must add another set of constraints, not present in
the transformational rules or the transformational rule operating principles
themselves. These constraints are associated with lexical entries dictating
the required argument structure of verbs and the Marcus parser's "packet
system" that fixes canonical base phrase structure order. This knowledge is
lumped together in the original Marcus parser but may be separated out so
that grammar rules themselves state only Lasnik and Kupin type operations.

2.5 Principle Clustering and Logic Grammars
There is plenty of evidence for automaticity in fluent parsing—recall
Fodor, Bever, and Garrett's (1974) heuristics that allowed for such statements as "Take the pair N–V as a sentence unless there is a surface sign of
an embedding." Frazier (1986) provides other psycholinguistic evidence
pointing to such automaticity in parsing, which is after all a quite natural
assumption.

All of these examples, anecdotal or otherwise, point in the direction of
source-to-source translation, or compilation. As section 1 pointed out,
compilation can mean many things, from simple variable substitution, to
partial evaluation, to reaxiomatization—the construction of some complicated, specific program that carries out some arbitrary mapping of the
original principle set to a new one. We have already seen how one can
multiply out the principles in a logic grammar by simple substitution and
partial evaluation, as in the three-part definition of *properly_governs*. In this
section we will examine this issue in more detail, taking a closer look at
how logic grammars might help us delimit the space of principle-based
parsers.

First note that what one regards as theorems is grammar relative. One can always build a new system that includes old axioms plus the derived theorems as axioms. However, it is easy to exclude this case simply by requiring that our axiom set be primitive in the sense that no axiom be derivable from any subset of the other axioms. We might also replace old axioms with derived theorems, but then we must be careful that the proposed representational units are just as explanatorily adequate as before. These restrictions have a particularly clear interpretation in the case of rewrite systems. Consider the following example. Suppose we had this grammar:

$$S \rightarrow S_1$$
$$S_1 \rightarrow S_2 a$$
$$S_2 \rightarrow abc.$$

A direct parser must use the representational units as given by the grammar: the symbols S, S_1, S_2, and the push and replace parsing actions corresponding to each rule as described above. As before, we would construct a derived parser that uses the rule $S \rightarrow abca$ directly. Now, we could add the new derived rule $S \rightarrow abca$ to our old rules and claim a direct implementation. But this would violate the condition that representational units be respected. Or, we could replace rules (1)–(3) with this single new rule. The new axiom would be independent, and our parser now direct. But we must be careful that this single rule is all that is required. Our grammatical representation now excludes the units S_1, S_2, and so forth. If such representational units are required on independent grounds, then we cannot exclude them. All this means is that our new system is subject to the usual demands of descriptive and explanatory adequacy.

Considering the results of the previous section, then, we may distinguish at least three distinct notions of principle-based implementation, the first direct, and the second and third indirect:

- *Direct implementation*: The principles are used for parsing as represented, without any intervening recoding. We may imagine the principles to be represented and consulted as if they were written down directly inside the parser itself and consulted on-line.
- *Indirect parsing by weak translation*: The principles are preprocessed by an interpreter that works on-line, so that principles can be processed only on a principle-by-principle basis (in essence, a metagrammatical approach).
- *Indirect parsing by strong translation*: The principles are preprocessed ("compiled") by a (perhaps arbitrary) computational procedure into a form that is actually used for parsing. For example, this is what

happens in so-called LR parsing: a (context-free) grammar is processed to output a set of parsing tables that are actually used, and the grammar then may be discarded.[15] We may take this preprocessing to range all the way from systematic partial evaluation of the metagrammatical interpreter to its wholesale replacement (by whatever means at our disposal—for instance, a human programmer's inspection).

We will return to the logic-based view below, but first let us cover some general points and some specific observations about implemented systems.

The compilation (source-to-source translation) issue is an important and delicate one. As Shieber (1985:145) notes, in the case of systems with complex features, "compilation" in the sense of full expansion into atomic features, usable by Earley's algorithm, may be problematic: one may fail to obtain closure with the *predict* operation of Earley's algorithm or in the standard LR parsing algorithm, for example. Shieber suggests restricting feature expansion in the *predict* step of Earley's algorithm, so that the parser may still operate.[16] In essence, this is the key to how principle-based parsers are designed: they explicitly cut off theorem derivations beyond a certain point so as to get working parsing algorithms. The problem is that this leaves open just how compilation is to be done. Just what are the reliable derived or clustered principles to use? Do they vary from language to language?[17]

In practice, implemented principle-based parsers most often use three kinds of simple techniques. The first two operate *within* a given linguistic level of representation, like S-structure, and include parameter fixing and variable substitution (fleshing out an $\overline{X}$ skeleton tree by setting the head to the values noun, verb, preposition, and so forth). The third commonly used technique is partial evaluation: the basic axioms are multiplied out, generally *across* linguistic levels like D-structure and S-structure, to give, for example, all possible positions for movement within a single sentence or within the range of two sentences. Fong (Berwick and Fong 1989, 1990) has carried out the most detailed experiments along these lines. The answer is complex; there is no single strategy that is uniformly optimal; counterintuitively, multiplying out principles can sometimes result in *slower* performance (this result runs counter to Johnson's (1988) experience with a more limited principle-based system, for instance). But not always. Fong's results are reviewed just below, but let us see intuitively why they might hold.

The basic point is this. Parsing in a principle-based system is, in general, nondeterministic: many possible alternative paths must be pursued to find a "proof" that a given sentence can follow from the given axioms. Suppose we collapse certain predicates, off-line. For instance, suppose we combine (1) the predicates that check whether an NP-trace is c-commanded by its antecedent, (2) the predicate that assigns the NP its antecedent index, and

(3) the predicates that actually build tree structure. Then this new super-predicate must be applied along *every* path the parsing system attempts, including the failed ones. If the cost of predicate application is high, then the overall cost of testing for such complex superpredicates may outweigh the benefits of predicate combination. This is because superpredicate applications are wasted if they are applied to proof paths that do not succeed. Note that this cost depends on the inherent branching factor in the search space, so that if parsing were purely deterministic, then predicate combination would always be beneficial. But in general, Fong's tests show that $\overline{X}$ parsing is not deterministic in this sense. On the other hand, if the combined predicate tests are local ones, so that the application cost is low, then combination may be worthwhile. For example, in contrast to index antecedent assignment, the test to check for case assignment is purely local, since we need only look immediately to the right or left to see if a governing element (like a verb) is present. Then the benefits of combination may always outweigh the costs, because even though some predicates are applied to structures that will never lead to valid "proofs" that a sentence is derivable from the axioms, the application cost is low. In short, there is no single answer to whether predicate combination improves parsing efficiency. It depends on two things: the branching factor of the search space, and the cost of combined predicate application. The cost of predicate application, in turn, depends on whether the predicate can be computed entirely locally (hence off-line) or whether it must look at arbitrary portions of the tree structure (as in the case of antecedent index assignment). Fong has confirmed experimentally that "folding together" all such complex predicates results in a *slower* parser than before.

As a concrete example of this effect, consider combining the representations of S-structure and Logical Form (not logical form in the logician's sense, but the level at which elements are coindexed or linked to their antecedents). Now consider a sentence that is unambiguous syntactically but has two coindexed representations, such as *John thinks that he likes ice cream*, where *John* might or might not be linked to *he*. If we combine the S-structure and LF predicates, then we must apply all the structure-building predicates twice, once for each possible coindexing. If we leave the predicates uncombined, then we build one S-structure representation for each coindexing and *then* apply the coindexing predicate. This turns out to be cheaper (contra Johnson 1988).

2.5.1 Compilation in a Modular Theory   The many principles in a full-fledged modern grammatical theory admit a variety of source-to-source translation possibilities, since in general these systems are richly deductive. For example, given six distinct but connected axioms, one can multiply out any one of these six possibilities and apply any one of the remaining modules as a filter in any order. As suggested earlier, all one is required to do is respect the proprietary *vocabulary* of their principles (their information structure) and certain logical dependencies (almost like dataflow dependencies) between the principle modules.[18] One can still combine them temporally in different ways and get a principle-based parser. It is by no means clear just which of these is "correct." Below we will address the question of whether the logic-as-grammar view helps clarify matters.

What does seem common to almost all schemes is that X theory (either in an underspecified form or in the form of fully projected lexical items) serves as a basic template on which to rest the remaining parsing principles. Just below we will see why this is so: it follows the logical dependencies of principles-and-parameters theory.

On the other hand, it is apparently not necessary to build complete $\bar{X}$ skeletons before filling in other licensing relationships. Consider Abney's parser. It works by analyzing two words at a time, determining whether one element case-marks its neighbor or not. In effect, it builds an $\bar{X}$ skeleton at the same time as it computes case relationships and movement.[19]

Let us examine some actual examples to see what the range of possibilities for principle-based parsers might be, keeping to models that build $\bar{X}$ skeletons first. We will defer the complications introduced by word frequency effects, intonational contours, and the like, although these certainly are other approaches worth investigating.[20]

The paradigmatic example of an uncompiled principle-based system is direct, bottom-up $\bar{X}$ projection from lexical items. The idea is a simple one and has been proposed by Berwick (1982, 1985), Pinker (1984), Abney (1986), Frazier (1986), Correa (1987), and many other researchers. In its clearest form, direct $\bar{X}$ projection has three steps:

- Encounter a lexical item in the input;
- Create a maximal projection based on the features of the item;
- Assemble projected phrases (bottom-up) based on licensing from case marking, theta theory, or whatever other principles one might import.

Note that there are many variations on just what lexical features might be projected, leading to different $\bar{X}$ parsers and different psycholinguistic predictions. Following Shieber's point about restriction, we might not want to project all features from the lexicon (indeed, the lexicon itself might be structured in a complicated way so as to force this choice). The possibilities range from the most underspecified to the least underspecified:

- Project nothing about categorial features. This leads to a "pure" $\bar{X}$ skeleton parser.
- Project just categorial features, but not detailed verb subcategorizations.

- Project categorial features and verb subcategorizations. This can lead to *Aspects*-style phrase structure rules (Chomsky 1965), as Frazier (1986) notes.
- Project all features, including agreement features.

The most literally minded principle-based $\overline{X}$ parser is the first. This model has been adopted by Kashket and (nearly) by Dorr (see sections 3 and 6).[21] Not unexpectedly, there seems to be some trade-off here between parsing speed and use of pure $\overline{X}$ skeletons: if we use just bare $\overline{X}$ skeletons, then Dorr's research shows that parsing is slowed down, because we have to wade through many dozens of illegitimate tree structures. To get around this problem, Dorr coroutines the skeleton parser with principles.

If we project topological structure and some modest amount of lexical information, we build up trees with NPs and VPs in them, but no information on subcategorization. Based on psycholinguistic evidence, Frazier (1986) proposes this as one possibility for what she dubs a non-principle-based parser: one that would reflexively build VPs without looking at whether a verb is transitive or intransitive. Evidently, there is some evidence (from verb-final languages like Dutch and from psycholinguistic experiments in English) that reflects this compilation choice. Frazier aims to "multiply out" the $\overline{X}$ choices for a particular language at least down to the level of N, V, A, and P.[22]

But this is not *necessary*. If we used Dorr's parser, we could simply coroutine the tree-building routine with filtering constraints (figure 4.4b). The parser works using any ordinary context-free parsing algorithm— Earley's algorithm, Cocke-Kasami-Younger's (CKY's) algorithm, a left-corner scheme (for English). Whenever Earley's algorithm gets stuck at *scan, push,* or *pop* time, the principle module is accessed to filter, extend, or refine the parse, then passing control back to the context-free parser itself. Since this scheme works with relatively underspecified $\overline{X}$ skeletons (Dorr's system), there is no reason why it should not work with NPs and VPs as well.

How should the other principle modules be carved up? Clearly, there are some logical dependencies: for instance, since binding is computed in terms of c-command, we must first establish structural dependencies before proceeding to binding.

These dataflow-like dependencies can be calculated by considering module input and output: which representational levels each module uses (its inputs) and constructs (its outputs); see Berwick and Fong 1989, 1990. To be concrete, consider a government-binding grammar with three representational levels (Phonetic Form (PF), S-structure, and D-structure) and six modules ($\overline{X}$ theory, theta theory, Move α, a Case Filter, Logical Form (LF) movement, and a lexicon). There are 57 possible combined modules. $\overline{X}$

theory builds D-structure and needs no other input. Theta theory takes D-structure and filters it. Move α takes D-structure as input and builds S-structure; the Case Filter takes S-structure as input and filters it; the phonetic component takes S-structure as input and outputs PF; and a logical form component takes S-structure as input and outputs LF. From these relationships one can conclude that theta theory and Move α apply after X̄ theory and that the Case Filter, PF, and LF apply after Move α. This implies that certain module combinations are ill formed: for instance, the X̄ and Case Filter modules cannot be combined by themselves, since the full effects of the Case Filter cannot be computed without movement being factored in. In all, 14 out of 57 combinations are illicit; each one attempts to combine modules across S-structure while omitting Move α. We have thus verified that Move α indeed plays a central role in the familiar version of principles-and-parameters theory.

More generally, the following combinations are possible:

- Combine X̄ principles with a few parameters from trace theory (choice of trace) to parse with underspecified X̄ skeletons; the remaining principles are in separate modules and are all accessed separately on-line, with binding theory accessed after (in particular, subcategorization is accessed on-line). Example: Dorr's parser (see section 6).
- Combine an underspecified X̄ parser with subcategorization information held in common between lexical items. Example: Barton and Berwick 1985.
- Combine X̄ principles, case theory, and theta theory; this leads to old-style phrase structure rules (for example, VP → V NP), with disjuncts allowed. Major category names are accessed and projected. Example: Frazier 1986.
- Compile out X̄ principles, case theory, theta theory, and subcategorization apart from other principles. No existing principle-based system does this exactly, and the analysis above shows why.
- Compile out subcategorization information apart from case and theta theory, and apart from wh-movement, building X̄ subtrees after case and thematic relationships are established. Example: Abney's parser (section 5).
- Keep all principle modules distinct. Example: Kashket's parser (section 3).[23]

How does module combination affect parsing time? Dorr's results for her particular way of multiplying out principle components show that although a completely uncompiled system runs too slowly, because there are too many X̄ possibilities to weed out, a completely multiplied-out system is also in the same boat, because its grammar size is too large.

2.5.2 Experimental Testing of Module Combination   Evidently this result holds only for Dorr's particular system. As discussed above, whether a combined system is faster or not is difficult to assess in general. The optimal combination depends on one key factor: how fast ill-formed structures are weeded out, as investigated by Fong (Fong 1990; see also Berwick and Fong 1989, 1990). It is easy to see informally why this should be so. For example, combining $\bar{X}$ theory with theta theory cuts down the number of structures considered, since theta theory filters out some D-structure representations that would otherwise have to be considered separately. But adding in Move α again increases parse time because movement can only add to the set of possible output structures. Similarly, factoring an LF movement possibility into $\bar{X}$ and theta theory increases parse time, because the parser must check for a whole set of multiplicative possibilities: quantifier scope ambiguity with or without moved NP elements, at any possible landing site. If these constraints are left in their original, encapsulated form, then the parser can sort through a much smaller set of possibilities in an additive fashion: first check NP movement, and then check for quantifier scope possibilities.

In order to more fully explore this idea, Fong constructed a logic-based parser to demonstrate the effects of principle ordering.

This parser was built in a highly modular fashion to allow for maximum flexibility in exploring alternative orderings of principles. For instance, each principle is represented separately as an atomic parser operation. A structure is deemed to be well formed only if it passes all parser operations. The scheduling of parser operations is controlled by a dynamic ordering mechanism that attempts to eliminate unnecessary work by eliminating ill-formed structures as quickly as possible. (For comparative purposes, the principle-ordering parser also allows the user to turn off the dynamic ordering mechanism and to parse with a user-specified (fixed) sequence of operations.)

Although it was designed primarily to explore the computational properties of principles for building more efficient parsers, this parser is also designed to be capable of handling a reasonably wide variety of linguistic phenomena. The system was designed to follow the text of Lasnik and Uriagereka 1988 as a reference. Parser operations implement principles as described earlier in section 1.

How important an issue is the principle-ordering problem in parsing? An informal experiment was conducted by Fong using the parser described in the previous section to provide some indication of the magnitude of the problem. Although he was unable to examine all the possible orderings, it turns out that order-of-magnitude variations in parsing times are possible.

The parser has about twelve to sixteen modules. Given a set of one dozen operations, there are about 500 million different ways to order these operations. Only some of these, about half a million, are actually valid, due to logical dependencies between the various operations, as shown in figure 4.3. However, this is still far too many to test exhaustively; Monte Carlo sampling was used to test a uniform selection of possible orderings.

From Fong's experiments with the parser we have found that dynamic principle ordering can provide a significant improvement over any fixed ordering. We have found that speed-ups varying from three- or fourfold to order-of-magnitude improvements are possible in many cases.

2.5.3 Explaining the Variation in Principle Ordering   The variation in parsing times for various principle orderings that was observed can be explained by assuming that overgeneration is the main bottleneck for the parser. That is, in the course of parsing a single sentence, a parser will hypothesize many different structures. Most of these structures, the ill-formed ones in particular, will be accounted for by one or more linguistic filters. A sentence will be acceptable if there exist one or more structures that satisfy every applicable filter. Note that even when parsing *grammatical* sentences overgeneration will produce ill-formed structures that need to be ruled out. Given a goal to minimize the amount of work performed during the parsing process, we would expect a parse using an ordering that requires the parser to perform extra work compared with another ordering to be slower.

Overgeneration implies that we should order principle filters to eliminate ill-formed structures as quickly as possible. For these structures, applying any parser operation other than one that rules it out may be considered as doing unnecessary work. However, there is no globally optimal ordering, as described in Berwick and Fong 1990:

> The impossibility of the globally optimal ordering follows directly from the "eliminate unnecessary work" ethic. Computationally speaking, an optimal ordering is one that rules out ill-formed structures at the earliest possible opportunity. A *globally* optimal ordering would be one that always ruled out every possible ill-formed structure without doing any unnecessary work. Consider the following three structures (taken from Lasnik and Uriagereka (1988)):
>
> (a)   *John$_1$ is crucial [$_{CP}$[$_{IP}$ e_1 to see this]]
>
> (b)   *[$_{NP}$ John$_1$'s mother] [$_{VP}$ likes himself$_1$]
>
> (c)   *John$_1$ seems that he$_1$ likes e_1
>
> Example (a) violates the empty category principle (ECP). Hence the optimal ordering must invoke the ECP operation before any other operation that it is not dependent on. On the other hand, example (b) violates a Binding Theory principle. Hence, the optimal ordering must

also invoke this principle as early as possible. Given that the two operations are independent, the optimal ordering must order the binding principle before the ECP and vice-versa. Similarly, example (c) demands that a variant of the Case filter must precede the other two operations. Hence a globally optimal ordering is impossible. (pp. 319–320)

2.5.4 Heuristics for Principle Ordering   Berwick and Fong (1990) also describe a heuristic strategy for ordering:

> The principle-ordering problem can be viewed as a limited instance of the well-known conjunct ordering problem (Smith and Genesereth (1985)). Given a set of conjuncts, we are interested in finding all solutions that satisfy all the conjuncts simultaneously. The parsing problem is then to find well-formed structures (solutions) that satisfy all the parser operations (conjuncts) simultaneously. Moreover, we are particularly interested in minimizing the cost of finding these structures by re-ordering the set of parser operations. ...
>
> This heuristic mechanism can be subdivided into two distinct phases which are discussed in turn. First, the dynamic ordering mechanism decides which principle is the most likely candidate for eliminating a given structure. Then the parser makes use of this information to reorder parser operation sequences to minimize the total work performed. (p. 320)

2.5.5 Predicting Failing Filters   Berwick and Fong (1990) then go on to describe how to predict the optimal failing filter:

> Given any structure, the dynamic ordering mechanism attempts to satisfy the "eliminate unnecessary work" ethic by predicting a "failing" filter for that structure. More precisely, it will try to predict the principle that a given structure violates on the basis of the simple structure cues. Because the ordering mechanism cannot know whether a structure is well-formed or not, it assumes that all structures are ill-formed and attempts to predict a failing filter for every structure. In order to minimize the amount of work involved, the types of cues that the dynamic ordering mechanism can test for are deliberately limited. Only inexpensive tests such as whether a category contains certain features are used. Any cues that may require significant computation, such as searching for an antecedent, are considered to be too expensive. Each structure cue is then associated with a list of possible failing filters. (Some examples of the mapping between cues and filters are shown in [table 4.1].) The system then chooses one of the possible failing filters based on this mapping.

Table 4.1
Some of the heuristic cues used for testing which filter will block a given sentence

Structure cue	Possible failing filters
Trace	Empty Category Principle, and Case Condition on traces
Intransitive	Case Filter
Passive	Theta Criterion
	Case Filter
Nonargument	Theta Criterion
+ Anaphoric	Binding theory Principle A
+ Pronominal	Binding theory Principle B

The correspondence between each cue and the set of candidate filters may be systematically derived from the definitions of the relevant principles. For example, Principle A of the Binding Theory deals with the conditions under which antecedents for anaphoric items such as *each other* and *himself* must appear. Hence, Principle A can only be a candidate failing filter for structures that contain an item with the + anaphoric feature. Other correspondences may be somewhat less direct. For example, the Case Filter merely states that all overt noun phrases must have abstract Case. Now, in the parser the conditions under which a noun phrase may receive abstract Case are defined by two separate operations, namely, Inherent Case Assignment and Structural Case Assignment. It turns out that an instance where Structural Case Assignment will not assign Case is when a verb that normally assigns Case has passive morphology. Hence, the presence of a passive verb in a given structure may cause an overt noun phrase to fail to receive Case during Structural Case Assignment—which in turn may cause the Case Filter to fail. [FN: It is possible to automate the process of finding structure cues simply by inspecting the closure of the definitions of each filter and all dependent operations. One method of deriving cues is to collect the negation of all conditions involving category features. For example, if an operation contains the condition "not (Item has_feature intransitive)," then we can take the presence of an intransitive item as a possible reason for failure of that operation. However, this approach has the potential problem of generating too many cues. Although it may be relatively inexpensive to test each individual cue, a large number of cues will significantly increase the overhead of the ordering mechanism. Furthermore, it turns out that not all cues are equally useful in predicting failure filters. One solution may be to use "weights" to rank the predictive utility of each cue with respect to each filter. Then an adaptive algorithm could be used to "learn" the weighting values, in a manner reminiscent of Samuels (1967). The failure filter prediction process could then automatically eliminate testing for relatively unimportant cues. This approach is currently being investigated.]

The failing filter mechanism can been seen as an approximation to the Cheapest-first heuristic in conjunct ordering problems. It turns out that if the cheapest conjunct at any given point will reduce the search space rather than expand it, then it can be shown that the optimal ordering must contain that conjunct at that point. Obviously, a failing filter is a "cheapest" operation in the sense that it immediately eliminates one structure from the set of possible structures under consideration.

Although the dynamic ordering mechanism performs well in many of the test cases drawn from the reference text, it is by no means foolproof. There are also many cases where the prediction mechanism triggers an unprofitable re-ordering of the default order of operations. (pp. 320–322)

2.5.6 Logical Dependencies and Reordering   In fact, Berwick and Fong (1990) show that the reordering procedure has several subtleties.

Given a candidate failing filter, the dynamic ordering mechanism has to schedule the sequence of parser operations so that the failing filter is performed as early as possible. Simply moving the failing filter to the front of the operations queue is not a workable approach for two reasons.

First, simply fronting the failing filter may violate logical dependencies between various parser operations. For example, suppose the Case Filter were chosen to be the failing filter. To create the conditions under which the Case Filter can apply, both Case assignment operations, namely, Inherent Case Assignment and Structural Case Assignment, must be applied first. Hence, fronting the Case Filter will also be accompanied by the subsequent fronting of both assignment operations—unless they have already been applied to the structure in question.

Second, the failing filter approach does not take into account the behavior of generator principles. Due to logical dependencies it may be necessary in some situations to invoke a generator operation before a failure filter can be applied. For example, the filter Principle A of the Binding Theory is logically dependent on the generator Free Indexing to generate the possible antecedents for the anaphors in a structure. Consider the possible binders for the anaphor *himself* in *John thought that Bill saw himself* as shown below:

(a)   *John$_i$ thought that Bill$_j$ saw himself$_i$

(b)   John$_i$ thought that Bill$_j$ saw himself$_j$

(c)   *John$_i$ thought that Bill$_j$ saw himself$_k$

Only in example (b) is the antecedent close enough to satisfy the locality restrictions imposed by Principle A. Note that Principle A had to be applied a total of three times in the above example in order to show that there is only one possible antecedent for *himself*. This situation arises because of the general tendency of generators to overgenerate. But this characteristic behavior of generators can greatly magnify the extra work that the parser does when the dynamic ordering mechanism picks the wrong failing filter. Consider the ill-formed structure *John seems that he likes e* (a violation of the principle that traces of noun phrases cannot receive Case). If however, Principle B of the Binding Theory is predicted to be the failure filter (on the basis of the structure cue *he*), then Principle B will be applied repeatedly to the possibilities generated by free indexing. On the other hand, if the Case Condition on Traces operation was correctly predicted to be the failing filter, then Free Indexing need not be applied at all. The dynamic ordering mechanism of the parser is designed to be sensitive to the potential problems caused by selecting a candidate failing filter that is logically dependent on many generators. (pp. 322–323)

2.5.7 Source-to-Source-Translation in Logic Grammars   We can now summarize the various source-to-source translation approaches to principle-based parsing.

A first approach would be simply to adopt the paradigm of logic programming. To do this properly, since the constraint filters of principles-and-parameters theory apply to trees or subtrees, we would use the usual approach to record the structure of a proof as we go, by adding an extra dummy predicate (as originally proposed by Cordell Green); this will store the derivation tree. The declarative principles-and-parameters constraints would be applied to this derivation tree.

However, this method would be extraordinarily time consuming—essentially like the old analysis-by-synthesis approach first proposed for transformational grammars. The example we looked at earlier with an unambiguous representation at S-structure but an ambiguous representation at LF shows why. Full sentences would be instantiated and then checked for all possible constraints, but most of the time this would be wasteful. For example, the system would check for an ECP violation even in sentences where no movement rules had applied, and therefore no traces were present.

To see how to get around this problem, it is worthwhile to examine implemented principle-based principles-and-parameters parsers, such as Dorr's or Correa's (1987) (Correa's system uses Prolog and so is particularly appropriate in this context). As noted earlier, these systems apply constraints as a parse tree is built up, subtree by subtree, and left to right. In Correa's system, this is done by passing up and constructing at appropriate mother nodes integer values that denote possible "chains" of NP- or *wh*-movement; this evaluation is done in a syntax-directed way, by pseudo-semantic evaluation as each NP or S subtree is completed.[24]

Finally, there is the possibility of "strong compilation": if we study exactly *when* constraints are applied, then, just as Marcus's parser contained an if-then rule to say exactly where a trace could be inserted, we ought to be able to see what constraints are applied at what steps in a derivation. For example, we know that the ECP will be applied only in trace-governed contexts, or that case is assigned only under government, so we can "factor in" this constraint to each rule that expands an NP to a trace by adding the ECP constraint clause (whatever that happens to be). Although this may well obtain the most efficient possible parser, just as in the Marcus parser case, it may leave us with a nonsystematic relation between our original axiom system and our compiled one—in the limit, we are left to our own devices and programming cleverness to figure out just what the right compiled representation ought to be.[25] For example, Marcus used a special sort of buffer-plus-stack data structure; if that is in fact the most efficient processor, somehow the logic grammar compiler has to output a device that simulates such a system. In general, this automation of data structure production seems quite difficult.

2.6 Reconciling Principle-Based Parsers with Psycholinguistic Models

There has been some debate about whether one can use experimental results to figure out whether people access rules or modular constraint systems in on-line processing. On the one hand, researchers like Frazier, Clifton, and Randall (1983) and Freedman and Forster (1985) argue for a modular, constraint-based system, basically one in which structures are computed before constraints like Subjacency are applied. On the other hand, Crain and Fodor (1985) have countered with experiments claiming to reveal certain shortcomings in the original experiments, such that one would not necessarily be able to conclude that constraints were being applied separately.

However, it is possible to show that principle-based parsers are still, at least, compatible with recent psycholinguistic evidence presented by Frazier (1986). Naturally, this does not resolve the dispute about rules versus constraints; as indicated above, we need a much deeper and more subtle analysis of the entire situation.

Turning first to the narrower points, Frazier (1986) has argued that principle-based parsing models make psycholinguistic predictions at odds with known psycholinguistic facts. Frazier presents two basic examples: (1) in head-final languages like Dutch the parser seems to blindly project NPs and do attachment, without first waiting to see what the verb is; this suggests that "pure" lexical projection is not carried out; (2) in some psycholinguistic experiments the human sentence processor apparently chooses transitive verbs blindly, without looking at lexical information. To comport with this evidence, Frazier argues for a slightly compiled-out rule system ($\overline{X}$ plus case plus theta theory). Actually, Frazier seems to be aiming for *Aspects*-style phrase structure rules rather than rules with full case and thematic constraints factored in, but that is irrelevant to the main point being considered here.

But neither of these psycholinguistic facts is really incompatible with a principle-based parser. Suppose we just use an underspecified $\overline{X}$ parser (perhaps constructing phrasal contours based on intonation, as some researchers have suggested). Whatever the details, we can certainly proceed with parsing, delaying access to subcategorization information until a verb is reached. This is exactly the way Dorr's parser works: the basic tree structure is built up before any other principles are consulted. Or, if one takes a more sophisticated view of what underspecification comes to, then Barton and Berwick's model (section 5) suggests another way around the problem. Both parsers are principle based.

Kashket's parser design for Warlpiri also answers at least one of Frazier's objections. Kashket's parser is bottom up in its basic operation and projects maximal phrases from the lexicon. Yet it does not delay projection of phrases until the verb is encountered (since the verb may be encountered almost anywhere). Instead, each phrase subtree is constructed as it is found in the input.

Frazier argues that the absence of delays (as indicated by misanalyses that the head would otherwise guard against) in processing head-final languages like Dutch argues against a direct projection of lexical items into $\overline{X}$ schemas. She also presents other intuitive and experimental evidence indicating that Dutch sentence-processing preferences argue against Kashket's "direct projection" strategy. Frazier considers a Dutch (verb-final) sentence like the following:

... dat het mesije van   Holland houdt.
     that the girl   from Holland liked

Frazier claims that when the preposition *van* is processed, it can only be projected to a PP and then attached to the preceding NP *het mesije*, since the verb has not yet been seen. But evidently this is not the route taken;

only if there is an additional PP, as in the following sentence, will the first PP be attached to the NP:

... dat het mesjie van Holland van Spans houdt.
that the girl   from Holland from Spain liked

But all this assumes Frazier's minimal attachment strategy: that nodes are attached as soon as possible to the phrase structure tree being built. This is not a necessary constraint (though it is classically argued that it reduces memory load in some fashion). Suppose, in contrast, that one opts for a more "wait-and-see" approach, like Marcus's—and by this I mean simply a bottom-up processing strategy like Kashket's. Kashket's approach for Warlpiri works well in this situation and is compatible with the Dutch processing evidence: it simply builds subtrees and waits until the main verb head is projected. Any structural attachment difficulties that arise in the Dutch examples can now be dealt with.[26]

It remains to see just what psycholinguistic evidence can be brought to bear on the question of principle-based parsing. Certainly the gap between surface measurements and internal principles may be large. More precisely, we do *not* want to repeat the derivational theory of complexity mistakes all over again and assume that logical divisions of principles must be temporally respected. A good example is Dorr's coroutined design. If one examines the operation of this parser from the outside, then it looks like case theory and trace theory are being computed almost at the same time as $\bar{X}$ skeletons, so one might conclude—erroneously—that these modules are all multiplied out together (thus *concretely* confirming Crain and Fodor's worry). In actuality they are kept distinct in this system. The problem is that we don't even know very much about what surface cues people actually use when they parse and how these are related to grammatical principles. Such cautionary tales suggest, unfortunately, that psycholinguistics may be even harder than it looks.

3 Principle-Based Parsing for Warlpiri

As a case study, let us compare how a context-free rule system and a principle-based parser might handle Warlpiri, a well-known free-word-order language. Again, the key idea is to develop a more flexible representational vocabulary so that the possible surface constructions in a language may be easily described by parametric variations in principles, rather than by a completely new and unrelated set of rules.

Warlpiri provides a good test bed for the principle-based parsing approach because it seems on the surface to look very different from English, German, and the Romance languages. Warlpiri word order is quite free. Even so, Kashket (1986) shows that the difference between a parser for

Warlpiri and one for English is roughly a parametric difference in case marking: when the verb marks case, as in English, then this tends to fix word order; whereas if other elements mark case, as in Latin, Warlpiri, and some parts of English, then word order tends to be free. Let's examine how Kashket's model works.

By using a vocabulary other than the *concatenation* and *hierarchy* that are blended in context-free rules, we can easily account for the free word order found in Warlpiri as well as that part of English that exhibits fixed word order (subject-verb-object) and those parts of English that are relatively free (prepositional phrases). One and the same parser will work for both. In contrast, since context-free rules can use only concatenation (linear position) to encode the more basic principles of case marking and case assignment, they ultimately fail to perspicuously describe the range of possibilities seen in natural languages. The result is that a rule-based parser for free-word-order languages almost invariably writes out all possible word order sequences, leading to a corresponding increase in grammar size.

3.1 Warlpiri and Rule-Based Parsing

To begin, let us consider some variations in a simple Warlpiri sentence. All permutations are legal. (Hyphens are added for readability.)

> Ngajulu-rlu ka-rna-rla punta-rni   kurdu-ku karli.
> I   AUX   take-NONpast child   boomerang
> 'I am taking the boomerang from the child.'
>
> Kurdu-ku ka-rna-rla ngajulu-rlu punta-rni   karli.
> child   AUX   I   take-NONpast boomerang
> 'From the child I am taking the boomerang.'
>
> Karli   ka-rna-rla kurdu-ku ngajulu-rlu punta-rni.
> boomerang AUX   child   I   take-NONpast
> 'It is the boomerang I am taking from the child.'
>
> (Plus 21 other possibilities)

Although phrase order is free except for the rigid auxiliary-verb-like element in second position (as in German), phrasal variations lead to different emphasis in topic and focus, as the translations indicate. In contrast, morpheme order is fixed: at the level of words, Warlpiri is in argument-function form, or what is called a *head-final* language, with markers *rlu* (ergative), *rni* (tense, nonpast), and *ku* (dative) appearing in word-final position. (The absolutive case marker is null and so does not show up explicitly on *karli* 'boomerang'. Also, there are basically just two lexical categories: nouns and verbs.)

How could we write a traditional context-free rule system to describe these constructions? Let us consider several possibilities and discuss their deficiencies.

First, aiming at mere string coverage, we could explicitly write out all possible phrasal expansions. (Here, the tags *S* and *O* stand for subject and object and we ignore the AUX element; *NP* stands for a noun phrase.)

S → NP-S NP-O V

S → NP-S V NP-O

S → NP-O NP-S V

S → NP-O V NP-S

S → V NP-S NP-O

S → V NP-O NP-S

Plainly, this is an unperspicuous grammar that also suffers from computational defects. By explicitly writing out the rules, we have missed the basic fact that the phrase order is free. To put the same point another way, the grammar would be almost as simple (almost as small) if we omitted the last rule S → V NP-O NP-S. And the grammar is large, because it contains more rules, and will thus run more slowly using standard context-free parsing algorithms.

Perhaps more importantly though, this approach ignores the basic and well-known asymmetry between subjects and grammatical functions like direct objects and indirect objects. (See Laughren 1987 for discussion.) For instance, it is the subject, not the object, that can be empty in constructions such as *I wanted to leave*, which does not have a counterpart *I wanted Bill to leave* meaning I wanted Bill to leave me. This asymmetry leads directly to positing a certain hierarchical structure that explicitly represents the domination of the object by the verb, with the noun phrase subject external to the verb phrase. Thus, a better context-free grammar would be something like this:

S   → NP-S VP

VP → V NP-O

But as is plain, this sort of grammar cannot parse the sentence order V NP-S NP-O that is observed in Warlpiri:

Punta-rni   ka-rna-rla ngajulu-rlu kurdu-ku karli.
take-NONpast AUX   I   child   boomerang
'Taking am I the boomerang from the child.'

To get over this hurdle, various proposals have been made: invisible verb phrase nodes, movement rules, and the like. What these rescue operations have in common is some way to break apart the linear phrasal concatenation forced on us by context-free rules. (Not even allowing the permutation of right-hand sides of context-free rules, as in the ID/LP format, will work here, because that format admits only sister permutation of phrases, not intercalated phrases as in Warlpiri.)

One could resort to a change in algorithm in order to overcome this hurdle. One such proposal that has been made in the context of a functional unification grammar for Finnish (Karttunen and Kay 1985:298–305) is to say simply that one particular phrasal order is stored and the permutations that actually appear are generated on demand. The base grammar would remain small. As Karttunen and Kay put it, "The opportunity is to work with a much smaller grammar by embodying the permutation property in the algorithm itself."

As we will see, in effect this is the approach adopted to parse Warlpiri via principles. There is a key distinction. In the Warlpiri system the difference lies not with some special algorithm, put probably where it ought to lie: with the statement of the grammar of Warlpiri. In fact, *nothing special* need be said about the Warlpiri parsing algorithm at all; it does not have to embody some permutation procedure, except implicitly as allowed by the principles of the grammar. Further, the very same parser will work for English as well—crucially, as mentioned, the only changes that have to be stated are the *linguistic* differences between English and Warlpiri, which have to be stated anyway.

3.2 Japanese and Context-Free Parsing

Free phrase order is not just a parsing problem in Warlpiri. The same problem arises in Japanese. Tenny (1986) reports on her experience in writing a context-free parser for Japanese (using a modified LR(k) parser that can return all possible parses, dubbed the "Malone parser"):[27]

> The free word order of Japanese syntax presents a major problem for a rule-based parser such as the Malone parser. Each rule must express a possible fixed word order—of which there are a great many in Japanese. This means that coverage of even a small number of basic structures requires a large number of rules, reducing the overall efficiency of the parser. This problem was in part circumscribed by labeling several different kinds of constructions with one name ('ARG'), but this solution has reduced efficiency elsewhere in the system. For example, some extra machinery is required to distinguish ARG's that are required by verbal case frames from those which are not. (1986:2)

As one example of the extra machinery Tenny refers to, we can take a look at Tenny's rule for sentences with one overt argument. (The annotation below the rule is a LISP function that runs at the time the LR parser is about to complete the right-hand side of a rule; in this case it checks that the sentence in fact has one overt argument.)

S → Smod? ARG Smod? verb
sent1-arg

The rule collapses all ARGs together, but they must then be distinguished later on, as Tenny makes clear in her discussion of this rule:

> This [rule] parses a sentence with one overt argument. A case frame is created, the verb entered as the predicate, and the argument entered as Nominative (*ga*), Dative (*ni*), Accusative (*o*), or Instrumental (*de*), depending on the case marker of the argument and the case frame of the verb. (If the verb belongs to the verb class vst [stative verbs] the semantic specifications in the case frame must determine which *ga*-marked ARG goes in which case slot.) If the ARG has the node type Sbar, it is entered into the case frame as having clause case. If there are ARG's left over after the case frame is filled, they are entered into the case frame as mod[ifiers] and labeled postpositional phrase.
>
> If there is a topic-marked ARG, do not enter it in the case frame until all the other ARG's have been entered. The topic is entered in the case frame in the following way:
>
> • The rule only applies if the topic is the first ARG in the clause. Otherwise, reject the parse.
>
> • Call a function to check whether there are any empty case slots in the case frame. If there are, fill the topic ARG into that slot. If there are not, fill the topic ARG into the case frame as a mod[ifier].
>
> • Label the parent S with the feature Topic.
>
> (1986:6)

It is evident that what we gain in being able to generate free phrase order—by having just one type of node, ARG—we lose again when we have to distinguish ARGs. Thus, although this method is workable, it is unwieldy.

Tenny notes a second problem with context-free rule-based Japanese descriptions, for NPs. We cannot allow free NP recursion because Japanese NPs constrain what possible constructions there can be at each level of recursion:

• At level 1, simple noun and adjective recursion is permitted (*yasui hon* 'inexpensive book').

• At level 2, NPs may be joined by conjunctions (*hon to zasshi* 'book and magazine'; *kuruma ya jitensha* 'car and such a thing as bicycle').

• At level 3, NPs may be followed by nominal quantifiers (*gakusei igai* 'nonstudent'; *gakusei inai* 'within students'; *gakusei dake* 'only students').

• At level 4, an NP may be followed by a particle (*gaikoku kara* 'coming from a foreign country').
• At the ARG level, an NP is followed by some general postposition marker (*gakusei wa* 'as for students').

As Tenny notes (1986:29), "All of these constructions may appear in one NP (*binboo na gakusei to kanemochi-no roojin igai ni wa* ['as for those other poor students and rich old people']) ... but the hierarchy of NP levels may not be violated." The upshot of these constraints is that a rule-based system must include five distinct NP types: NP1–NP4, plus the ARG NP itself. (It remains an open question how to handle these distinctions in a principle-based parser, but the difficulty with the rule-based approach is clear enough.)

Finally, Tenny notes her rule system eliminates hierarchical structure, yet that is probably needed in Japanese: "No word order is more basic than any other, yet some facts about how pronouns are construed with noun phrases within a sentence point to the idea that the word order Subject-Object-Verb is most basic in Japanese. To build this into the rule system would increase the number of rules dramatically" (1986:5).[28]

3.3 The Limitations of Context-Free Rules

To summarize, for Japanese we see that context-free rules fall short in two respects, as they did for Warlpiri: on the one hand, in order to accommodate free word order, they must "flatten" hierarchical structure, increase grammar size, and blur distinctions that are then postponed for later ("semantic") processing; on the other hand, if they try to accommodate the hierarchical structure demanded in Japanese (and, in some accounts, in Warlpiri), they cannot describe all sentences.

All of this suggests some underlying flaw in the context-free rule format itself. As mentioned, various extensions have been proposed to patch things up: one can change the parsing algorithm, incorporating permutation directly; one can introduce "invisible" VP nodes for Semitic verb-subject-object languages (Aoun 1979); one can propose "discontinuous" constituents; and so forth. In a certain sense, all of these proposals try to do the same thing: they try to break apart how context-free rules strictly tie phrasal hierarchical information to word precedence information.

This immediately suggests that a solution to the free-word-order problem is to recast the context-free account of word order and phrase hierarchy in terms of a different vocabulary of autonomous, modular principles. The central idea is identical to Halle's (1986) view of autosegmental representations as a kind of "spiral notebook" (see figure 4.7): the "surface" phonological form is like the spiral part of the notebook, resulting from the intersection or projection onto one plane of several independent, non-

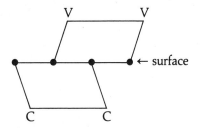

Figure 4.7
Halle's spiral notebook view of autonomous segmental components. The line labeled with a "V" stands for a level of vowels, whereas "C" indicates a consonant level, or plane. Individual consonant and vowel planes do not interact except to intersect at the surface level where a construction is ultimately observed.

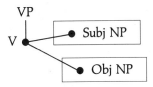

Figure 4.8
By dividing grammatical relations into separate "planes," we can describe a verb-subject-object language without crossing lines.

interacting "leaves": vowel sequences, consonants, rhythmic patterns, and the like. This "multidimensional" viewpoint is exactly what is implied by Aoun's invisible VP analysis to handle verb-subject-object order in Arabic. To make the comparison explicit, suppose we wrote the verb-NP-object connection in one plane and the NP-subject connection in another, disjoint plane. Then the VP can dominate the object NP in one plane and be linked with the subject NP in another, without any "crossing" of lines (see figure 4.8). Put another way, both NPs and VP can participate in domination relationships, without saying anything at all about precedence; precedence is established when the two planes are projected to a single phonological line. (Another key information-processing feature of this proposal is that it attempts to reduce all grammatical relationships to adjacency: whatever looks like a "long-distance" relation at the suface is in fact an adjacent one at a projected level of representation.)[29] But note that this is just a *graphical* way of saying that we have broken apart the grammatical relationships between VP, subject NP, and verb into autonomous, distinct modules that interact—in a word, we have broken up the context-free rules into principles. The whole idea of the principle-based approach is to abandon the straightjacket imposed by context-free rules to find a new vocabulary that will factor apart the constraints of word order and hierarchical phrases in such a way that they can operate independently, combining to produce the full range of free word order to rigid word order found in natural languages.[30]

Having stated our goal, let us see how we can discover the right principles to use and how we can get them to work directly for parsing Warlpiri (and English).

3.4 Parsing Warlpiri with Principles

Kashket's key insight is to apply case-marking and case assignment principles for Warlpiri at two autonomous representations. One representation requires precedence-ordered trees and one does not, and this bifurcation allows us to account at the same time for the rigid morpheme order in Warlpiri along with its free word order:

- *Precedence* structure: This level expresses, among other things, precedence relations (one morpheme precedes or follows another).
- *Syntactic* structure: This level expresses hierarchical relations (one phrase dominates another). The phrasal elements bear no precedence relations to one another.

The claim, then, is that phrasal syntax really needs only hierarchical information, not precedence information (as is reflected quite generally in the order-free nature of almost all principle-based predicates for syntax).

Having split apart the representations, Kashket proposes to split apart case marking and case assignment along these very same representational fault lines. It is this division of principles that will allow us to capture the full range of free-/fixed-word-order phenomena.

Case marking is taken to be an essentially word-based (or phonological) process, hence one that logically ought to be represented at the level of precedence structure. Therefore, case marking depends upon precedence information, since this is encoded at the morphophonemic level. As expected, it is directional and operates completely locally, under adjacency.

In particular, in Warlpiri case marking is to the left. This makes Warlpiri a head-final language at the morpheme level: case markers must appear at the end of words. Let us see how this works in an example.

In the word *ngajulu-rlu*, the ergative case marker *rlu* case-marks *ngajulu* 'I' to the left, so this word is well formed; we may imagine it comprising a complete "case phrase" unit ready to be analyzed at the phrasal level, as indicated in figure 4.9.

Crucially, in Warlpiri verbs are *not* case markers. We will see that this forces an essential difference between a so-called "configurational" language like English and "nonconfigurational" languages like Warlpiri. The

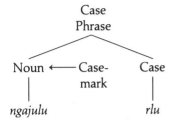

Figure 4.9
Directional case marking forces fixed internal word order in Warlpiri. The "heads" of Warlpiri words are final, with case marking to the left.

parser need only know that in English, a verb *is* a case marker, and that in Warlpiri, a verb *is not* a case marker.

Case *assignment* is carried out at the phrasal level under sisterhood, but with one crucial difference: since phrases do not even encode precedence information, case assignment cannot refer to order or adjacency at all and is nondirectional. This is what will allow Warlpiri phrases to be order free.

Let us consider another example to see how this works. Take the word sequence *Ngajulu-rlu punta-rni karli* 'I took the boomerang'.[31] This is first parsed as three separate word-level units: *ngajulu-rlu* is a noun-case combination that is case-marked as usual to form what Kashket calls a C̄ unit; *punta-rni* is a verb-tense combination that forms what Kashket calls a V unit; *karli* has a null absolutive marker at its end and thus is case-marked (as usual) to form a C̄ phrase. Note that all three words are in argument-function (head-final) form and thus well formed; if, for example, the tense marker had a noun to its left, then such a structure would be rejected.

The verb morpheme unit is now projected into syntax under the usual X̄ format: it contains a V node, a V̄ node, and a V̿ node. Under Kashket's model, the V̄ node assigns absolutive or dative case (in either direction); since *karli* is marked for absolutive case, it receives this case no matter whether it is to the left or to the right of *punta-rni*. Similarly, V̿ case-assigns ergative (either to the right or to the left). Finally, the association between thematic roles and cases is rigid in Warlpiri, so *karli* is identified as THEME and *ngajulu-rlu* as AGENT:

AGENT ↔ ERGATIVE

THEME ↔ ABSOLUTIVE

PATH   ↔ DATIVE

Figure 4.10 shows the resulting syntactic tree. It is important not to be misled by the order of the subtrees shown in this structure. Though one

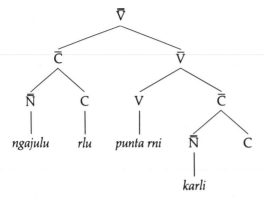

Figure 4.10
A Warlpiri syntactic structure for *I took the boomerang*. It is important to note that the order of subtrees is not encoded at this level, even though the picture must show some order on the page.

must write the subtrees in some order, in fact the first $\overline{C}$ could have been written to the right of the $\overline{V}$ instead of to the left.

By splitting up case-marking and case assignment principles—via adjacency and dominance—and using these principles in parsing, we can account for the difference between Warlpiri and English. In English a verb *is* a case marker, so position matters: the verb case-marks subject and object at the morpheme level where linear precedence is encoded. (More precisely, it is the verb's tense that marks the subject's nominative case to the left.) The result is that we usually get the order subject-verb-object in English.

Note that English also exhibits some phrase order freedom: prepositional phrases may appear relatively freely after a verb. Under the current account, that is because case assignment is carried out internally by the preposition. There is no ordering among phrases.

3.4.1 The Warlpiri Parser Accesses Principles, Not Rules   With this overview behind us, we can now look at the details of Kashket's parser and cover some fine points omitted earlier.

The parser consists of two stages: one for precedence structure and one for syntactic (hierarchical) structure. These two operate in tandem. Input sentences are passed to the precedence-based lexical parser, which breaks words into morphemes and outputs an ordered forest of trees. Every morpheme is also sent to the hierarchical parser, which projects information based on the lexicon and the lexical parser's output and attempts to produce a single hierarchical structure with unordered subtrees. No context-free rules or rules of any kind (in the usual sense) are accessed. The dictionary contains basic syntactic category information as well as *actions* (for a case or tense marker) that say what kind of element the case or tense marker selects (noun or verb), and, in the case of a verb, what arguments it case-assigns. Figure 4.11 shows how the actual Warlpiri dictionary transparently encodes the case selection (marking) and assignment actions illustrated earlier; these properties are directly accessed by the parser. (Some of the details are omitted here.)

The lexical parser determines the well-formedness of words according to morphophonemic constraints. Basically, this stage operates on groups of two morphemes at a time. After the first morpheme is input, no action can occur. The second input morpheme prompts word construction: the parser looks at the unit immediately to its left to see whether it may be combined (selected) by the case marker. For example, if the case marker is the tense element *rni*, and the unit to the left is not a verb, then the structure is ill formed, and the two units remain detached; but if the unit to the left is a verb, then combination can occur and a verb node can be produced, as described earlier. A dictionary is consulted here, as is typical. In addition, if a verb projection (predicate) is being formed, the dictionary will supply case assignment actions to be associated with the projections of the verb, as appropriate. (Note that if there is a null case marker, as with the absolutive, then we assume that morphological analysis supplies a null second morpheme.)

As each word is completely constructed, it is fed to the second stage, the phrasal parser. This stage's job is simply to carry out case assignment, in effect "linking" arguments to any predicate and thereby licensing them. Recall that we associate case assignment actions with each V node projection, as retrieved from a dictionary. The phrasal parser will execute *all* applicable actions, globally, *until no more actions apply*, but, plainly, a case-marked argument must be present before case assignment can take place. Note that the actions consider all possible directional case assignments, across all subphrases; this permits free phrasal order.

Finally, we note that the auxiliary is handled specially: its dictionary entry says that it takes a verb projection as an argument. (The AUX-second constraint receives no explanation on this account.)

3.4.2 An Example Parse   An example parse should make the algorithm clearer. Consider an object-verb-subject-object sentence form, such as *Kurdu-ku ka-rna-rla punta-rni ngajulu-rlu karli* 'from-the-child AUX am-taking I the-boomerang'. At the word level, nothing happens when the first morpheme *kurdu* is processed. The second morpheme, *ku*, adds a dative case marker, and it selects the noun to its left (a directional, precedence selection), forming a complete word with case as the root of the phrase. The next morphemes constitute the auxiliary and are projected as an

RLA: actions: SELECT: (OBJECT ((AUXILIARY . SUBJECT)))
             data: MORPHEME: RLA
                         NUMBER: SINGULAR
                         PERSON: 3
                         AUXILIARY: OBJECT

RNA: actions: SELECT: (SUBJECT ((AUXILIARY . BASE)))
             data: MORPHEME: RNA
                         NUMBER: SINGULAR
                         PERSON: 1
                         AUXILIARY: SUBJECT

KA: actions: SELECT: (AUXILIARY ((V . +)(N . −)))
             data: MORPHEME: KA
                         TENSE: PRESENT
                         AUXILIARY: BASE

RNI: actions: SELECT: (+((V . +)(N . −)(CONJUGATION . 2)))
                         ASSIGN: ABSOLUTIVE
             data: MORPHEME: RNI
                         TENSE: NONPAST
                         TNS: +

PUNTA: actions:
             data: MORPHEME: PUNTA
                         THETA-ROLES: (AGENT THEME SOURCE)
                         CONJUGATION: 2
                         N: −
                         V: +

RLU: actions: SELECT: (ERGATIVE ((V . −)(N . +)))
                         MARK: ERGATIVE
             data: MORPHEME: RLU
                         PERCOLATE: T
                         CASE: ERGATIVE

KU: actions: SELECT: (DATIVE ((V . −)(N . +)))
                         MARK: DATIVE
                         ASSIGN: DATIVE
             data: MORPHEME: KU
                         PERCOLATE: T
                         CASE: DATIVE

Figure 4.11
The Warlpiri dictionary directly encodes $\bar{X}$ features, case marking, and case assignment.

NGAJULU: actions:
            data: MORPHEME: NGAJULU
                       NUMBER: SINGULAR
                       PERSON: 1
                       N: +
                       V: −
KURDU: actions:
            data: MORPHEME: KURDU
                       N: +
                       V: −
KARLI: actions:
            data: MORPHEME: KARLI
                       N: +
                       V: −

Figure 4.11 (continued)

auxiliary phrase by a procedure not described here. Third, the verb *punta* with its tense marker *rni* is encountered. The tense selects the verb to its left, forming a verb unit, which is passed to the phrasal parser. At the phrasal level, the tense marking itself is attached to the A(uxiliary) unit. Also at the phrasal level, the verb unit is projected to a $\bar{V}$. Now the morpheme *ngajulu* enters the input and is processed; it is noted as a noun, but no actions can apply to it because it is not yet case-marked. The next morpheme, *rlu*, combines to its left with the noun to case-mark it ergative and form a $\bar{C}$ phrase; this is passed to the phrasal parser. Figure 4.12 gives a snapshot of the hierarchical structure built so far, where I have deliberately placed *ngajulu-rlu* to the left of the V projection node to indicate the order-free character of phrasal structure. Note that the tense element *rni* has been removed from the verb (it is attached to the auxiliary unit at this level of representation). Now any actions attached to the V projected nodes apply if possible. Since there is an ergative case-marked argument, ergative case assignment applies, linking $\bar{C}$ to the V phrase. Similarly, dative assignment is possible and *kurdu-ku* is attached. See figure 4.13.

Since no more actions apply, *karli* enters the lexical parser; with its null absolute case marker, it is a well-formed word and is passed as a $\bar{C}$ to the phrasal parser. Once again, a V projection action can now apply to this case-marked argument. This action assigns *karli* absolutive case (the THEME of the sentence). Figure 4.14 shows the final result. "PS" refers to the level of word structure, or precedence structure; "SS" is hierarchical phrase structure. The figure also shows how the tense marker *rni* is attached as part of the auxiliary or inflection phrase that dominates the entire phrase structure.

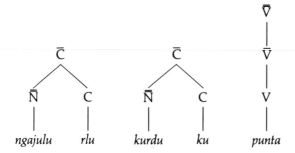

Figure 4.12
Starting to parse a Warlpiri sentence. The first three words, up through the verb and to the subject that follows it, have been analyzed. This figure represents hierarchical structure, so in fact the tense element *rni*, which is part of the verb at the precedence structure level, does not appear here.

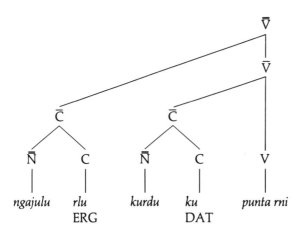

Figure 4.13
Linking the ergative subject and dative object in a Warlpiri sentence. These actions are forced by the dictionary entries associated with projected verb elements.

PS:

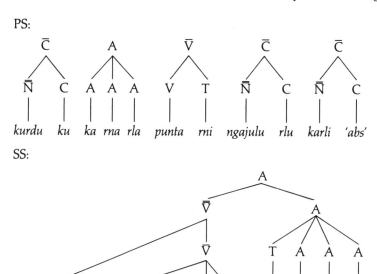

Figure 4.14
Linking in the Absolutive argument—which is phonologically absent—in the Warlpiri
example sentence gives us the THEME of the sentence. The figure shows both the final
precedence structure (PS) and syntactic structure (SS).

Kashket's implemented parser can handle a far wider range of constructions than shown here, including compound nouns. These show a particularly interesting interaction between lexical parsing and phrasal parsing and indicate the flexibility of a rule-less system. Given a string of nouns in the form

Noun Noun Noun Noun ... Case,

there might be some ambiguity about whether the unmarked nouns receive absolutive case. But this does not occur; the case at the end of the phrase is transmitted to all the nouns. The reason is that when nouns appear in this kind of group, they are all part of a single intonational phrase and therefore can be phonologically recognized as a single unit. We may assume this preprocessing to take place prior to or at the time of morpheme processing, as part of speech analysis. In contrast, if compound nouns appear discontinuously, then they must all be case-marked with the same marker, and again there is no parsing ambiguity. In this way, Kashket's system can quite easily accommodate additional information sources that are superimposed on his basic constraints.

Let us summarize why a principle-based approach succeeds where a context-free rule approach fails. Kashket's principled division into two distinct representations, a morphemic level obeying adjacency and linear precedence, and the phrasal level obeying just dominance relations, forces rigid morpheme order and permits free phrase order. At the same time, the case-marking/case assignment vocabulary lets us state the difference between languages like English and languages like Warlpiri in a straightforward grammatical way as a difference between which elements case-mark and which do not, all without resorting to novel parsing procedures for either language.

Kashket's parsing algorithms for English and Warlpiri will look exactly the same. Nothing need be said other than what minimally must be said anyway about the difference between the two languages: that verbs case-mark in English, but not in Warlpiri. In this way, a uniform principle-based system can significantly advance our understanding of the free-word-order/fixed-word-order continuum and show us how one kind of parser can handle many different kinds of languages.

Free word order is one place where principles have an advantage over construction-particular rules. We now turn to another example of the same kind: so-called ungrammatical sentences.

4 Ungrammatical Sentences and Principle-Based Parsing

Perhaps one of the clearest ways to see the difference between rule- and principle-based parsing is to investigate how the two approaches treat "ungrammatical" or "ill-formed" sentences. There are two distinct issues here: one that has to do with what have traditionally been dubbed ungrammatical sentences, and another related issue that centers on the (largely GB-based) distinction of core grammar versus periphery—that is, sentences that are somehow central or basic to grammatical theory versus those that are stylistically marked.

One important topic that will not be addressed in detail is the thorny one of what *people* do when they process ill-formed sentences. It's an important issue, because, as Freedman and Forster note, if their experimental results bifurcating grammar constraint violations like Subjacency versus phrase structure and agreement violations are correct, then that indeed "presents problems for any theory that has no notion of degree of generability" (1985:125). A principle-based theory tackles the whole notion of degree of generability head on.

The problem here is that the psycholinguistic evidence is still under debate. This section will be limited to the strictly engineering differences between rules and principles. Almost all "working" parsers that have tried to deal with ill-formed sentences—from ATNs on—have tried to modularize their constraint systems and not fold all rules together into a single system. The obvious example is agreement violations: since these are parceled out into register checks in an ATN, one can readily imagine the parse going through, but relaxing (separately) the register checks on agreement. (This would even fit what Crain and Fodor ultimately say about such cases, namely, that there's a longer matching time for such sentences because there's a search for a suitable grammatical alternative.)

4.1 Parsing Ill-Formed Sentences: Rules versus Principles
Parsing ill-formed sentences has always been a problem for rule-based systems. If we build a context-free grammar that can generate exactly the structural descriptions of a certain set of sentences, then how do we account for the perfectly human ability to assign structural descriptions to sentences not in this set? Indeed, grammaticality judgments would seem to demand that people build some kind of representation for ill-formed sentences, if only to be able to judge how they are ill formed. There's no doubt that people parse sentences such as *What do I wonder John likes*, even though such sentences are difficult to interpret. Further, ungrammaticality can range from pure word salad (violations of basic phrasal order, as in *Book the John put table on*), to thematic role violations (as in *John hit*), to binding violations.[32]

A principle-based approach accommodates the possibility of so-called ill-formed input naturally and directly in a way that a rule-based parser does not. Evidently, we might say that the parser assigns an interpretation to every string of sounds x—even if the sounds are Chinese for an English speaker.[33]

This causes problems for a rule-based parser built from the start to handle just a distinguished set of strings. What are we to do with strings not in the language? It is instructive to see how ill-formed input has been dealt with in rule-based systems. Essentially two approaches have been used: first, one can add new rules that parse the ungrammatical strings, while assigning scoring values to these parses; second, one can adopt a constraint relaxation model.

The first approach was adopted in the DIAGRAM system (Robinson 1980). For example, the following DIAGRAM rule scores a sentence fragment such as *I saw boy* lower (giving it the feature "unlikely") than a fragment such as *I saw the boy*. (The LISP-like style of the DIAGRAM rules has been replaced with a more English if-then format.)

If
> there is an NCOMP node

Then
> set the NBR feature to the intersection of the NBR of the Determiner, Nominal Head, and NCOMP;

Otherwise,
> set the NBR feature to the intersection of the NBR of the Determiner and Nominal Head;

If
> the Nominal Head is singular and not a mass noun

Then
> label the NP with the FACTOR UNLIKELY, because no determiner

(1980:60)

Because this approach is rule based, it is up to the rule programmer to notice ill-formed inputs, develop rules to parse them, and score them. For example, the same rule system rejects NPs such as *two boys than that* or *many water*. This is typical of a construction-oriented method. There are no general principles that explain why a particular construction fails to pass all grammatical constraints, aside from the descriptivist statements like mass/count noun disagreement.

The second approach is typified by the work of Weischedel and Black (1980) and Kwasny and Sondheimer (1979). Weischedel and Black were working within a foreign language instructional system, in which ill-formed inputs made by beginning students were to be expected; for instance, they cite the example of English-speaking students forgetting "to put past participles at the end of a clause" in German (1980:99), thus using *Ich habe gegessen das Fleisch* 'I have eaten the meat' rather than *Ich habe das Fleisch gegessen* 'I have the meat eaten'. They offer, first of all, to simply add more rules (the first approach described above): "If particular forms are anticipated, they may be explicitly included in the syntactic model.... The path in the augmented transition net (ATN) corresponding to the incorrect form computes a message to tell students of the mistake" (1980:99).

They also propose that one simply relax the predicates attached to network transitions:

> A straightforward example of the use of such predicates is for subject-verb agreement. It is easy for a user to make mistakes in long English sentences, resulting in parser failure. A solution would be simply to remove the predicate from the rule. However, Grishman (1973) reports from their experience ... that the predicates effectively eliminate a large number of spurious parses.
>
> We suggest that, instead of forcing all predicates to be satisfied or ignoring the information inherent in them, that the designer should designate that *certain predicates can be relaxed*, with a record being kept of each predicate not satisfied during parsing. Only parses yielding the fewest unsatisfied predicates are completed. Since the number of predicates that evaluate to false in a partial parse is a non-decreasing number, only those partial parses with the fewest unsatisfied predicates have to be continued....
>
> The notion of allowing certain predicates to go unsatisfied is much more general than the highly special environment of the German tutor.... several predicates were made optional or "failable". By "failable" we mean that the predicates ought to be true for the pattern to match, but could be false without preventing the pattern from matching if there would be no parse with all such predicates true. In addition to subject-verb agreement, pronominal case was also made failable. The two together allow a sentence such as "me think him win often" to be parsed, even though the parser has a model of correct language. (1980:99–100)

Note that this model comes closer to the principle-based ideal: in effect, a surface construction is allowed if it passes all well-formedness constraints; thus, by relaxing constraints one by one, we get a graded set of surface sentence possibilities. What is missing is a principled way to know what constraints to relax. In addition, models of this sort generally limit themselves to the obvious predicates placed on ATN arcs—agreement and cooccurrence restrictions—and not the full range of constraint violations (like island violations or thematic violations). For example, Kwasny and Sondheimer's (1979) model for handling ill-formed input similarly works by "selectively relaxing predicates to deal with co-occurrence violations and relaxation of expected word categories." In short, these construction-oriented approaches do not give a *theory* for ill-formed input; nor would we expect them to.

A principle-based approach confronts the problem of ill-formed input directly by saying what constraints are violated by any particular sentence. As a concrete example, suppose we take the modules in figure 4.3 as typical. We can now classify sentences according to whether they pass all or some of these constraints. Parsing so-called ill-formed sentences amounts to applying the well-formedness conditions above; the more constraints a sentence violates, the more ill formed it is. Of course, matters are more complicated than this; for example, simple agreement violations seem to cause more problems than they ought to. Given this, Crain and Fodor (1985) argue that the real problem has to do with confusability: subjects are looking for a near-miss grammatical example, and that's possible with agreement violations and not possible with violations such as *Who did you see Picasso's picture of.* Therefore, in the agreement violation case, processing will be longer as the subject searches for a possible alternative; in the second, constraint-violating example, the subject gives up rapidly. Freedman and Forster (1985) attempt to lay this matter to rest by trying to show that correctability does not account for all such results, but from my point of view the entire matter still seems unclear.

In any case, we do know that certain constraint violations don't disrupt processing fluency and others do. Perhaps the answer depends on how the information modules are temporally wired together: (1) $\overline{X}$ processing does occur rapidly and autonomously, and violations of such constraints force major disruption; (2) agreement violations cause processing hiccups because of the correctability effect, but this processing is still done modularly (as nearly everybody in computational linguistics wants it done);[34] (3) case and thematic violations are next worst; (4) locality and binding constraint violations cause the least processing disruptions because processing has already passed to a second stage of interpretation by that point. However matters work out, Freedman and Forster (1985) discovered that nongenerable strings are processed less fluently than strings that pass some, but not all, constraints, and we should now abandon the whole notion of generation and replace it with constraint satisfaction.

As one might expect, since some principles (like binding) depend upon calculations that other licensing principles provide, one might expect that some constraint violations are less harmful than others. For example, an $\overline{X}$ violation may prevent one from even being able to compute structural relationships among the elements in a sentence and so tends to result in a completely uninterpretable sentence. Similarly, theta theory violations can't be as easily interpreted since missing arguments can't be supplied. On the other hand, agreement, binding, and bounding violations must be calculated relative to an already licensed structure and so are usually interpretable. For example, *John seems it is certain to like ice cream* and *Bill thought Mary likes himself* are both parsable and interpretable. In this way, a principle-based account provides a *theory* of ill-formed sentences in a way that a rule-based approach does not.

- Violation of theta theory: *John hit; Bill hit John Joe.*
- Violation of trace theory: *John hit t.*
- Violation of bounding theory: *The man$_i$ who pictures of e$_i$ are on the table.*
- Violation of $\overline{X}$ theory: (more than one head in a phrase) *John Mary kissed Sue.*
- Violation of Projection Principle: *John hit e$_i$.*
- Violation of Empty Category Principle: *Who$_i$ do you think that left e$_i$.*
- Violation of Case Filter: *John's destruction the city; I bought quickly the book* (adjacency violation in English).
- Violation of binding theory: *John said that Mary thought that washing himself would be OK.*

Freedman and Forster (1985) also want to find out where such violations are processed—at S-structure, LF, D-structure, or somewhere else. Their tentative answer pins it down to a blend of S-structure and "plausibility." This is such a rough-cut answer that it would fit almost any model. For example, one could take S-structure to be just that provided by a completely multiplied-out set of GPSG rules, and "plausibility" to be whatever it is. Clearly, much more work must be done here: can one use quantifier effects to dissect out different levels in LF, for example, as Hornstein (1986) proposes?

How would a parser accommodate these constraint violations? Freedman and Forster (1985) observe that a rule-based parser—for them, Marcus's parser—would be hard pressed to maintain an account of sentence overgeneration. But if we follow Kashket's model described in section 3, then nothing special need be said at all, though the parser may fail at various points because it winds up with incomplete subtrees at the lexical level or with an unattached subtree at the phrasal level. For example, if Kashket's parser is given a sentence with a verb that must assign DATIVE case and there is only one NP case-marked ABSOLUTIVE, then case assignment fails and the NP remains detached. Thus, this NP is not licensed, even though the sentence is partially analyzed. Exactly as much of the structure as can be built is built.

The nonhomogeneity of principle-based systems assists here as well. If we assume that *wh*-movement well-formedness is checked by a separate parser component (as in fact most systems do: consider ATNs, Marcus's parser, and Abney's licensing model described in section 5), then we would expect there to be sentences that can be completely analyzed phrasally, but cannot be assigned correct *wh*-empty category indexings, such as *What do you wonder who likes*—roughly because all the parsing machinery aside from the separate *wh* components works fluently.

This is not to say that a rule-based system cannot reproduce the effect of graded unacceptability. After all, the ATN system and Marcus's system are "rule based" in the traditional sense of the term. But I would argue that to the extent that they factor out a distinct operating unit with its own behavior that is imposed on top of the basic parser operation—be it hold cell or *wh*-comp mechanism—these parsers slide at least part of the way into the principle-based domain. Note further that this is also true of agreement violations: since agreement is typically imposed nonhomogeneously on top of otherwise well-formed tree structures, agreement violations may be understood as principled violations of well-formedness conditions, precisely because they can be factored apart from phrasal well-formedness. Indeed, to the extent that we break apart a surface construction into the interaction of several components, we adopt a principle-based view.

Once again, then, the difference between rules and principles here is not so much one of formal distinction as it is one of practice: how easy is it to accommodate ill-formed sentences in a given framework? If we have not factored apart the distinct constraints that are contributing to an unacceptable sentence, then it may be particularly hard to unravel their effects, and this is why a principle-based parser gains in handling such cases. By way of example, consider what one must do with a traditional context-free grammar to parse a sentence such as *Mary to like ice cream is nice*. One must add a new rule that allows *for* to appear optionally in a sentential NP, along with some flag so that we know that such a sentence is not perfectly well formed:

Sentential NP → $\overline{\text{S}}$

$\overline{\text{S}}$ → for NP INFL-tns VP

INFL-tns → to

VP → like NP

$\overline{\text{S}}$ → NP INFL VP

   new rule (score 0.7)

The problem is that the new rule really doesn't say *why* the sentence is bad—it's just mixed in with the other rules. It's another example of having the wrong vocabulary to talk about cause and effect: what we'd really like to say is something to the effect that *Mary* needs to be case-marked by *for* (given the absence of a tensed verb). On this principled account, we don't have to add a new rule at all. Furthermore, consider what happens when we try to extend the two systems to encompass a closely related example like *Mary likes ice cream is nice*. On the context-free rule approach, we have to add another new rule that would permit the absence of *that*. This rule would be completely distinct from the rule to handle an optional *for*—yet we know that the two problems are closely allied, since the same constraint that is being violated when we omit *for* is at work when we omit *that*. A full context-free system to handle all possible unacceptable sentences would be enormous. Note that it could not simply say that all sentences are acceptable—this would take a very small grammar, of course—because we would still like to recover the proper structural descriptions of completely well formed sentences, and judge gradations in unacceptability. The scoring functions would have to be quite carefully hand-tailored to achieve this goal. In contrast, a parser using case-marking principles would be able to report back immediately where and why such sentences are unacceptable, with no additional machinery.

Principle-based handling of unacceptable sentences is not confined to the principles-and-parameters model, of course. The same remarks apply to any theory—like GPSG—that possesses well-formedness constraints. Figure 4.15, taken from Sells (1985:79), outlines the major GPSG components.

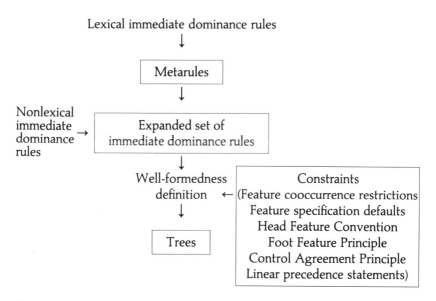

Figure 4.15
GPSG also builds up surface constructions by superimposing a set of constraints on a set of tree structures. (From Sells 1985:79.)

We see that although GPSG does contain rules (although they are in fact admissibility constraints on well-formed subtrees, hence closely allied to constraints), it also contains a variety of principles that apply to an expanded set of immediate dominance rules and relate these to well-formed syntactic structures: feature cooccurrence restrictions, feature specification defaults, the Head Feature Convention, the Foot Feature Principle, the Control Agreement Principle, and linear precedence statements. By factoring apart the well-formedness of individual constructions into several components, GPSG can also isolate unacceptability into one or another component and produce a parser that can automatically handle ill-formed sentences by relaxing one or another of the constraints. The information flow inherent in the GPSG picture also leads to a natural (though perhaps incorrect) picture like the GB one: certain constraints lead to gross unacceptabilities, because they do not even license correct phrasal trees; other constraints violate only agreement conventions and so permit phrasal construction to proceed unhindered all the way through to the bottom of the GPSG information flow diagram. Nothing bars GPSG from developing a principle-based treatment of unacceptable sentences.[35]

In short, when we have a principle-based parser, we need state a constraint only once, and we know why an unacceptable sentence is unacceptable. With a rule-based system, we in effect work with the theorem-like results of deductions from more basic axioms, and so we lose the intermediate steps that tell us why such sentences are unacceptable (other than the scoring function that is left behind). Given a construction-oriented approach, there is a further temptation to simply dump in another rule to cover each unacceptable case that comes along, without recognizing the systematic patterns that lie behind the unacceptabilities. As is well known, simply adding more rules to a context-free grammar can have unintended consequences (ask anyone who has written a large context-free grammar). Finally, readers familiar with artificial intelligence expert systems should recognize immediately the superiority of a system that can reason from first principles in order to understand what has gone wrong.

4.2 Principles and the Role of Core versus Periphery in Grammar

How might we expect the distinction between core and peripheral constructions to be reflected in a principle-based parser? Should stylistically marked or idiosyncratic constructions be more or less difficult to process? Since the basic information flow of the principle-based model leads us to first establish licensing conditions, given a principle-based parser like Kashket's (or the Abney or underspecified $\bar{X}$ model described in section 5), we would expect sentences that meet basic licensing conditions to be relatively easy to process, whereas more "marked" constructions would be those that violate basic licensing conditions (government and the like). The implications for processing complexity are unclear. For example, infinitival sentences with lexical subjects (*I want John to win*) meet all the basic licensing constraints, and I would not expect them to cause any extra processing difficulty. This prediction contrasts with that offered by Frazier (1986), who implicitly argues that a direct, principle-based parsing system would predict an extra processing load in such cases.

I see no reason why this extra processing load should necessarily follow. Though it's true that examples such as *I want John to win* are more unlikely, that doesn't mean that they're hard to parse via direct X̄ projection. Section 5 shows that simply by projection, in turn, maximal phrases for *John*, the inflectional element *to*, and the verb *win* will do the trick: the expectation that *want* takes a case recipient will permit it to actually assign case to either *John* or the full sentence, depending on which sequence of words actually appears. Such an example should be just as hard to parse directly as *John wants ice cream*—which is what Frazier claims to be the case (1986:24).

In fact, Frazier would like to say more generally that there is no processing distinction between core and peripheral constructions (1986:24)—and that this provides an argument for a "compiled" rather than a "direct" use of grammatical principles:

> . . . we might expect infinitives with lexical subjects to be difficult to understand. Presumably derived nominals with "of" inserted (e.g., destruction of Rome) should also be perceptually complex, assuming "of"-insertion is idiosyncratic and thus peripheral (i.e., we can't simply list it and let it apply to any caseless noun phrase such as "John" in "It was hit of John" or "I tried of John to win.") Similarly phrases with idiosyncratic order ("someone clever" cf. Emonds 1986) should be difficult to parse, on the view being considered.
>
> There is evidence suggesting many so-called 'stylistically-marked' constructions are relatively difficult to parse, at least in isolation. But in every case I'm aware of, the complexity of such constructions can either be attributed to independent parsing principles and/or its complexity is eliminated when the sentence is presented in the appropriate discourse contexts. (1986:41)

The problem with Frazier's point here is that her examples of "marked" constructions really aren't marked with respect to a principle-based parser. We have already covered the example of lexical subject infinitivals. For *of*-insertion, it also seems likely that licensing processing will proceed normally: the parser will recognize a nominal form, as in *destruction*, via projection from the lexicon; the next token, *of*, assigns case normally to the NP to the right, and no unusual processing at all takes place. On the other hand, *It was hit of John* will cause the processor to balk (as expected and as seems true on introspection), since *was hit* will not be processed as a nominal ($+N$) form. It does not seem outlandish that this idiosyncrasy would be encoded in the lexicon and accessed as such directly by the parser, demanding a caseless NP to the right.

5 Parsing Models for Principle-Based Systems

We turn next to parsing models for principle-based grammars, contrasting them with rule-based systems. We have already seen how Kashket's parser works by imposing well-formedness conditions on words as they enter a hypothetical input stream. The chief difference from a rule-based parser, as one might expect, is that a principle-based parser proceeds by checking a variety of heterogeneous well-formedness conditions as it goes along, rather than "matching" against a storehouse of uniform individual rules. (A context-free rule system represents a paradigm example of such a matching system.)

But there are other issues. Since a principle-based parser need not recover phrase structure, this leaves open the question of exactly what kind of information structure must be built. Here there are many open possibilities; this section will consider just a few. First, as in Abney's system, one might simply recover licensing relations directly. Second, as in Kas..ket's parser, one could just recover adjacency relations at one autonomous level and hierarchical relationships at another. Third, one could assume a predicate such as *government* to be basic to the parser's job. On this model, government relations could be built via skeletal (topological) projections from $\overline{X}$ theory, supplemented by intonational phrasings (as supplied by the speech stream). We will look briefly at this in section 5.2. Fourth, one could assume a basic pushdown stack model that extensionally provides the equivalent of c-command, as suggested in Berwick and Weinberg 1984. If we take government to be mutual c-command, then such a model would already have at its disposal much of the apparatus to compute the well-formedness conditions for syntax. (In a sense this is what Abney's parser does.) Fifth, one can interleave $\overline{X}$ projection along with application of other well-formedness constraints; this is the approach that Dorr takes for parsing, described in section 6.

In this section we will see via explicit case studies that direct principle-based parsing need not slow things down, contrary to some expectations. Indeed, principle-based parsing appears to resolve certain problems that plague deterministic parsing. In addition, it opens up a wider range of parsing techniques than variations on context-free parsing methods like Earley's algorithm, CKY parsing, or its Prolog-based analogues. In part, this is because we may eschew traditional tree-based predicates in favor of whatever predicates are needed to compute well-formedness conditions—

such as c-command and government. We may in fact take the hallmark of a principle-based parser design to be its avoidance of traditional phrase structure, since this is largely subsumed by other predicates in such a system.

At the conclusion of this section we will turn briefly to the second part of an answer to the processing speed question: Are principles transformed into rule-like form? We will see that an autonomous processing theory for principles—grounded on Halle's spiral notebook conception for linguistic structure—actually suggests more efficient parallel processing schemes for modular, principle-based parsers. The information structure of principles does suggest, however, that there are deductive clusters that may *look* like "compiled" rule systems.

We will cover only two basic ways to organize a principle-based parser here, forcusing in detail on two specific proposals. There are other possibilities that we will not consider. Sharp (1985) and Thiersch (1986) have built GB parsers using Prolog to encode the required well-formedness predicates (axioms), while relying on Prolog as a backtracking proof procedure to deduce whether a given sentence can follow from the axioms. Wehrli (1984) has built a Pascal implementation of a principles-and-parameters parser that we will not look at here.

Since Prolog-based designs were discussed earlier, in section 2.3, we will not explore them further here. Instead, we will analyze two other alternatives that grapple with the issue of principle-based processing: Abney's licensing model and Barton and Berwick's $\overline{X}$ parsing model.

5.1 Parsing as Licensing: Abney's Model

Abney (1986) has developed a GB-based parser quite similar to Kashket's in the sense that it is grounded on the notion of *licensing*: every element in a sentence appears there because it is fulfilling some grammatical role—entering into a grammatical relationship on either the giving or the receiving end—and a sentence is well formed if and only if every one of its elements is licensed. Also, just as in Kashket's parser, case relationships are assigned essentially under sisterhood, without necessarily having to first build $\overline{X}$ skeletons. We saw how case assignment licensed elements in Kashket's Warlpiri parser. In fact, Abney's parser never really builds phrase structure at all. Figure 4.2 showed how Abney's licensing relations of thematic assignment (θ), subjecthood (S), functional selection (F), and modification (M) work to validate every element of a simple sentence.

In particular, for Abney licensing relations are (1) unique, (2) local (in effect, operating under sisterhood, just as Kashket claims), and (3) lexical (particular verbs assign particular thematic roles). Importantly, Abney's model shows how one can apply case and thematic principles *before* phrasal structure is completely fixed; indeed, in his system, it is case and thematic

will:	⟨← NP S⟩
	(*will* assigns Subjecthood relation to NP to its left)
will:	⟨→ V F⟩
	(*will* functionally licenses a V to its right)
like:	⟨→ NP THEME⟩
	(*like* thematically licenses an NP theme to its right)
pictures:	⟨→ [genitive] THEME⟩
	(*pictures* thematically licenses a genitive theme to its right)
of:	⟨→ NP F⟩
	(*of* functionally licenses (case-marks) an NP to its right)

Figure 4.16
Assignment of licensing relations to lexical items in Abney's system

licensing that fix phrasal structure. Additionally, his parser includes a blend of heuristic-like principles (it analyzes roughly two words at a time) that are presumably derived from the competence grammar itself. Thus, Abney's parser is not a "direct" principle-based parser. Nonetheless, it is clearly principle based.

5.1.1 Abney's Parser in Action   We can review in more detail the operation of Abney's parser on the sentence *John will like pictures of Mary*. Like Kashket's parser, Abney's works on basically two words at a time, without referring to any explicit phrase structure rules. Abney assumes the assignment of licensing relations to lexical items shown in figure 4.16. (S, F, and M stand for the three varieties of licensing besides theta assignment; when theta assignment is mentioned, the particular thematic role involved is listed. The directionality of assignment—since Abney is talking about English—is also listed.)

As Abney then points out,

> We can parse our sample sentence by means of a very simple algorithm: proceeding from left to right, examining two words at a time, assemble them by assigning whatever relations can be assigned. The parse would proceed as follows.... *John* has no roles. Only the first of *will*'s roles is assignable to *John*; the second matches in neither directionality nor description of receiver.... At each point, exactly one role is assignable, making for a rather trivial parse. (1986:5)

Figure 4.17 shows the snapshot sequence for the parse. What is more, as Abney states,

Step 1: John   will
       [N]   [I]
         $\langle \leftarrow N\,S \rangle$
         $\langle \rightarrow V\,F \rangle$

Step 2: John $\xleftarrow{\text{license}}$ will   like
       [N] $\leftarrow$ N S   [I]   [V]
             $\langle \rightarrow V\,F \rangle \, \langle \rightarrow N\ \text{theta} \rangle$

Step 3: John $\leftarrow$ will $\xrightarrow{\text{license}}$ like   pictures
         [I]   [V]   [N]
             $\langle \rightarrow N\ \text{theta} \rangle \, \langle \rightarrow \text{[gen]}\ \text{theta} \rangle$

Step 4: John $\leftarrow$ will $\rightarrow$ like $\xrightarrow{\text{license}}$ pictures   of   Mary
         [I]   [V]   [N]   [P]   [N]
                   $\langle \rightarrow NP\ F \rangle$

Step 5: John $\leftarrow$ will $\rightarrow$ like $\rightarrow$ pictures of $\xrightarrow{\text{license}}$ Mary
         [I]   [V]   [N] [P]   [N]

Figure 4.17
Parsing by two-word licensing, using Abney's model. N = noun, V = verb, P = preposition, I = inflection.

Once the licensing structure of the sentence has been recovered, phrase structure follows straightforwardly.... It is also reasonable to suppose that licensing relations, taken as a group, are nonreflexive and noncyclic: i.e., no element can be licensed by itself, and no element can be licensed by another which it itself licenses (directly or indirectly). This guarantees that licensing relations, taken together, define a finite tree. If we assume that all relations are associated lexically with their assigners, then only words can be assigners of licensing relations ... Finally, assume the relevant locality condition on licensing relations to be strict government: mutual c-command. If we eliminate, or at least ignore, intermediate-bar-level categories, this locality condition is simply phrase-structural sisterhood. (1986:5–6)

If licensing relations are so very much like phrase structure rules—akin to McCawley's well-formedness templates for depth-one trees—then the right question to ask is whether this principle-based approach is any different. The answer is yes: licensing relations are stricter than phrase structure templates because certain $\bar{X}$ constraints are enforced—there is a unique head and "all nonheads are maximal categories." Abney observes that licensing, as expected, also works better across languages: though there need be no connection between the phrase structure rules from one language to another, this is not true for licensing. Because the licensing vocabulary is so restricted, the only thing that can change is basically the direction of licensing (right or left). This greatly narrows the possible class of licensing relations (hence phrase structure realizations).

It is also interesting to compare this system with a much older framework: categorial grammar. In a certain sense, categorial grammar does the same work, telling us what can combine with what. As expected, a key difference is that Abney's system is grounded on principles: we do not have arbitrary combinatory rules, but we do have a more restricted vocabulary of licensing direction and licensing relationships. This eliminates the need for any kind of complex cancellation "arithmetic." (On this view, categorial grammar superficially reflects these more basic combinatory principles.)

As one can see, Abney's parser assembles subtrees in a roughly bottom-up fashion. No rules are used, however—only general admissibility constraints. To deal with a wider range of sentences, Abney's full parser includes a much richer array of processing techniques, which we will review only briefly here.

One of these deals with top-down expectations. For these, Abney adds *templates*, basically, partial government fragments. The problem arises because the parser must sometimes wait until a licenser appears: for instance, an adjective following a determiner must wait until it sees its noun licenser. To handle such cases, one can add to the determiner a template [Adj Noun]—the expectation that the adjective will indeed be (ultimately) followed by a noun. This template is assigned by the determiner to the adjective. (Presumably this would also hold for multiple adjectives.) Abney observes,

> Templates have an obvious similarity to phrase structure rules. In fact, they perform precisely the function which phrase structure rules perform. The important difference between this system and systems based on phrase structure rules is that in such systems, the phrase structure rule format is used as a homogeneous rule format for all aspects of parsing. Here, templates are only one segment of a larger system, and are highly specific to a certain task, rather than being used for tasks for which they are not suited. (1986:14)

Frazier (1986:17) argues that Abney's use of templates really means that one isn't using grammatical principles directly at all any more. But surely this is a matter of degree. Templates are quite limited in their activity— they apply in only very special, isolated circumstances. In this respect, they may indeed reflect heuristic parsing residues.

A second set of additions center on structural revisions necessitated by incorrect parses—Abney's parser backtracks to rectify incorrectly assembled licensed structures. This will happen, for example, in well-known sentences where a verb can subcategorize for either an NP or a sentence, such as *They knew the solution to the problem would be easy*. Abney hypothesizes that such seemingly fluently processed cases are corrected by purely adjacent, local reorganizations of the licensing structures. I think this view to be largely correct, and in section 5.2 we will take another look at such examples.

Third, Abney uses his licensing principles to resolve some notorious cases of attachment ambiguity. His approach here does not bear directly on the issue of principle-based parsing, except to point out that the licensing vocabulary may provide a better account of such cases than previous, purely structural (and essentially context-free rule based) approaches. If more than one node in the preceding near edge can license the current node (as in *I ate the ice cream on the table*), then Abney's parser chooses one based on the following ranking:

- theta-licensers preferred over non-theta-licensers;
- verbs preferred over other categories;
- low attachment preferred.

This ranking is partially principled because theta-licensers and verbs play a central role in validating a fully licensed structure: without a verb, or theta-licenser, arguments are not assigned case. Finally, the third action may be regarded as a default that is taken when no licensing priorities apply. Thus, unlike systems that aim at purely descriptive statements of attachment preferences (such as minimal attachment or processing strategies such as ordering PUSH versus SCAN operations in an ATN), this ranking is highly rationalized. Again, the point is not that processing strategies can't simulate these effects; the point is that principles guide us to the appropriate solution. And Abney's ranking fares reasonably well: as he points out, it correctly predicts the preferences in examples such as *I could interest the mayor in a new Volvo* (theta-licensing wins over modification); *I thought about his interest in the Volvo* (theta-marker *interest* wins out); *I sang to the cat in the kitchen* or *I wrote a letter to a friend* (both candidates theta-mark but the verb wins out); and *a gift to a boy in a box* (both theta-licensers are nonverbs, so default low attachment wins, even though the fragment is semantically anomalous interpreted this way).

Finally, Abney's parser does what all principle-based systems ought to do: it contains several different devices to follow the constraint-satisfaction view of sentence constructions, rather than attempting to shoehorn everything into a single kind of rule format. In particular, like many previous parsers, Abney's contains a distinct device for handling displaced constituents. However, he has turned this into a separate movement module, which is not concerned with licensing or structure building at all, aside from inserting empty categories. In this Abney follows Berwick and Weinberg's two-stage approach to parsing: the first stage builds correctly licensed structure (phrase structure in Berwick and Weinberg's sense, though this is replaced here with licensing structure); the second stage uses that structure as a scaffolding on which to assign filler-gap relations.

The constraint that an antecedent c-command its gap is quite transparently encoded via the licensing relations. Abney does not take this view, but, recalling that our goal is to reduce all grammatical relationships to adjacency, consider a sentence like *Who did you think Bill saw*. Abney's model will license the following grammatical relations, where *IP* stands for an inflection projection and *CP* for a complementizer projection:

[who $\rightarrow$ IP-did]   [NP-you $\leftarrow$ Infl-did]   [Infl-did- $\rightarrow$ think-V]

[think-V- $\rightarrow$ CP]   [C-e- $\rightarrow$ Infl-saw]   [NP-Bill $\leftarrow$ Infl-saw]

[V-saw- $\rightarrow$ e]

We note that there is an unbroken chain of *adjacent* licensed grammatical relations extending from *who* down to the gap after *saw*. Put another way, the composed, adjacent licensed relations are the reflex of what has been called a path or a chain in the theory of filler-gap relations. The licensing principles transparently enforce the c-command condition.

When this chain of adjacencies is broken, this corresponds to an (ill-formed) sentence where an antecedent does not c-command its gap, as in Abney's example *Who$_i$ Bill saw surprised e$_i$*. Here, there is no grammatical relation linking *who* with the chain leading from CP through the verb *surprised* down to a gap.

[who- $\rightarrow$ IP-saw]   [NP-Bill $\leftarrow$ Infl-saw]   [V-saw]

[CP $\leftarrow$ Infl-surprised]   [V-surprised- $\rightarrow$ e]

If this approach is correct, once again no additional rules need to be added in order to represent the correct licensing structure for long-distance dependencies; only the basic principles themselves are needed. We may contrast this approach with one that attempts to multiply out into the rule system itself the required chains. As before, attempting to do this using *one* kind of rule results in (1) blowing up the number of required rules enormously (see Barton, Berwick, and Ristad 1987, appendix B, for an estimate in English) and (2) folding together two distinct phenomena: local licensing and filler-gap dependencies. This is no different from trying to encode agreement relations in context-free rules: the result is a multiplied-out rule system that tries to do too much with a single rule format. In principle-based parsing, the ideal is to operate a number of distinct modules, each with its own particular informational constraints and independence.

5.2 Direct Parsing of $\overline{X}$ Rules

As our third example of principle-based parsing, we will consider what it means to parse using $\overline{X}$ theory directly. Our goal will be a familiar one: to show that if one embeds $\overline{X}$ theory *directly* into a parser instead of using multiplied-out context-free rules, one in fact gets a better deterministic parser. The model here is based on Barton and Berwick 1985 and Berwick and Weinberg 1985.

- The direct use of $\overline{X}$ theory permits one to delay parsing decisions so as to retain the advantages of deterministic parsing without any special machinery of the kind proposed by Marcus (1980). In particular, no special "attention-shifting" mechanism is required.
- The new parser design does not use any lookahead, yet remains faithful to human processing of "garden path" sentences. It fails naturally on "short" garden path sentences (such as *The boat floated sank*) that were perfectly well parsable using the Marcus 3-cell lookahead design. At the same time, the $\overline{X}$ format succeeds on sentences that seem to require lookahead, such as *I know that guy likes ice cream.*
- The new parser design does not recover tree structure; instead, it builds up a modified *phrase marker* representation. This representational format directly encodes the coidentification of lexical and phrasal heads (following $\overline{X}$ theory). Interestingly, the representation is formally constrained in such a way that only certain grammatical operations can be stated, and these correspond to what is actually required in current theories. For instance, Chomsky adjunction, but not sister adjunction, is possible.
- The new parser design is completely modular. Information from a variety of sources may be folded together to yield the output representation, in a layer-cake fashion. Syntactic ambiguity is easily encoded, with extrasyntactic resolution of ambiguity requiring minimal additions to the output representation.

To begin, we discuss the new parser design. We use roughly the same bounded-context design outlined by Marcus (1980) and modified by Berwick and Weinberg (1984). At any given point in the analysis of a sentence, the parser has access to certain bounded left and right context information; this is used to fix the parser's next move. The parser is deterministic, in a sense made precise below. The left context represents the analysis of the sentence seen so far; the right context holds words. In Berwick and Weinberg's model, left context could consist of at most a single constituent domain plus at least one additional cyclic node domain;

within these constituent domains, only nodes c-commanding the current token scanned are accessible. Thus, the left context is literally bounded in this model. We will adopt these restrictions here.

In Marcus's design, and in Berwick and Weinberg 1984, the right context was taken to be at least the current word being analyzed plus (usually) two lookahead symbols. In the new model, there will be no lookahead; only the current token scanned is visible. In this way the model follows Kashket's and Abney's designs. We could replace its explicit operations by licensing as well, but I have not done so here.

The new parser will be deterministic, in the following sense. At any step i in a parse we denote the representation of the sentence analysis at that point by A_i. A parser will be said to be *deterministic* if and only if the sequence of sets $A_1, A_2, \ldots$, is monotonically increasing in an information-theoretic sense: each set in the sequence is either the same as or a refinement of its predecessor. This means that one cannot *remove* information from an analysis set once it is placed there; one may, of course, refine this information. We will see that this constraint has important implications for what grammatical operations can and cannot be represented in the new parser design, as well as for the resolution of ambiguous sentence examples.

So far, aside from the lack of lookahead, the parser design we have sketched is identical to that in Berwick and Weinberg 1984. We now turn to the key difference between the two models. Instead of reconstructing explicit tree structure as a part of its left context representation and as its final representation of sentences, the new parser will build as its output representation a *phrase marker* in the original sense used in transformational grammar: a set representing all and only the *is-a* and *left-to-right precedence* relations in a sentence. This representation is augmented to directly encode the key $\overline{\text{X}}$ constraint identifying heads of phrases with lexical heads and the indexing of, for example, traces. Given Kashket's design, it would probably be more correct to parcel out the levels of precedence and dominance into two distinct representations, but we will not do that here (we will deal only with English).

An example that will be used later on will help to pin this notation down and show its similarity to the usual context-free parsing analysis. Suppose we have the sentence *I know that block supports the pyramid*. First, number the positions between the word tokens:

$_0$ I $_1$ know $_2$ that $_3$ block $_4$ supports $_5$ the $_6$ pyramid $_7$ ● $_8$

Here is the output set for this sentence (using traditional *is-a* symbols for now). Each element of the set is a triple, consisting of first the phrasal name followed by its *start* and *stop* positions. (Nothing crucial hinges on the exact details of this phrasal analysis.)

{(S 0 7) (NP 0 1) (PRONOUN 0 1) (INFL 1 1)

(V 1 2) (VP 1 7) (DET 2 3) (NP 2 4) (NBAR1 3 4)

(NOUN1 3 4) (S 2 7) (INFL 4 4) (V 4 5) (VP 4 7)

(NP 5 7) (DET 5 6) (NBAR 6 7) (NOUN 6 7)}

Note that this information will allow one to reconstruct hierarchical relationships among the elements, if desired, though remaining ambiguous in the case of nonbranching domination, since then we would have, for example, (NP 1 3), (NP 1 3). (Indeed, in the output representation these two NPs would be merged and thus be quite literally indistinguishable.)[36]

Moving closer to our desired $\overline{X}$ representation, let us now replace the conventional symbols NP and VP with their coidentified lexical heads. That is, let us say that the features of a maximal projection are coextensive with those of the lexical item that heads it. We indicate this by an index on a maximal projection identical to that of its lexical head. The index actually corresponds to a feature bundle, but is used simply as an abbreviation.[37]

{(X-max i (= INFL) 0 7) (X-max j 0 1) (I j 0 1) (INFL i 1 1)

(know k 1 2) (X-max k 1 7) (that 2 3) (X-max l 2 4)

(NBAR1 3 4) (block l 3 4) (X-max m 2 7)

(INFL m 4 4) (supports n 4 5) (X-max n 4 7)

(X-max o 5 7) (the 5 6)

(NBAR 6 7) (pyramid o 6 7)}

This is the *output* available at a parse's end. Of course, at intermediate stages of sentence analysis only intermediate portions of this set are available. The parser consults a bounded left context representation of this set plus the current input token scanned in order to fix its next move. This context is placed on a pushdown stack in the manner described in Berwick and Weinberg 1984.

Note that at any stage the analysis is simply a *set* of assertions comprising *is-a* and left-to-right precedence relationships compatible with the input seen so far. In fact, this is entirely equivalent to the *prefixes* of phrase markers, in the traditional sense (only prefixes, of course, since the parser cannot tell us anything about input that it has not seen so far). By the end of the parse, the assertion set will simply be the phrase markers compatible with the input string.

Information recorded at every step in the parse will be monotonically preserved. Once a recorded decision about the *is-a* or start and end points of an element can no longer be refined, this commitment will not be revoked. That is, once we have fixed that an element of the assertion set is an NP, that cannot be changed to VP. Similarly, a decision that the NP extends between positions 1 and 3 of the input cannot be retracted once it is made. However, it is possible to *refine* a decision in an information-theoretic sense, in three ways: first, we may add features to an *is-a* element, using the $\overline{X}$ features (for instance, changing an XP, with no features, to a $+N$ item, to a $+N$ $-V$ item, provided that the element is still part of the left context); second, we introduce a special asterisk notation, *, indicating that the *end* of a constituent has not yet been seen (this is apparently inevitable in a left-to-right analysis); third, we may *add* a new assertion, provided that the relevant portion of the phrase marker set is accessible. The asterisk, since it represents *no* information about the end position of a constituent, may be refined by replacing it with a specific numerical value, but of course, once this is done, the numerical value may not be retracted.

Unlike Marcus's machine, the parser will not use lookahead. Instead, its parsing decisions are based entirely on the current word token scanned and the representation of the input built up so far (the so-called left context of the parse). We may restrict the left context, as Berwick and Weinberg do, to a literal encoding of what amounts to one S, but this will not be necessary in the sequel here. At each step in the parse, the assertion set of triples maintained will simply be the intersection of all triples compatible with the input seen so far. Thus, at each step the assertion set will encode just what is *known for certain* given the input processed so far. (This is a precise way to formulate the "wait-and-see" approach suggested by Marcus.)

Finally, the parser will be able to make top-down predictions (as in Marcus's parser) based on, for example, subcategorization information, as when the lexical entry for a verb of a certain type sparks an expectation that a certain argument structure will be encountered. And, as in Marcus's design, the parser can certainly create assertions based on the actual words it finds in the input.

5.2.1 The $\overline{X}$ Parser in Action   Now consider some examples that might seem to require lookahead. Note that our current design doesn't use lookahead at all—just the current token of the input. We will see that using $\overline{X}$ theory directly comes to the rescue—that a principle-based approach, using the right grammatical vocabulary, does better than an explicit rule system.

In English, words such as *for* and *that* are ambiguous. *For* can be either a preposition or a complementizer; *that* can be a pronoun, determiner, or complementizer. What must happen for a parser to successfully distinguish between these various uses?

I know that block supports a pyramid. (*that* is a determiner)

I know that blocks support the pyramid. (*that* is a complementizer)

Examples such as these lead one to argue that one cannot parse deterministically without looking one or more tokens ahead into the input, to see whether *blocks* is singular or plural.[38] If we cannot use lookahead, and we must decide whether to parse *that* as part of a noun phrase or a new sentence, we are stuck. This is also true of our explicit rewrite rule approach, as used in the new parser design. If the only nonterminal names are objects such as Complementizer and NP, and if we must choose between these without retraction, then we are in trouble.[39]

Suppose, though, that the $\overline{X}$ representational format is directly incorporated in the parser. Then parsing can proceed deterministically, or, rather, monotonically. In particular, suppose that we adopt the idea that a verb such as *know* subcategorizes a case recipient argument (NP or S) and that all heads project to form phrases of some kind. Now let us see what happens when the parser analyzes a sentence like *I know that the block supports a pyramid*. We pick up the action at the time just after *know* is scanned. Since *know* predicts that a case recipient starts in the position just after it, we add the assertion triple (Case Recipient, 2, 8) to the assertion set. (We might just use a diacritical x here instead of *Case Recipient*; this doesn't really matter.)

Now what? Reading *that*, the parser's compatible assertions include (*that*, with no features, or perhaps (+ N 2 3)); (X-max 2 *) (projected from *that*, now assuming the $\overline{X}$ theory); (Case Recipient 2 *); and the remainder from the earlier portions of the parse. Note that the features of the X-max and *that* remain underdetermined; this is the best the machine can do at this point.

The parser now scans *block*. We add the triple (block + N − V 3 4); but we can now also *refine* the earlier triples, (X-max 2 *) to (X-max + N − V 2 *). Finally, by scanning *support*, we can add whatever refinement we want to the Case Recipient triple, turning it into an $\overline{S}$ (or S, as one might wish in some cases). Eventually, the X-max (NP) will span positions 2 through 4; the Case Recipient, 2 through 7.

Now let us try *I know that blocks support the pyramid*. Again we predict a (Case Recipient 2 *) triple after *know*, and (X-max 2 *); (*that* 2 3). Now the parser sees a plural Noun, *blocks*. Based on this information, it can now refine the X-max triple to (X-max + whatever feature complex $\overline{S}$s have, 2, *); (*that* + features for COMP 2 3); and (Case Recipient + features for $\overline{S}$ 2 *). We also add the new projection (X-max + N − V 3 *) (for the NP headed by *blocks*), and one for an S; note that this is always allowed. Eventually, the $\overline{S}$ will span positions 2 through 7; the S, positions 3 through 7.

Note that no lookahead is required to resolve these cases, nor any abnormal rule that attaches items in a peculiar fashion. The "wait-and-see" or "attention-shifting" behavior of Marcus's parser does not need to be stipulated; rather, it falls out of the normal behavior of the parser, operating with $\overline{X}$ principles and assertions. Where the $\overline{X}$ system underdetermines feature complexes, we get the *effect* of wait-and-see behavior, but it is part and parcel of the normal operation of the machine—nothing special at all need be said in order to get this effect.

The same approach resolves many *for* and *to* ambiguities.[40] If the grammar has to use the categories PP, $\overline{S}$, and so forth, then our deterministic parser must fix this categorial status correctly, without extra lookahead in the proposed model. But then the parser cannot correctly decide between *for* as the head of a prepositional phrase and *for* as a Complementizer—the Head of an $\overline{S}$, in some theories. Now suppose that the $\overline{X}$ schema is directly used by the parser. Then, given that *for* is a Head of some kind, the parser can create a maximal projection, with a kind of "operator" status (the Head element). The features of this projection can remain partially determined until the following material is analyzed as either an NP followed by verbal material (then *for* heads an $\overline{S}$) or just an NP (*for* heads a PP). In fact, on this alternative, there is no "PP" or "$\overline{S}$" at all, just the Head with whatever features it has.

Next consider *to* ambiguities. No matter whether *to* is a preposition or inflection, it is a case-marking operator; this is what the underdetermined $\overline{X}$ machinery projects. The same holds for *have* considered as either an auxiliary verb (Inflection) or a main verb. In either case, *have* forms a maximal +V projection. One can delay a decision to insert an NP in a sentence such as *Have the students take the exam* until *after* the NP is processed, since this will involve simply *adding* a new assertion, not destroying any old assertions. Thus, no lookahead is required in this case either.

Let's take a more complicated example. Consider another sentence type where a verb can subcategorize for either NP or $\overline{S}$, for example, *I expect John/I expect John to leave*. Exactly the same approach will work here as before. In the first sentence, the X-Case Recipient triple will eventually be coidentified with the N-max projection, via refinement. In the second, the X-Case Recipient will be refined to be an $\overline{S}$ spanning positions 2 through 5, whereas the N-max will stretch only from position 2 to position 3 in the input. Refinement occurs automatically as each token is scanned: when the infinitive *to* is reached, the N-max is closed off at position 3 and its N-max features not percolated to the X-Case Recipient. No lookahead is required.

At the same time, because no lookahead is ever used, "short" garden paths, such as *The boat floated sank* are at least possible to envision: Marcus's parser had to deliberately ignore its own lookahead information in an ad hoc way in order to garden path in such cases. Note that this is in contrast to the ambiguous subcategorization of *know*, where we had a particular alternative that could later be refined. In the present sentence, there is no obligatory argument after *floated*, so none can be safely posited. Unless extra information is provided that sets up an alternative that may safely predict an operator, then the parse will fail. This would be true, for example, if *that* were present. But now note that we have reconstructed—in a *principled* way—the canonical surface sentoid strategy of Fodor, Bever, and Garrett (1974): "Take N–V as a main sentence unless there is a surface mark of embedding."

5.2.2 Imposing Constraints in the $\overline{X}$ Parser   The set-based model lends itself to a rather different picture of parsing, essentially equation based: each proposition adds an additional constraint set to be imposed on the initial analysis provided by the parser. These constraints might include lexical, intonational, or word frequency effects, or even (after syntactic processing is complete) plausibility filtering. A modular view makes this possible.

To see how this might work, we will draw on some examples from Barton and Berwick 1985 and Berwick and Weinberg 1985:[41] one dealing with PP attachment ambiguities, and one with so-called readjustment rules. The point is simply that the direct use of $\overline{X}$ rules in a set format makes adding constraints easy.

Consider first the typical PP ambiguity sentences:

$_0$ I $_1$ saw $_2$ the $_3$ guy $_4$ on $_5$ the $_6$ hill $_7$ with $_8$ the $_9$ telescope $_{10}$

What can the parser say for certain here? The individual NP and PP phrases are positively known:

(NP 2 4) (PP 4 7) (NP 5 7)

(PP 7 10) (NP 8 10)

This base can be easily augmented to incorporate lexical or intonational effects—the point being that all we need are monotonic refinements. For example, if we add the assertions (NP 2 10) and (NP 5 10), then we get a completely right-branching analysis. Adding just (NP 5 10) gives us the reading where *on the hill with the telescope* modifies *see*; adding just (NP 2 7) gives us [*guy on the hill*] [*with the telescope*], and so forth.

Intonational effects may be easily incorporated as obligatory constraints laid on top of the base set. Suppose that clause-final lengthening and onset stress provide the cues for clause boundaries (XPs) but nothing more:[42]

I saw the guy on the hill ↓ **with** the telescope.

Then we would expect the intonational component to propose the following assertions: (X-max 2 7) (X-max 7 10). We may now impose this constraint on our base set, yielding (NP 2 4), (PP 4 6), and (X-max 2 6). Since every maximal projection must be coidentified with some lexical head, our remaining choice is to make the X-max an NP or a PP. A head-first constraint makes it the NP.

A similar analysis works well for proposed cases of so-called readjustment rules, but in this case we can again give a *principled* account for them—that is, they are a side effect of our more basic $\overline{X}$ parser. Consider the classic Chomsky-Miller example where intonational contours run counter to syntactic contours: *This is the cat that chased the rat that ate the cheese.* Suppose we take intonations as providing us with the following surface analysis of such sentences, with extraposition of relative clauses:

[the cat$_j$ t_i] [that t_j chased the rat$_k$ t_l]$_i$ [that t_k ate the cheese]$_l$

From this we can construct the following assertions (where an empty category is in the form (NP x x), dominating no phonological material in the string):

(NP$_j$ 0 2) (Det 0 1) (N$_j$ 1 2)

($\overline{S}_i$ 2 2) ($\overline{S}_i$ 2 6) (that 2 3)

(NP$_j$ 3 3) (VP 3 6) (V 3 4)

(NP$_k$ 4 6) (Det 4 5) (N$_k$ 5 6)

($\overline{S}_l$ 6 6) ($\overline{S}_l$ 6 10) (that 6 7)

(NP$_k$ 7 7) (VP 7 10) (V 7 8)

(NP$_m$ 8 10) (Det 8 9) (N$_m$ 9 10)

The intonational evidence is compatible with the assertions as listed; for example, there is an XP between positions 0 and 2 and between positions 6 and 10. More importantly, in order to "readjust" the structure to reconstruct the right S-structure, one only needs to *add* certain statements, such as (NP 0 6), as indicated by the indices. No special readjustment rules of any sort are called for.

5.2.3 Summary of $\overline{X}$ Parsing

In short, the $\overline{X}$ parser and principled assertions, combined in a "layer-cake" model, work well together and better than simple context-free rules to accumulate evidence in a monotonic way for parsing. The most important moral is that all this works naturally *if* one is willing to parse using $\overline{X}$ principles directly, rather than indirectly. In addition, the framework sketched here is compatible with constraints that allow the order among complements to a verb to be free, if there is no other constraint on them. That is, in order to establish what constituents are to be expected after a verb, we simply project, directly, the lexical subcategorization frame of the verb as it is found; there is no need for an ordered right-hand side as in a traditional context-free rule. Whatever assertions are compatible with the (unordered) subcategorization frame will simply be made as before. Of course, if there *are* constraints, such as case assignment/adjacency considerations, these may be enforced and the resulting assertion sets filtered; no change in the basic parsing machinery is required.

To summarize: in this section we have examined an $\overline{X}$ parser that uses underdetermined features in order to monotonically analyze sentence structure. The essential idea is that many locally ambiguous parses have the same topological structure, so we can force the parse foward, deterministically, until resolving lexical information is found. The parser is more "compiled" than Dorr's or Kashket's designs, since it projects categorial and, if need be, case features; yet it is still firmly wedded to $\overline{X}$ principles.[43]

6 Principle-Based Translation

We next turn to principle-based parsing for a different domain: language translation. We will look at a particular principle-based translation system, implemented by Dorr (1987, 1990). Dorr's system successfully overcomes the difficulties of a rule-based approach. It also illustrates a coroutine design for principle-based parsing that interleaves generators and filters. We will see how this works on a Spanish example sentence that would ordinarily require a number of complex rules for its description:

¿Qué vio?
'What did he/she see?'

This short sentence is deceptively simple. It actually shows three interesting phenomena: a null (missing) subject; inversion of the verb; and movement of *qué* to the front of the sentence. A traditional rule-based system would describe each of these explicitly. As we will see, Dorr's system can describe them all via the same parameters that are required for English.

Dorr's parser works by using a standard context-free parser, Earley's algorithm, on very slightly expanded $\overline{X}$ skeleton tree structures. These skeletons guide the Earley algorithm parser working in tandem with other principles. By modularizing the principles in this way, significant computational efficiencies are realized.

Dorr assumes that $\overline{X}$ theory provides the basic phrase configuration possibilities (across all languages). The basic rules

$\overline{\overline{X}} \Rightarrow$ Specifier $\overline{X}$

$\overline{X} \Rightarrow X$ Complement

are combined with two rules to handle adjuncts,

$\overline{X} \Rightarrow$ (Adjunct) $\overline{X}$ (Adjunct)

$\overline{\overline{X}} \Rightarrow$ (Adjunct) $\overline{\overline{X}}$ (Adjunct),

where the parenthesized symbols are optional.

Some terminology is useful here. A *specifier* is simply a word like a determiner that further specifies the properties of a phrase. A *complement* is just what we have been calling the *arguments* of a verb or a preposition. An *adjunct* is an optional phrase that need not be part of a verb's thematic structure.

In addition, Dorr sets a parameter so that adjuncts may occur before or after the specifier and before or after the complement (in a specifier-head-complement language). Finally, if we vary the order of specifier and complement with respect to the head, we have (assuming just one level of recursion) the $2^2 = 4$ possible tree topologies shown in figure 4.18, where the topology in the upper left-hand corner corresponds, for example, to English phrase structure order. What Dorr has done, then, is to partially "compile out" information about skeletal phrase structure possibilities. Note that these skeletons do provide topological information for parsing but do *not* provide any detail about categorial identity or verb selection information—for instance, whether *eat* must take an object or not. However, the system can access on-line lexical category information—whether a word is a noun or a verb, or its binary feature equivalents. It also knows about a few other parameters in each particular language and multiplies these into the $\overline{X}$ skeletons: choice of specifier, what a possible empty category can be in a particular language.

To summarize, the following information is precompiled in Dorr's system:

- The $\overline{X}$ order for a language
- Specifier choice (for example, determiner for $\overline{N}$ in Spanish)
- The adjunction possibilities (for example, clitic *le* can adjoin to $\overline{V}$ in Spanish)
- Default values for nonlexical heads (for example, $\overline{\overline{V}}$ complement for I(nflection) in Spanish)

(Here, Inflection simply means an element bearing tense, like the auxiliary verb *will* or *would* in English.)

To get the actual context-free rules for Spanish, we simply instantiate the $\overline{X}$ template with values for X = {N, V, P, A} *at the time parsing occurs* plus two rules for I(nflections) and C(omplementizers), following details that are irrelevant here. For Spanish, the system knows that the choice of specifier for $\overline{C}$ may be a *wh*-phrase like *which* or *what*; and it also knows that if a COMP head is absent, then the complement of C is $\overline{I}$. Finally, it knows that a V(erb) and $\overline{N}$ are adjunction possibilities. Note that these

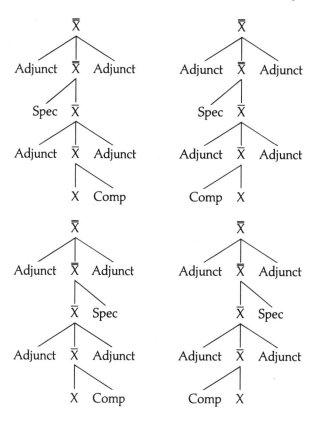

Figure 4.18
Dorr's X̄ theory provides for four basic X̄ skeleton structures on which to base further computation.

Table 4.2
Earley's parser works in tandem with principle-based constraints in Dorr's parsing design. Each standard parser action (start a phrase, scan a token, complete a phrase) runs one or more different constraint checks or structure-building routines.

Action	Earley's parser	Principle Constraint Module
Push	Expand nonterminal	Predict empty category
		Check empty category and bounding
Scan	Traverse terminal	Determine argument structure
		Perform feature matching
Pop	Complete nonterminal	Assign thematic roles
		Check Theta Criterion

rules do not form a complete description of Spanish, and are not intended to: they are indeed underconstrained. The entire $\overline{X}$ skeleton system multiplies out to a hundred or so context-free rules.

Dorr's full parser works by using the $\overline{X}$ skeleton rules as a driver program coroutined with all remaining principles, as sketched in table 4.2. The $\overline{X}$ component vastly overgenerates; it builds underspecified phrase structure because it does not access details of the thematic roles each verb demands. The actual parser is simply an Earley parser, using the context-free rules given by $\overline{X}$ expansion. As each word is processed, the parser uses the standard Earley algorithm PUSH, SCAN, or POP actions until no more actions trigger. It then calls on the remaining principles like the Case Filter or the Theta Criterion. These principles also call on the PUSH, SCAN, and POP actions, but in a much more complicated way. In effect, the skeletal parser has only a vague idea of the actual structure of sentences, which is used just to keep the Earley algorithm's PUSH-SCAN-POP sequence going. By splitting up the computational work in this way, we can vastly reduce the size of the context-free component needed, because we do not multiply out the rules used.

The principle module component has three tasks, accessed on demand: first, it weeds out bad parses (for example, a parse that calls for a complement when the verb does not need one or if bounding conditions are violated); second, it tries out possibilities that the $\overline{X}$ skeletal parser does not know about (for example, it can PREDICT that an empty category must be present at a certain point); and third, it tries to extend the Earley parse to a point where skeletal parsing can take over again (for example, by assigning and checking thematic roles, it can get the parse to the point where a phrase is complete, and so Earley's algorithm can execute a POP action).

Table 4.2 summarizes how work is split between the $\overline{X}$ component and the remaining principles. The overall effect is to implement a back-and-forth flow of information between the Earley parser actions and the filtering constraints and actions. (All parsing possibilities are carried along in parallel, as is typical with Earley's algorithm.)

For each particular language, there will also be a set of parameterized choices in the $\overline{\overline{X}}$ and constraint modules. For example, Spanish permits $\overline{N}$, *wh*-phrase, V, I, *have*-aux, and *be*-aux as empty categories; English permits only $\overline{N}$ and *wh*-phrase. These are used for predicting an empty category at PUSH time.

To see how this all fits together, consider the simple sentence *Qué vio?* 'What did she/he see?'. Figures 4.19 and 4.20 show the parsing sequence and final results. There are four final generated trees, labeled (a)–(d), of which just one, (b), is valid. The figure carries this labeling through several steps to show where each tree comes from.

As mentioned, this sentence exhibits three interesting syntactic phenomena of Spanish: a null subject; inversion of the verb; and movement of *qué* to the front of the sentence. All of this can be captured *without* explicit rules.

Morphological analysis first reduces this to the actual parsed form *¿Qué ver?* + features past, singular, third person (with the root form for the verb, as is typical). The parse itself then begins.

In step 1 as shown in figure 4.19, the parser first accesses the $\overline{\overline{X}}$ skeleton for $\overline{\overline{C}}$, which is simply C-spec–C–C-comp (in Spanish), where C need not be overt. A precompiled parameter particular to Spanish forces selection of $\overline{\overline{I}}$ to be the complement of C, since there is no head present. *Qué* is then scanned (attached) to $\overline{\overline{C}}$ as its (optional) specifier (note once again that this may lead to overgeneration since no conditions are checked at this point to determine whether this attachment is in fact correct).

Next, the expansion of $\overline{\overline{I}}$ has two $\overline{\overline{X}}$ precompiled possibilities, both of which are pursued by Earley's algorithm.

First, $\overline{\overline{I}}$ may be expanded as V–$\overline{\overline{I}}$ (with V filling the adjunct slot of $\overline{\overline{I}}$); let us continue to call this parse (a). (Here, V is one of the adjunction possibilities that has been compiled out beforehand; adjunction is assumed to occur at the $\overline{\overline{X}}$ level.) Second, $\overline{\overline{I}}$ may be expanded to contain $\overline{N}$ in I-spec (parse (c), step 1). At this point, the parser has access to the next word, *ver*, a verb. This rules out any expansion of $\overline{N}$ as its usual spec-head-comp sequence. For this parse, then, no further $\overline{\overline{X}}$ actions can occur and the parser consults the principle constraint module.

Moving on to step 2 of the parse, the constraint module determines that the next symbol to operate on for parse (c) is a nonterminal; hence, a PUSH is required. The corresponding action is to predict an empty category. There are two types of empty categories in the system: a *trace*, the position of a moved noun phrase, and *pro*, an empty pronominal. Both are predicted here: there is a possible antecedent that is not too far away, and the subject position (first $\overline{N}$ under $\overline{\overline{I}}$) is still open. (Several principles come into play

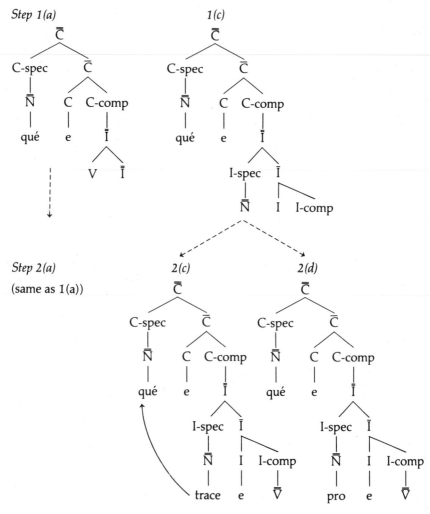

Figure 4.19
Beginning of the parse of *¿Qué vio?* in Dorr's system. This simple Spanish sentence has four possible parses, but only one is valid. This figure shows parsing steps 1–2. Parsing steps 3–7 are continued onto the next figures. (There are no trees 1(b), 2(b), 3(b), or 1(d) since possibilities (b) and (d) will arise from the splitting of tree hypotheses in later steps. The *e* nodes stand for absent nodes, not empty categories.)

here, notably bounding; each is checked separately on-line.) We will call these two ongoing possibilities parses 2(c) and 2(d). (For parse 2(c), the binding module links the trace to *qué*; for parse 2(d), the system knows that only one special kind of empty category can be placed in the relevant position.) The principle constraint module has nothing to say about parse possibility 1, and parsing is returned to the $\overline{X}$ component.

Finally, still in step 2, the precompiled $\overline{X}$ skeleton notes that I is currently absent, and so adds the (precompiled) complement possibility of $\overline{V}$ for parses 2(c) and 2(d).

We proceed to step 3 (figure 4.20). The parser next scans *ver*. It can be attached to the V slot for parse 3(a). The constraint module is then called upon: its job is to determine the argument structure for the verb *ver*. The lexical entry for *ver* predicts an $\overline{\overline{N}}$ complement.[44] For parses (c) and (d) this prediction may be realized only as an empty category trace linked to the antecedent empty category, because there is no more input available; for parse (a), however, the subject position, known to be (precompiled as) $\overline{\overline{N}}$, is still open, so either of two possible empty category types may be predicted here, yielding parse 4(a) and a new parse 4(b). In all, there are now four parses. (In the course of these steps the parser rules out many possible realizations of the specifier position for I, but we will not cover these here.)

All words are now scanned, so the principle constraint module is called on to check for any additional actions (step 4). For parses (c) and (d), all that remains is thematic checking: the Theta Criterion says that each argument receives one and only one thematic role. However, both parses (c) and (d) violate this condition since two semantic roles are assigned to the object position: the object is both goal and, via its antecedent linking, agent. These parses are thrown out.

For parses (a) and (b), additional actions are possible (steps 5–7, figure 4.21). The complement of $\overline{\overline{I}}$ is precompiled as a $\overline{V}$ (as dictated by a pre-compiled parameter, not a rule, since I is empty) (step 5). Since there is no word present, this $\overline{V}$ may be expanded (in Spanish) by a precompiled $\overline{X}$ template as an empty verb (since verbs may be traces), linked to *ver* plus (via on-line accessed subcategorization facts because of linking to *ver*) an $\overline{\overline{N}}$ complement (steps 5 and 6, parses (a) and (b)). Finally, the constraint module must again be accessed at this point, since the parser has just predicted an $\overline{\overline{N}}$ complement. Constraint principles dictate that the $\overline{\overline{N}}$ may be realized only as an empty category trace in this position, and the results are shown in 7(a) and 7(b). Transliterated, parse (a) means "What saw"; parse (b), "What did she/he see"; parse (c), "What did what see itself"; and parse (d), "What did she/he see himself, herself".

Note that of the remaining two possible parses, (a) and (b), (a) is ruled out by feature checking, since *ver* demands an animate subject. This leaves only parse (b) as valid, "What did she/he see" (with the null subject parameter

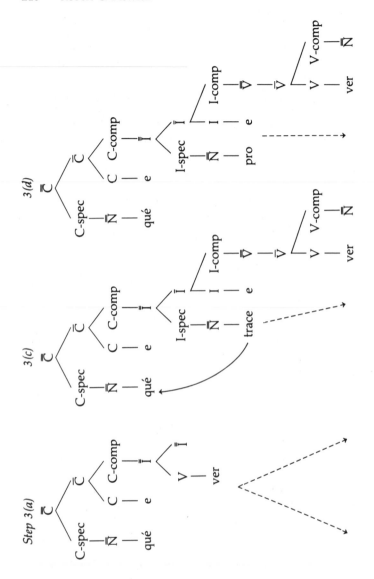

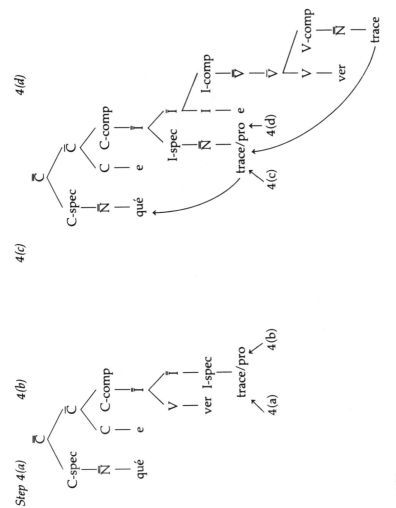

Figure 4.20
Continuation of the previous parse of *¿Qué vio?*, steps 3–4. This simple Spanish sentence has four possible parses, but only one is valid. Parses 4(c) and 4(d) remain the same through the next steps 5–7.

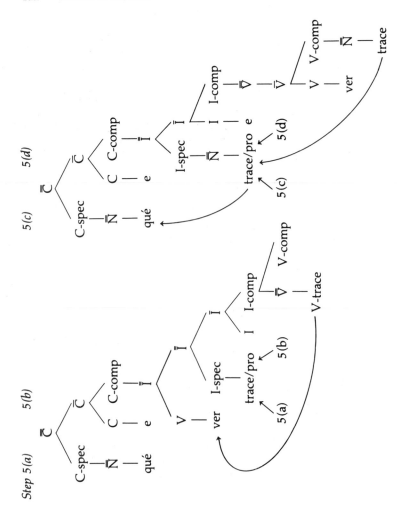

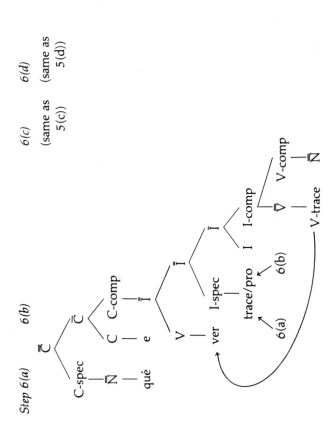

Figure 4.21
Conclusion of the parse of *¿Qué vio?*, steps 5–7. Only parse 7(b) passes all conditions, corresponding to *What did she/he see.* Parse 7(a) corresponds to the ill-formed *What saw.* Parses (c)–(d) are the same as they were in step 4 and correspond to the ill-formed sentences *What did what see itself* and *What did she/he see herself/himself.*

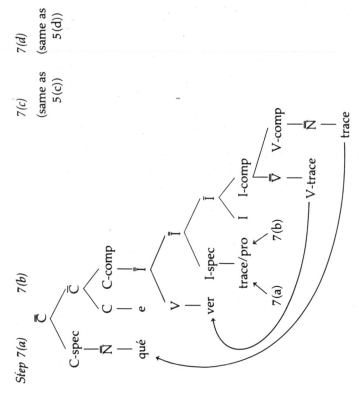

Figure 4.21 (continued)

in Spanish permitting an empty category in subject position). Note that the three syntactic phenomena of null subject, inversion, and movement are covered by filtering principles guiding the $\overline{X}$ parse, rather than by particular rules.

7 Modularity and the Computational Implementation of Principle-Based Parsers

The previous sections have given several working examples of principle-based parsers. One thing almost all have in common is modularity: they divide up grammatical representations into different vocabularies, parceling out the computational work that must be done into several different formats instead of a single, monolithic representation.

One question that deserves to be raised pertains to the computational efficiency of principle-based approaches. Though the implemented parsers justify themselves on this score—they seem about as efficient as large context-free grammars, or Marcus's parser—one might wonder whether such modularity makes sense on more general grounds. In particular, we have seen that principle-based theories often posit a many-step derivation between principles and surface sentence, and this might take an equally long time for a parser to unwind. Fong's (1990) analysis shows that the general problem for principle-based systems is overgeneration: too many hypotheses are generated, only to be ruled out later on, and this wasted effort cannot be fixed by any simple method of predicate ordering or predicate folding.

To conclude this survey of principle-based parsing, then, it is interesting to speculate why in another sense modularity might be more efficient than a monolithic representational format.

There is one simple point to make and one deeper, relatively newer speculation. The simple point is that modularity makes for smaller grammars: smaller, because we can replace a multiplied-out rule set with an additive principle set. This obvious point needs little explanation. It has an interesting formal language theory backing; see, for example, the work of Plátek and Sgall (1978), who show how a cascade of linear pushdown stack transductions of simple languages can give fairly rich strictly context-sensitive languages—but not all context-sensitive languages—as output. This argues for a stratified, multiple-level linguistic theory. This formal point is echoed in the parser construction business; one need only take a look at a worked-out example of how large a multiplied-out rule set can become.[45]

The deeper point centers on the power of modularity used in conjunction with parallel processing. Roughly speaking, if a problem can be written down as a highly modular, planar graph, it can be solved by superfast parallel circuits. If this property holds of subportions of a modular linguistic theory, then we might expect parallel speedup advantages here also by using so-called *constraint propagation* methods. It is not clear whether these properties hold of modern, principle-based theories of whatever model; however, it is at least clear that they do hold in certain domains, such as autosegmental theory, or in the two-level version of LF proposed by Hornstein (1986), and so we can expect significant parallel speedup, at least in principle.

Barton, Berwick, and Ristad (1987) summarize the relationship between modularity and parallel speedup this way:

> Intuitively, the easier it is to divide a graph into distinct and roughly equal pieces, the easier it is to use more efficient divide-and-conquer algorithms instead of combinatorial backtracking. Intuitively, a graph's *separability* tells us how many vertices we have to remove in order to obtain two roughly equal sets of nodes with no connections between them. For example, trees are highly separable; by removing a single vertex we can divide any n-vertex tree into two parts, each with no more than $2n/3$ vertices. Therefore, we would expect divide-and-conquer methods to be especially efficient on tree structures.... Divide-and-conquer algorithms carve the original problem into two or more smaller problems. The subproblems are then solved by applying the divide-and-conquer algorithm recursively; the solutions to the subproblems are then combined to form the solution to the original problem. Divide-and-conquer methods work best when the subproblems are significantly smaller than the original problem.
>
> Similarly, certain separable 3SAT [3-satisfiability] problems can be solved more quickly than general 3SAT problems, though the algorithms still take exponential time. In recent work, Kasif, Reif, and Sherlekar (1986) show that planar 3SAT problems—roughly, the class of 3SAT problems representable in a plane so that truth assignments don't cross—can be solved in serial time $O(2^{c\sqrt{n}})$ by a divide-and-conquer algorithm. This is still not polynomial time, but is much better than "brute force" backtracking with its $O(2^n)$ complexity. (On a parallel random access machine, they show this approach takes time $O(\log^3 n)$ using $O(n^2 \cdot 2^{O(\sqrt{n})})$ processors.)
>
> When the modularity of a 3SAT problem is even stronger, so that we can split a graphical 3SAT representation into about two equal pieces by removing only a *constant* number of vertices, then we can do even better: these problems are in $\mathcal{NC}$ and so can be solved by superfast parallel algorithms (taking only logarithmic time). (Kasif, Reif, and Sherlekar 1986).

These examples may be linguistically relevant. Chapter 6 [of Barton, Berwick, and Ristad 1987] develops an account of morphological analysis that relies on the algorithm known as constraint propagation. Constraint propagation is usually fast, but it can compute only local satisfiability constraints based on consistency between adjacent elements, not the global consistency and satisfaction properties.…

What is more interesting, however, is that while constraint propagation cannot always give correct answers to NP-hard problems of the sort that certain morphological or [grammatical] agreement frameworks may provide…it *does* appear to solve rapidly the modular problems that arise in natural morphological systems—at least for the examples described in chapter 6. In this respect, it corresponds more closely to natural grammatical systems than to morphological frameworks that are NP-hard or worse. We speculate that the separable character of natural morphological systems may yield this result. For example, one current line of phonological research known as *autosegmental theory* favors highly separable feature analyses; given our speculations, such grammatical systems may be more amenable to nonbacktracking and fast parallel algorithms than the two-level morphological system described in section 5 is.

To summarize, graph separability may provide a formalization for the notion of problem modularity that leads directly to efficient parallel algorithms. If this speculation is on the right track, then modular grammatical representations—whose components are separable in this way—may have precisely the right sort of structural characteristics for efficient parallel processing. If correct, such a view would direct us away from monostratal grammatical systems that attempt to characterize sentences at a single level of constraint and toward separable constraint systems such as ID/LP grammars…, the constraint modules of government-binding theory, or autosegmental theory in phonology. However,…, not every kind of modularity supports modular processing; thus it is not an immediate result that separable constraint systems of this sort have significant advantages for parallel processing. (pp. 85–86)

The caveat at the end is very important. If systems are highly intertwined in a deductive way—the kind of property usually highly prized in a principle-based theory—then planar separability may not ensue, and speedup may be impossible. Thus, the richly deductive structures *within* syntactic levels may not be susceptible to superfast parallel speedup. Even so, nobody has really investigated this possibility; it may be that there are still relatively autonomous subparts of principle-based theories that can be attacked by divide-and-conquer methods, or else subparts like autosegmental theory that use autonomous representational levels and so are efficiently analyzable.

On the other hand, there certainly are well-known autonomous representational levels in the usual T-model, and even some arguments (see Hornstein 1986) for autonomous subdivisions within the usual T-diagram at the level of LF. On this account, further subdivisions of Move α into distinct, ordered subcomponents would be computationally favored.

Considering parsing models, a natural one is the two-stage division into structural assembly of phrases followed by binding.[46] This sort of autonomous modularity is highly separable, hence amenable to superfast parallel speedup of the sort that Kasif, Reif, and Sherlekar have explored. It remains to be seen just how the circuit models they propose can be turned into workable parallel implementations for grammatical theories, of course, but on balance, it appears that the modularity now appearing in most modern grammatical theories—from GB Theory to GPSG—would have much to recommend it.

One must be cautious, however: so far as we know, just because a theory *is* highly interdependent does not mean that it is not amenable to parallel speedup, though this is an interesting possibility briefly discussed in Barton, Berwick, and Ristad 1987.

Whatever the outcome of these speculations, it is clear that our study of principle-based parsing has only just begun. Many parsing models are possible if one is willing to give up context-free rules; the relationship between modularity and computational complexity is only partially understood. Many topics in principle-based parsing have not even been addressed. But the moral should be plain: principle-based parsing *works*. Principle-based parsers open up a whole new range of possible parsing algorithms—including those that don't even build phrase structure. As we better understand the representations and principles that underlie grammars, it seems more and more certain that we will see more parsers like these, providing a wealth of new parsing ideas and psycholinguistic predictions for many years to come.

Notes

1. See Jaeggli 1986 for discussion of passive constructions described this way.
2. See chapters 1 and 4 of Halle and Vergnaud 1988 for additional discussion on this point; evidently, empirical evidence suggests that phonological principles should not be stated in a purely declarative manner, but should reflect the possibility of ordering.
3. This was recognized as far back as Chomsky 1955: here at least some argument was made that the primary grammatical corpus was related in some way to language acquisition. In most later work in generative grammar, attempts at justifying the initial set of grammatical strings were simply dropped.
4. This is the point of view adopted in Chomsky 1955.
5. "Nearly autonomous" would be a better word here, since it is plain that certain constraint modules depend on others; for example, bounding theory applies only to chains or structured elements otherwise licensed by $\overline{X}$ theory.

6. Berwick and Weinberg (1984) propose a two-stage parsing division that distinguishes principle clusters (1) and (2) from (3). Frazier's (1986) discussion of principle-based parsing and its psycholinguistic implications is also relevant here. Frazier brings up many of the same points discussed below, and I will draw on some of her psycholinguistic insights. In particular, she suggests a tripartite division of principles grounded on the fundamental notion of a "chain." Although one can raise substantial disagreements with some of the specific points Frazier raises, the general point is quite intriguing and again shows how a shift to a principle-based view leads to quite different ideas about the information structures required for parsing.

7. This observation comes from comments due to Stuart Shieber, though in fact this tripartite distinction is quite standard in the logic programming literature; see, for example, Bowen and Kowalski 1982.

8. Note that this account would allow a parser to make *finer* distinctions than the grammar.

9. There is still admittedly a sense in which even this first parser will be indirect: namely, it will use a stack, just as the second parser does. Now, one might argue that this already involves auxiliary, nonlinguistically sanctioned data structures and hence is an indirect implementation. We might be able to dodge this by building a tree and using that instead of a stack. But we will sidestep this point here; there is still a clear sense in which the second parser pays even less attention to the individual rules of the grammar.

10. Thus, we see that in certain cases the notion of "strong equivalence" is in fact too weak for some purposes: we cannot discriminate between these two strongly equivalent, but otherwise quite different systems.

11. Note that even here the grammar is "used"—namely, to derive the original theorem—but once so used, the grammar may be discarded. The connection to language learning should be plain.

12. This distinction differs from other proposals that attempt to sort out the explicit/implicit rule spectrum. Dennett (1983) proposes three categories of rules: explicit, implicit, and tacit. For Dennett, *explicit* rules are those that are literally enscribed, accessed, and causally figure in the operation of a process. In clear cases of rule-following behavior, a representation of a rule is empowered by its very shape as a causative agent of the process in which it participates. To use Matthews's (1984) terminology, in this case we say that a representation "figures in the etiology of . . . behavior." The system actually consults a representation of a rule in order to figure out what to do next. A simple example: one might produce simple sentences by consulting the literal enscription, "Sentence → Noun Phrase Verb Phrase."

In contrast, Dennett defines *implicit* knowledge just as that word would suggest: as knowledge that can be implied by knowledge that is stored explicitly. For example, my knowledge of whether a certain English sentence 100 words long is grammatical or not is presumably derivable from my knowledge of the grammar of English, hence is implicit knowledge.

Finally, for Dennett, *tacit* knowledge is knowledge simply "built into" the operation of a process—the brute "know-how" that cuts off any Rylean infinite regress. On the familiar terrain of Turing machines, this will correspond to whatever machinery it is that knows how to interpret the instructions such as "Move the tape head one square to the left"; for an ordinary computer, this will be its built-in ability to decode an instruction (in binary form) and respond appropriately (updating its program counter, and so on).

On this account "tacit knowledge" comes out sounding very much like physical reductionism pure and simple. Consider the computer's ability to execute instructions. Even this description introduces entities that do not exist under our attribution: for instance, physically speaking, there need be no literal "program counter" at all in a computer. Of course, some machines *do* possess a physically distinct piece of hardware that serves as a program counter, but this is by no means necessary; other micro-processors simply use a distinguished memory address, or register. Entities like *program counter* and *instruction register* serve to regularize our theories of the behavior of the machine; without assuming them, the machine's step-by-step operation may be quite mysterious. Indeed, it would seem that the description of the machine in terms of program counter, instruction register, and the like, is on a par with theoretical descriptions in other sciences, and, by extension, on a par with theories of cognitive processes. At bottom, all behavior is presumably "tacit" in Dennett's sense, since it is physical regularities and primitives that fix behavioral capabilities. It is an uninteresting fact that we can replace any program description—any set of rules, if you will—with an equivalent version that is simply "wired" to behave in just the way prescribed by the rules, because the description in terms of voltages and wires is not the crucial one. The true theory of the machine—the counterfactual supporting description—uses terms like *program counter* simply because the regularities of the computer mesh with this theoretical vocabulary. This should be no surprise, since the designer probably used this vocabulary in the first place. Similarly for grammars. We introduce the terms S, NP, $\overline{X}$ level, and constraints like the Projection Principle, Subjacency, and so forth, for exact-ly the same reason, so as to best account for the facts of natural grammars.

13. Another simple example drawn from logic grammars—which incidentally provides one of the simplest possible examples of source-to-source translation or "compiling"—is how one deals with terminal words within a Horn clause translation of a phrase structure rule. For example, assuming that $A.U$ stands for a list with a single head element A and a tail U, then McCord (1987:318) initially writes the context-free rule

NP → Det Noun *that* VP

as

np(X, V) ← det(X, Y) ∧ noun(Y, Z) ∧ ($Z = that.U$) ∧ vp(U, V).

But, as he notes, we can just substitute for Z directly, obtaining the simpler expression

np(X, V) ← det(X, Y) ∧ noun(Y, $that.U$) ∧ vp(U, V).

Note that this substitution obeys the representational boundaries of the original princi-ples, the single phrase structure rule.

14. Another possibility here is to introduce the usual sort of complexity metrics in order to quantify derivational complexity and so measure the "distance" between axioms and derived predicates. This would be a worthwhile alternative to pursue, but is beyond the scope of this survey.

15. Note that the compilation procedure might result in an incomplete parser, that is, one that does not work on all inputs without some kind of external oracle; this is what can happen when an ambiguous context-free grammar is compiled into LR parsing tables.

16. This is done by lumping a possibly infinite domain of nonterminals into one of a finite number of equivalence classes, deemed relevant for parsing.

17. Note that the choice of the restrictor function in Shieber's proposal is really left open to the grammar programmer; there may be arbitrarily many possibilities.

18. Crain and Fodor (1985) have carried out experiments, which, as they say, do rule out some possibilities: it looks as if constraints are being consulted before the entire sentence is being processed; at the same time, it looks as if information is sometimes accessed on an "as needed" basis. What one needs to do, as will be emphasized below, is to carry out a much more detailed and careful dependency analysis of the modern theories, from GB Theory to GPSG, which all possess quite subtle and not so subtle

interrelationships between their modules. This would tell us something more detailed about which constraints need to be considered when.

19. There is at least a hint that whatever the derived or compiled relationships are, they seem to be grounded on binary relations. For example, there is no tripartite relation where a dative verb selects one NP argument, which in turn selects another NP argument; instead, selection is mediated just through the verb. To take another example, even parasitic gaps may be described as the intersection of two chains with the same head; chains are themselves composed of binary-related elements. If this observation is correct, then all derived facts about surface constructions used in compiled principle-based parsers might be restricted to binary relations in some fashion.

20. Berwick (1982) shows how government and precedence parsing might be related, and Chomsky and Miller (1963) give the classic account of how intonational phrasing might be used to guide an initial skeletal parser that is only later refined. Note that in Chomsky and Miller's model the initial parser does not even build the same structures as those demanded by the competence grammar.

21. Dorr actually factors in some information about trace and adjunct possibilities.

22. Frazier also wants to multiply out into individual rules case theory and theta theory, but it is hard to see exactly where these principles are used, so I will put this question aside for now and just consider the projection of lexical category information.

23. Other government-binding parsers, like Wehrli's (1984), appear to lump together subcategorization information, case, and theta theory, but not enough detail is available in published form to be sure.

24. The use of such derivation chains to record movement history is remarkably similar—though with important variation—in theories as diverse as GPSG, Lexical-Functional Grammar (LFG), and GB Theory. This is the sense in which derivation structure is still crucial to syntactic theory, even though derivational history, in the sense of the order in which the mapping from one level to another is carried out, seems less crucial. It remains to formalize this notion of chain or path to see whether there are real differences between the various accounts. It is also important to note that this problem does not arise in simple-minded declarative GB reconstructions that axiomatize constraints only for single Ss or one-level embedded S-structure representations, because then there are no chains to reconstruct. Thus, the results from such simple analyses often belie the real complexity of a full declarative formulation of GB Theory, or even of GPSG.

25. A glance at the Prolog compilers actually found in the literature will confirm this intuition; see, for example, the system of Dahl and McCord (1983), which handles conjunction.

26. This is not to say that there are no difficulties in using Marcus's rule-based approach in a language like German. Indeed, experience in writing a large Marcus-type system for German, as part of the Athena Foreign Language project at MIT, has shown quite clearly that the verb-final character of the language caused problems, because important subcategorization information was not available.

27. Of course, one might question whether Japanese is truly "nonconfigurational" in the same sense as Warlpiri. Tenny observes that Japanese is actually "configurational" on some accounts. On the view presented in this chapter, the distinction between "configurational" and "nonconfigurational" languages is meaningless; rather, some languages allow freer phrase order than others (for example, the order of adjunct prepositional phrases in English is largely free). Whether Japanese is considered configurational or not, its free phrase order presents difficulties for a traditional context-free parser where such ordering is explicitly spelled out in advance.

28. The evidence that subject-verb-object order is most basic in Japanese is drawn from Saito 1985.

29. Verb-particle constructions exemplify the same phenomenon: if we "project" the verb-particle pair to a separate tier, then in fact they are adjacent even if not appearing so on the surface.

30. Modularity also has suggestive advantages for parallel processing, as we will see in section 7.

31. The AUX unit will be ignored for these and all remaining examples.

32. For an early attempt to describe the problem of ungrammatical sentences via a notion of *levels of grammaticality*, see Chomsky 1955. In effect, this approach makes no distinction between "grammatical" and "ungrammatical" sentences and so does not even admit to a distinguished set of strings called a language. This work was of course written before the real advent of formal language theory.

33. Note that this renders irrelevant the whole idea of weak generative capacity. Thus, although there is *something* correct in saying that natural languages are a lot like context-free languages, plus agreement augmentations and *wh*-movement, this statement is correct only insofar as it redescribes at a superficial level the more fundamental fact that natural languages follow $\overline{X}$ theory plus other constraints like case assignment, agreement conventions like the Foot Feature Principle (if that is what one believes in), and so forth. Weak generative capacity is completely derivative, a side effect of more fundamental principles.

34. Since this is not an exhaustive list, certain "ungrammatical" sentences—in particular, agreement violations that are not accommodated by any of the modules listed above—are not captured. Presumably, simple subject-verb agreement could be encoded in the usual way as (atomic) feature unification between Inflection and Subject in English.

35. Of course, there may well be more subtle cases where the distinct vocabularies used by the two theories lead to a different taxonomy of unacceptable sentences. This may well be true in the case of long-distance dependencies, if they are handled by passing SLASH features through phrasal trees in GPSG.

36. This representation, in fact, is exactly that used by so-called tabular parsing methods, such as Earley's algorithm. At every step in a parse, we simply *assert* which phrasal analyses are compatible with the input seen so far. In this regard, the representational format is quite like Kaplan's General Syntactic Processor (1973). Kaplan, however, aimed to build a tree once the assertions had been completely built. But this is unnecessary; indeed, as we will see, it is the source of parsing difficulties, not a solution.

37. The features $\pm$*lexical*, $\pm$*maximal* could be used to denote lexical (X^0) and maximal projections respectively; other combinations of these features yield intermediate bar levels.

38. One can construct real garden path examples in the worst case: *I know that blocks support for the pyramid is failing.*

39. In fact, Marcus's "diagnostic" rule to handle *that* is among the most baroque in his entire grammar: it specifically violates the general left-to-right operating principle of his machine, attaching the *first* item in the input buffer to the *second*.

40. It is interesting to speculate about the existence of function word homonyms of this kind; are these accidental or not?

41. The set-based representation also bears a close relationship to the proposals made by Marcus regarding a representation using just the predicates *precedes* and *dominates*. The similarities are plain enough, so they will not be spelled out here.

42. Matters become more complex if we have to introduce certainty factors into this information, but this could be done as well.

43. It may even suggest why sentences like *The students knew the solution to the problem would be easy* might result in an additional processing load as compared to sentences like *The students knew the solution to the problem*: the parser has a bigger refinement job (adding a new element rather than just refining one) in the first kind of sentence. But these details remain to be worked out.

44. This is actually done in a more principled way, by projection from lexical-conceptual structure, but we ignore this detail here.

45. See Ristad 1986, appendix A and B, and Barton, Berwick, and Ristad 1987, appendix B, for GPSG examples, including citations from working GPSG systems. But the same would be true for a multiplied-out principles-and-parameters parser.

46. Though binding may proceed S by S, or even word by word (that is, in a pipelined way, before the entire sentence is processed), as proposed by Berwick and Weinberg (1984) and in part confirmed by Freedman and Forster's (1985) work. Crain and Fodor (1985: 126) note that such modularity claims can indeed be controversial, since, as we have seen, modularity permits a greater variety of possible arrangements of logical information structures, hence a greater flexibility in adapting to almost any sort of experimental result. As they remark, "Frazier et al. have suggested that the constraints are in a different module than the rules, and are applied after the rules. But the constraints might be in a different module and yet applied simultaneously with the rules. And if they were, then the relative timing of processing operations would be indistinguishable from their relative timing in a nonmodular system."

References

Abney, S. 1986. A new model of natural language parsing. Ms., Department of Linguistics and Philosophy, MIT.

Aho, A., and J. Ullman. 1972. *The theory of parsing, translation, and compiling*, vol. 1. Englewood Cliffs, NJ: Prentice-Hall.

Aoun, J. 1979. Indexing and constituency. Ms., Department of Linguistics and Philosophy, MIT.

Bach, E. 1965. On some recurrent types of transformations. In C. W. Kreidler (ed.) *Sixteenth Annual Roundtable Meeting on Linguistics and Language Studies*. Washington, DC: Georgetown University Monograph Series on Language and Linguistics, 18.

Barton, E., and R. Berwick. 1985. Parsing with assertion sets and information monotonicity. In *Proceedings of International Joint Conference on Artificial Intelligence (IJCAI-85)*.

Barton, E., R. Berwick, and E. Ristad. 1987. *Computational complexity and natural language*. Cambridge, MA: MIT Press.

Berwick, R. 1982. Locality principles and the acquisition of syntactic knowledge. Ph.D. dissertation, Department of Linguistics and Philosophy, MIT.

Berwick, R. 1985. *The acquisition of syntactic knowledge*. Cambridge, MA: MIT Press.

Berwick, R., and S. Fong. 1989. The computational implementation of principle-based parsers. In M. Tomita (ed.) *First International Workshop on Parsing Technologies*. Pittsburgh, PA: Carnegie-Mellon University.

Berwick, R., and S. Fong. 1990. Principle-based parsing: Natural language processing for the 1990s. In P. Winston and S. Shellard (eds.) *Artificial intelligence at MIT: Expanding frontiers*, vol. 1. Cambridge, MA: MIT Press.

Berwick, R., and A. Weinberg. 1984. *The grammatical basis of linguistic performance*. Cambridge, MA: MIT Press.

Berwick, R., and A. Weinberg. 1985. Models for deterministic parsing. In *Proceedings of North Eastern Linguistic Society*. GLSA, University of Massachusetts, Amherst.

Bowen, K., and R. Kowalski. 1982. Amalgamating language and metalanguage in logic. In K. L. Clark and S.-A. Tärnlund (eds.) *Logic programming*. New York: Academic Press.

Chomsky, N. 1955. The logical structure of linguistic theory. Ms., Harvard University. (Segments published by Plenum, New York, 1975.)

Chomsky, N. 1965. *Aspects of the theory of syntax*. Cambridge, MA: MIT Press.

Chomsky, N. 1981. *Lectures on government and binding*. Dordrecht: Foris.

Chomsky, N. 1986. *Knowledge of language: Its nature, origin, and use*. New York: Praeger.

Chomsky, N., and G. Miller. 1963. Finitary models of language users. In R. Luce, R. Bush, and E. Galanter (eds.) *Handbook of mathematical psychology*. New York: Wiley.

Correa, N. 1987. An attribute grammar implementation of Government-Binding theory. In *Proceedings of the 25th Annual Meeting of the Association for Computational Linguistics*. Stanford, CA.

Crain, S., and J. D. Fodor. 1985. How can grammars help parsers? In D. Dowty, L. Karttunen, and A. Zwicky (eds.) *Natural language parsing: Psychological, computational and theoretical perspectives*. Cambridge: Cambridge University Press.

Dahl, V., and M. C. McCord. 1983. Treating coordination in logic grammars. *American Journal of Computational Linguistics* 9.2:69–91.

Dennett, D. 1983. On the notion of rule-governed behavior. In *Proceedings of the Oxford Philosophical Society*.

Dorr, B. J. 1987. UNITRAN: A principle-based approach to machine translation. Technical report 1000, Artificial Intelligence Laboratory, MIT.

Dorr, B. J. 1990. Principle-based translation. In P. H. Winston and S. Shellard (eds.) *Artificial intelligence at MIT: Expanding frontiers*, vol. 1. Cambridge, MA: MIT Press.

Emonds, J. 1986. *A unified theory of syntactic categories*. Dordrecht: Foris.

Fodor, J. A., T. Bever, and M. Garrett. 1974. *The psychology of language use*. New York: McGraw-Hill.

Fong, S. 1990. The computational implementation of principle-based parsers. Ph.D. dissertation, Department of Electrical Engineering and Computer Science, MIT.

Frazier, L. 1986. Natural classes in language processing. Paper presented at the MIT Cognitive Science Seminar, November 1986.

Frazier, L., C. Clifton, and J. Randall. 1983. Filling gaps: Decision principles and structure in sentence comprehension. *Cognition* 13:187–222.

Freedman, S., and K. Forster. 1985. The psychological status of overgenerated sentences. *Cognition* 19:101–131.

Grishman, R. 1973. Implementation of the string parser of English. In R. Rustin (ed.) *Natural language processing*. New York: Algorithmics Press.

Halle, M. 1986. Some speculations about the representation of words in memory. In V. Fromkin (ed.) *Phonetic linguistics: Essays in honor of Peter Ladefoged*. New York: Academic Press.

Halle, M., and J.-R. Vergnaud. 1988. *An essay on stress*. Cambridge, MA: MIT Press.

Harrison, P. 1988. A new implementation of Generalized Phrase Structure Grammar. Ph.D. dissertation, Department of Computer Science, University of Washington.

Hornstein, N. 1986. Semantics and quantifiers in a T-model. Ms., University of Maryland.

Jaeggli, O. 1986. Passive. *Linguistic Inquiry* 17:587–622.

Johnson, M. 1988. Parsing as deduction: The use of knowledge of language. In S. Abney (ed.) *The MIT parsing volume, 1987–88*. Cambridge, MA: Center for Cognitive Science.

Kaplan, R. 1973. A general syntactic processor. In R. Rustin (ed.) *Natural language processing*. New York: Algorithmics Press.

Karttunen, L., and M. Kay. 1985. Parsing in a free word order language. In D. Dowty, L. Karttunen, and A. Zwicky (eds.) *Natural language parsing: Psychological, computational and theoretical perspectives*. Cambridge: Cambridge University Press.

Kashket, M. 1986. Parsing a free-word order language: Warlpiri. In *Proceedings of the 24th Annual Meeting of the Association for Computational Linguistics.*

Kasif, S., J. Reif, and D. Sherlekar. 1986. Formula dissection: A divide and conquer algorithm for satisfiability. Ms., Department of Electrical Engineering and Computer Science, The Johns Hopkins University.

Kwasny, S., and N. Sondheimer. 1979. Ungrammaticality and extragrammaticality in natural language understanding systems. In *Proceedings of the 17th Annual Meeting of the Association for Computational Linguistics.*

Lasnik, H., and J. Kupin. 1977. A restrictive theory of transformational grammar. *Theoretical Linguistics* 4.3 : 173–196.

Lasnik, H., and M. Saito. 1984. On the nature of proper government. *Linguistic Inquiry* 15 : 235–290.

Lasnik, H., and J. Uriagereka. 1988. *A course in GB syntax: Lectures on binding and empty categories.* Cambridge, MA: MIT Press.

Laughren, M. 1987. The configurationality parameter and Warlpiri. In L. Maracz and P. Muysken (eds.) *Configurationality.* Dordrecht: Foris.

Marcus, M. 1980. *A theory of syntactic recognition for natural language.* Cambridge, MA: MIT Press.

Matthews, R. 1984. The Marcus parser and grammatical theory. Ms., Rutgers University.

Pinker, S. 1984. *Language learnability and language development.* Cambridge, MA: Harvard University Press.

Plátek, M., and P. Sgall. 1978. A scale of context-sensitive languages related to the context-free languages. *Information and Control* 38 : 1–20.

Pylyshyn, Z. 1984. *Computation and cognition.* Cambridge, MA: MIT Press.

Riemsdijk, H. van, and E. Williams. 1986. *Introduction to the theory of grammar.* Cambridge, MA: MIT Press.

Ristad, E. 1986. Complexity of linguistic models. S. M. thesis, Department of Electrical Engineering and Computer Science, MIT.

Robinson, J. 1980. Diagram: A grammar for dialogues. Technical note 205, SRI International, Menlo Park, CA, February 1980.

Rounds, W. 1988. LFP: A logic for linguistic descriptions and an analysis of its complexity. *Computational Linguistics* 14.4 : 1–9.

Samuels, A. L. 1967. Some studies in machine learning using the game of checkers. II— Recent progress. *IBM Journal.* November.

Saito, M. 1985. Some asymmetries in Japanese and their theoretical implications. Ph.D. dissertation, Department of Linguistics and Philosophy, MIT.

Sells, P. 1985. *Lectures on contemporary syntactic theories.* Stanford, CA: Center for the Study of Language and Information.

Sharp, R. 1985. A parser for GB theory implemented in PROLOG. S.M. thesis, University of British Columbia.

Shieber, S. 1985. Using restriction to extend parsing algorithms for complex feature-based formalisms. In *Proceedings of the 23rd Annual Meeting of the Association for Computational Linguistics.*

Slocum, J. 1984. METAL: The LRC machine translation system. ISSCO Tutorial on machine translation, Lugano, Switzerland.

Smith, D. E., and M. R. Genesereth. 1985. Ordering conjunctive queries. *Artificial Intelligence* 26 : 171–215.

Stabler, E. P., Jr. Forthcoming. *The logical approach to syntax.* Cambridge, MA: MIT Press.

Tamaki, H., and T. Sato. 1984. Unfold/fold transformation of logic programs. In *Proceedings of the Second International Logical Programming Conference.* Uppsala, Sweden: Uppsala University.

Tenny, C. 1986. A context-free rule system for parsing Japanese. Cambridge, MA: MIT-Japan Science and Technology Program.

Thiersch, C. 1986. A prolog GB parser for German (personal communication).

Ullman, S. 1979. *The interpretation of visual motion.* Cambridge, MA: MIT Press.

Weischedel, R., and J. Black. 1980. Responding intelligently to unparsable inputs. *American Journal of Computational Linguistics.* 6.2:97–109.

Wehrli, E. 1984. A government-binding parser for French. University of Geneva: Institute for the Study of Semantics and Cognition.

Index